Tall Man Talking

By Phil Heinricy

Tall Man Talking; by Phil Heinricy

Phil Heinricy asserts the moral right to be identified as the author of this work

This Edition: © February 2008

ISBN: 978-0-9562024-0-6

Much of the content of this book is based on the personal recollections of the author. Despite the author's best endeavours it is possible that inaccuracies may have occurred. If informed of any factual errors supported by appropriate proof the publishers will make every effort to correct such errors in future editions.

Publisher:
TPC GB & Ireland
Spectrum House
Dunstable Road
St Albans
Herts AL3 7PR

Printed by the MPG Books Group
in the UK

Cover Illustration: Charles Frost, © 1993

Contents

Part One

Me & the Club

Part Two

The Practical, the People, the Medical

Part Three

Some General Musings

Appendix

The Usual "Front of Book" Stuff

Acknowledgements

Rather than follow the Hollywood tradition of thanking everyone from family and friends to the therapist's nail technician's dog walker, I shall content myself with thanking all of those people who have enriched my life. Whether they realise it or not, they have all played their part, encouraging me when I needed to be encouraged, keeping my feet firmly on the ground when I was in danger of getting carried away, and giving me a kick up the backside when I stopped believing or trying.

There is no need to name each of them individually because I know that the people who matter don't mind, and the people who mind don't matter.

Naming Names

Within these pages I shall inevitably refer to many Tall Persons Club members by name. Inclusion should not be seen as a badge of honour, omission not as an insult.

I want to convey information, not compile a membership directory.

To Carol, the woman who has put up with me for more years than I had any right to expect, and who has supported all of my efforts for no reason I can surmise.

…and…

In Memory of my Sister
Herma Cumbes
10.1.1944 – 5.6.2008

———————————

Part One

Me & the Club

The Prologue

August 1st, 2007, 11.00pm. Exactly sixteen years ago today I was sitting at home, recovering from a hectic, tiring, and somewhat surreal day. It was one that would change not only my life but also, it would turn out, the lives of many other people.

I had not long returned from Glasgow, where I appeared on the live BBC television programme Garden Party and announced to the world that I was launching the Tall Persons Club GB, hereafter often referred to simply as "TPC". Little did I realise what was about to happen.

I would love to say that the day was the culmination of months of meticulous planning and careful research, but it wasn't. It was an accident, plain and simple.

Today, the Tall Persons Club GB & Ireland is sixteen years old (the Ireland was added a few months after the launch). It is now a Company Limited by Guarantee run by a board of directors and has been so since April 2000. In those sixteen years it has resulted in over forty weddings and at least fourteen children that I know of, probably more by the time you read these words. It has worked with Members of Parliament, both Westminster and Strasbourg, numerous corporations, medical and academic institutions, provided an expert witness to an industrial tribunal and much more besides. It has been influential in so many ways, but, above all, it has changed many lives for the better.

These days I am not involved with the active day to day running of the Club. Instead I act as a sort of informal consultant when requested to do so. It was during one of those consultations, a visit by two directors to our home in Hereford, that it became clear just how much information about the Club and about height in general is locked inside my head. It is not written down and, when I shuffle off this mortal coil, will be lost until someone relearns it all over again.

"You should write a book," said Jackie Timbs. Jim Briggs boomed his agreement; geez, that man has a loud voice!

"Nonsense," said I, "I wouldn't know where to start."

But start I did, and this volume is that book. However, I have no idea how it is going to turn out.

It cannot be an academic work, because my writing style is not suited to such things and the information is not all carefully detailed and structured. Most of the psychological stuff is what serious students of psychology dismissively refer to as anecdotal, but that does not make it any less relevant. Nor is it an entirely autobiographical work, although much of what went before and during, the experiences I had, the skills I acquired, contributed directly or indirectly to the success of the Club and to my personal views on height. A novel it most certainly isn't, because I couldn't have made up some of this stuff.

I shall do my best to make what follows relevant, interesting and entertaining. But I am no author, no great orator, and certainly no academic.

I am just a guy who had a dumb idea to start a club for tall people.

Starting Tall

Lewisham General Hospital in London will never erect a plaque to, nor accept the blame for, my appearance there on Sunday, 4th January 1953. At 8 pounds plus I wasn't small, but I wasn't particularly large or long at birth either.

I realised I was unusually tall from quite an early age, and I loved it when people thought I was much older than I actually was. However, it wasn't until many years later that I realised what effect my height had on my childhood and teenage. Yet so many other factors have played an important part that it is impossible to know just how large an influence my height has been on me.

There's only one thing for it: I'll have to start at the very beginning, it's a very good place to start...... (*Altogether now: "Doe, a deer, a fe-male deer..." – you'll have that tune in your head for the rest of the day now*)

My parents were German immigrants who met in London after the Second World War. My father was a prisoner of war who had stayed on after his release, my mother a refugee from the former East Germany. She had escaped her home town, together with her baby daughter, hours before it was occupied by advancing Russian troops. Living on her wits, she moved from town to town, finding work wherever she could. She eventually made her way to England, thanks to a refugee resettlement programme, arriving in Grimsby in 1949.

Of my father's past I know very little, other than that he was a highly intelligent man with a somewhat chequered past. A qualified pharmacist, he also spoke at least three languages. From what little I have been able to discover about him and his past, I know only that he was a compulsive gambler, had an uncertain relationship with the law and had therefore been disowned by his own family back in Germany. They even told his son that he had died in the war. I put that particular bit of misinformation right many years later, but that's another story. Let's just say that I went in search of an uncle and found a brother; more about that later.

In common with many former wartime soldiers, he found it difficult to settle back into civilian life. He was an alcoholic who could become physically abusive, and had trouble holding down a job for any length of time. We moved home a lot during those early years, and I recall at least nine different addresses by the time I was nine years old.

The regular moves meant that I never really established any firm or lasting friendships. There simply wasn't time. By the time I had got to know the local kids we were on the move again. I became accustomed to not getting too close to anyone, because we wouldn't be around long enough for it to be worthwhile. To this day I have few people in my life I would consider as close friends. I have plenty of acquaintances and mates, but friends are few and far between.

My sister resolved to leave home at the earliest possible opportunity. I was seven when she got married at the age of just 16 in 1960. Although her given name was Herma, her husband's family decided they preferred Helen, so Helen she became. Sadly, she recently died of cancer, but during her last days in the hospice she reverted emphatically to her given name once more.

From that time I was raised more or less as an only child. I learned to amuse myself, and was intensely curious about anything and everything. My favourite reading matter was an encyclopaedia, which I read the way other children read Enid Blyton and Beatrix Potter. I have no recollection of actually learning to read, but vividly recall reading comics and the school hymn sheets by the time I was five or six. I read Robinson Crusoe when I was eight, and it wasn't a special children's version either.

My father's dubious practices eventually caught up with him, and he became a guest of Her Majesty. As we were living in tied accommodation, a flat above the shop in North London which my parents managed, our tenancy came to an abrupt and untimely end. In one of life's ironies, my father ended up with a criminal record, a place to sleep and three square meals a day, while my mother and I were homeless. We spent a couple of nights in Trafalgar Square sleeping on a bench under a travel blanket, and a few more in assorted Salvation Army hostels and shelters for the homeless. At the same time I contracted a kidney infection, which caused me indescribable pain when passing water and which affected my health for years afterwards.

In an act of supreme kindness, the old lady from whom my father had embezzled kindly took us in. She had been a customer of the shop, and was an invalid who needed substantial care, which my mother gave in lieu of paying rent.

Soon afterwards my mother found work as a domestic assistant at Libury Hall, a care home in Hertfordshire. Accommodation was included for both of us. It was just two rooms in a shared cottage, the other half of which was occupied by one of the residents in a sort of sheltered housing arrangement, all part of the care home set up. We had no proper kitchen, and took all of our meals with the staff in their canteen.

Before long a new job as a housekeeper meant another move, this time to a cottage on a nearby farm. It was a two up two down, with a toilet and bath in an outbuilding across the small back yard. We had running water, but no hot water. If we wanted a bath, the water had to be heated on the old kitchen range, a huge black solid fuel affair which served for both heating and cooking, and then carried across the yard. A large garden provided plenty of fresh fruit and vegetables.

I mention all of this not because it has any great relevance to my height, but because living through those days taught me that material possessions are all well and good, but they don't really matter at all in the long run. It is surprising how little one can survive on. For some the experience would have led to a determination to succeed and to never experience such hardship again. In my case it strengthened a belief that life is to be enjoyed, and that something will always turn up when you need it.

I attended the school in nearby Little Munden, where I was known by my second name, David. There were already three other Philips in the class, so I suppose they thought enough was enough, and David I was. It was a small school with just one class of infants and one of juniors, where we worked at our own pace. I had started there while at Libury Hall, and our new home was close enough for me to continue to attend.

The school has grown a little since those days, but still has fewer than 100 pupils. The village website proclaims that "…each child will work at his or her own level, the teaching system being designed to cope with children of mixed ability and mixed age group". I'm glad to hear that some things don't change.

It was at Little Munden that I received the one and only caning of my academic career. The cane was about to be made illegal, and on the very last day that it could still be used Mr Dunsford announced that he wished to retire his trusty cane in style. The smile on his face told us that it was to be a largely ceremonial exercise, but we were on our guard all the same.

We were waiting for him in class after the morning break during which we had our daily milk – it was a time before "Thatcher, Thatcher, Milk Snatcher" had her wicked way with our daily calcium supplement. I was messing about with a classmate. Memory has faded the details, but I think it may have been William Knight, whose parents kept the Boot pub in Dane End. Enter Mr Dunsford, and our fate was sealed. He called us to the front of the class, and instructed us to clasp our knees which, full of trepidation, we duly did. He opened his desk drawer and pulled out a rather short greying piece of thin bamboo. This cane was a mere shadow of its longer and swishier former self. Even without a change in the law, its dignified retirement was long overdue. With great solemnity Mr Dunsford administered a gentle painless tap to our respective behinds, sighed, and tossed the cane into the waste paper basket. And that was that. It might not sound like much of a caning to you, but it still counts.

The school had close links with the neighbouring church, where I became a choirboy. Yes, I was one of those angelic wee souls.

It was here I learned how quickly one can gain status only to lose it again in an instant. Dressed for the Sunday service, we stood in our shiny white surplices while the vicar checked each of us, to ensure we looked our best.

"Where's Brian," he asked?

Brian was head choirboy. His outfit was distinguished by a large ornate cross on a red ribbon worn about his neck, and it was his job to lead out the choir, and take pride of place in the front pew of the choir stalls. To be head choirboy was the ambition of us all.

We waited until the last moment that morning, but still Brian did not appear.

"Someone else will have to take over," said the vicar, as he lifted the cross from its hook in the vestry,

I almost burst with pride as he smiled, and draped it around my neck. To an eight year old such things are of great importance. I took my place at the head of the line, ready to leave the vestry, knowing that my mother would be in the congregation to witness this proud moment in my young life.

Suddenly the door burst open and Brian rushed in, red faced and breathless. The vicar said: "Oh good, you're here," and quickly helped him to dress.

Then, to my horror and without a word, he took the cross from me and hung it around Brian's neck. He took my place, and I was sent back in the line of boys; I didn't even get to walk in second. I was crushed, and so was my relationship with the church.

I learned two things from that incident. First, that you could be late, could inconvenience others and still retain your rank and position. Second, that whatever exalted heights one might achieve in life, it can all be so fleeting. I had been head choirboy for less than a minute; how much more fleeting can it be?

I did well at school, and within a short time was doing the work required of candidates for the 11+ exam. A place at the nearby grammar school in Puckeridge beckoned. The headmaster applied to the education authority for me to take the exam a year ahead of schedule, as I was no longer finding my schoolwork a challenge. I was getting bored.

For the first time in my life I became aware that my height influenced the expectations of others because of the way they perceived me. My academic achievements did not appear to surprise many people. I was only nine years old, but over five feet tall, the height of most eleven year old boys. I performed as well as other children whose age I appeared to be, but the only real similarity was that we were similar heights. I was two years younger than any of them.

I didn't take the 11+ exam as planned. My mother was finding life difficult, raising me on her own without family support. The war was still within living memory, and that some of the local children referred to me as 'the Nazi kid' didn't help. It was 1961; the Berlin Wall had just gone up, America and the USSR were at loggerheads, the world was on the brink of war yet again and the strain told on my mother. Her Aunt Frieda, who lived in Hamburg, suggested that she should return to Germany, to more familiar surroundings and culture as well as family support. My mother told me that we were going on an extended holiday, for three months or so, and I was happy with that.

And so, in October 1962, we left England for pastures new.

I spoke very little German. My parents had often spoken it around the house, so the sound of the language was familiar, but I always had to ask to be taught certain phrases. By the time of my arrival in my new home I could request a glass of milk or a piece of bread with *leberwurst*, but that was about it.

Aunt Frieda and Uncle Johnny were very patient with me. Their son, Berthold, was a teacher. He supplied the German equivalent of several 'Janet and John' books, to help me learn my new language, and thankfully, as the human brain is wired to acquire language with ease in childhood, I made rapid progress.

I have been surprised at how useful my language skills have proven to be many times throughout my life, sometimes in the most unexpected way. Pardon me wafting off topic for a bit, but this is important to me.

We became involved with our local twinning association because a visiting rock band from Dillenburg, our twin town in Germany, needed accommodation with German speakers. We developed a close relationship with several of the band members, and are still in touch with some of them to this day. While I was working at a local factory, a team of German maintenance engineers had to attend to one of the machines on the production line. Guess who was called in to bridge the communication gap? The most bizarre incident occurred when, years later, I was running a limousine rental business. I picked up a family of Japanese tourists for a three day assignment. The two daughters spoke passable English, their parents however were more skilled in German. So there I was, driving an American stretched limousine on an English motorway with Japanese clients, chatting in German. Funny ol' life, innit?

Anyway, back to those early days in my new home.

I had been in Germany for just four weeks, and still living with my great aunt and uncle, when someone from the local school appeared at the front door. He delivered an official form which demanded that I attend school. Protestations about my still embryonic German needing to improve dramatically before that could be considered were ignored. The law was the law, and that is the German way.

Consternation was caused because I already had four years of school under my belt. In Germany, in 1962, children started school at the age of seven. I was nine, but academically I was in line with the fourth year pupils. It was decided that as I was as tall as they were, and had been at school as long as they had, I should join the fourth year class, even though I was two years younger than anyone else in that class.

Thrown in at the deep end, I knew no better, and simply absorbed everything I came into contact with. Within weeks my German was more than adequate to cope with the spoken parts of lessons. Written German took somewhat longer to reach the necessary standard, but by Christmas I was already well integrated into school life.

One little oddity arose in my first school report. All of my marks were acceptable, except one. In English, a compulsory subject, I was given an 'F' – a fail! How could I possibly have failed English when I was English, and it was my mother tongue? The teacher, with impeccable German logic, said that I had not demonstrated an ability to translate accurately into German and that, according to the rules, was a fail. In the end, thanks to intervention by Berthold and his teaching credentials, common sense prevailed and I was given a revised pass mark.

By the New Year my mother had found a place to live in a hostel for the homeless, the *Alsterdorfer Wohnlager*. It was considered an obligatory first step on the housing ladder, a stepping stone to a self-contained flat of our own. I joined her there soon afterwards.

Major redevelopment of that part of the city had already begun, so the hostel was already in its twilight years. The fifteen or so two storey buildings were spread across a large site. Each one consisted of four units, with four rooms per floor, allocated one room to a family. A small solid fuel stove served for cooking and heating. Two toilet cubicles and a single cold tap above a large sink on the landing were shared by the four families who lived on that floor. We lived, ate and slept in that one 4m x 3m room. It was my home for just over two years.

The one good thing about the hostel was that there were large open spaces between the buildings, so there was plenty of room for children to play.

One of the units was used as a childcare facility. We used to finish school at lunchtime, and because my mother worked full time this is where I would have lunch and do my homework, before returning home at 5pm.

When school broke up for the summer I spent all day there. It is also where I learned all about the facts of life.

Frau Wiechel, who was probably much younger than we thought her to be, and much less of a dragon than she at first appeared, was one of the carers. One day she overheard some of us boys telling 'rude' jokes, about subjects of which we knew absolutely nothing other than what we had heard from the older boys at school. She asked whether we would like to know where babies really come from. From our embarrassed mumblings she surmised that we were indeed extremely interested, and promised to explain all the next day, as soon as we had had lunch and finished our homework. Never in the field of human endeavour has lunch been eaten so quickly nor homework been done as diligently as it was that day.

We gathered in one of the rooms where Frau Wiechel had laid out books, charts and illustrations. She explained everything step by step, and answered all of our questions. She was so matter of fact that the whole business struck me as nothing out of the ordinary, and I neglected to mention it to my mother.

Some time later she and her then boyfriend, whom I didn't particularly like, thought it appropriate to broach the same subject. He braced himself for this momentous task by consuming more beer than was advisable before muttering about cows in the field climbing on each other's back and then handing me a copy of 'Fanny Hill' to read. His efforts were far from effective. My mother tackled the subject again a few days later and, thanks to Frau Wiechel, I was able to set her right on a few details.

While living in that hostel I was the butt of the 'weather' joke for the first time. Mother Guba, as she was affectionately known to all, was a grandmother who lived with her daughter and teenaged grandson in the room opposite ours. As wide as she was tall, she laughed as she asked, in German of course: "What's the weather like up there?"

I didn't actually get the joke at first. Yes, I was tall, heading as I was towards the six foot mark despite being only eleven years old, but to me it was normal. I had always been tall for my age, and saw nothing remarkable or unusual about it. It may have been the first time that I heard that joke, but it certainly wasn't the last.

The German education system is one which, in common with most other European countries, requires competence to be shown in a range of core subjects rather than excellence in a few selected ones. Although I was having no trouble with the academic content of lessons, my written German still had its weaknesses, in both spelling and grammar. It was therefore decided that I should attempt the entry exam for *Mittelschule* or *Realschule*, and aim for the *Mittlere Reife*. I was two years younger than anyone else taking that route, so in academic terms I was still way ahead of schedule. Although the entry exam for the upper school, the Gymnasium, wasn't that much harder, the academic, social and financial demands that would result from a pass were thought to be a little too much. Imagine the British equivalent as that of a boy from a local refuge attending a good public school on a financially unsupported scholarship, and you won't be far off.

I passed the exam and joined the *Sengelmannstrasse Realschule* in the spring of 1964, aged 11. The next youngest in class was eighteen months older than I, and yet I was nonetheless the tallest, albeit only just. The six foot mark was well within my sights, and I passed it the following year.

By this time my spoken German was such that no-one could tell that I wasn't a native. I had the local accent, which I still have to this day when I speak German. Nonetheless, I was still immensely proud of being British and holding a British passport.

My relationship with the class teacher, Frau Sass, was erratic, to say the least. I already had my own distinct opinions, and was not reluctant to express them. Few teachers found it easy to deal with a child who would constantly question accepted wisdom and want answers beyond those which lessons were meant to provide; Frau Sass most certainly didn't. She liked conformity, and that just didn't seem to happen with me. It wasn't always my fault either.

Occasionally I was summoned by a teacher of English in another class to translate a word that was not in their dictionary. I would stand in front of the class, translate the word, ensure that everyone had the pronunciation right, write it on the blackboard and return to my class. How many children do you recall being asked for help by other teachers? It didn't go down well.

My relationship with Frau Sass slowed my academic progress to a crawl. I did just enough to meet the minimum requirement to progress to the next class at the end of the school year. She was one of the old guard of teachers, one who liked things done the right way, i.e. her way. Any variance from this line resulted in her displeasure, and made school life generally uncomfortable.

I did display occasional flashes of excellence, but they were few and far between, occurring only when a particular subject or project interested me. One such was a talk each pupil was required to give on a particular species of bird. Most gave four or five minutes on whichever bird they had chosen, all of them domestic species; I chose parrots.

When my turn came, I took my place at the front of the class and spoke enthusiastically about the different species, their talents and abilities, their care as domestic pets, illustrating my talk with drawings and pictures. When I finished, I turned to Frau Sass who looked absolutely stunned. I thought for a moment that I had bombed totally, but after a few seconds she said: "I have no choice but to give you an 'A' for that." It was the pinnacle of my relationship with her.

Another teacher who did nothing to help my fragile confidence, and far from positive self-image, was our PE teacher, Herr Kölzow. He said that with legs like mine I should be able to run like the wind. But running the 100m, I would have had more use for a diary than a stopwatch. The only boy in class who was slower than I was Wilfried, who fought a constant battle with his weight. Those of us who lacked sporting or athletic prowess were not treated kindly.

The problem was that my muscle development simply couldn't keep pace with the rate at which I was growing. Imagine a twelve year old's muscles on a sixteen year old's body, and you're more or less there. I was gangly and uncoordinated, which meant I was also useless at basketball, providing yet another opportunity for ridicule by all and sundry. I could run around the court, or I could bounce and throw the ball, but mastery of both at the same time eluded me. To be fair, a couple of my classmates were sympathetic, and tried to be as supportive as they could, but it provided little comfort.

My mother's health had begun to suffer under the stresses and strains of recent years, and on two occasions she spent several weeks in hospital. I was delivered into the care of a children's home while she underwent treatment and convalesced afterwards.

The home was on the outskirts of the city, and so I attended a local school, where I experienced bullying for the first time. I outperformed everyone in the class, simply because the work they were doing I had done months before at my own school. This marked me out as a swot and teacher's pet. Being the tallest and the youngest in class, British, and a resident of the home completed the recipe, and after a couple of weeks of regular run-ins with one group of boys they decided it was time I was taught a lesson. They issued the threat of a beating, so I was naturally wary of venturing out alone that day for the journey back to the home after school.

Two boys came to my rescue, or so I thought. They offered to take me back to the home, one of them giving me a lift on the rear luggage rack of his bicycle. We set off, and all was well, until they came to a stop on a quiet lane still some way from the home. The group of boys stepped out from behind a hedge, and I was taunted and jostled until one of them pushed me to the ground, sat astride my chest and put in a couple of good punches to my ribs. Satisfied that their mission had been successfully completed they laughed and jeered as they all climbed back on their bikes and cycled off.

I don't remember much of the reaction back at the home when I told them what had happened. I recall only that I had never felt so lost and alone in my entire life.

In that home I also learned a distrust of anyone in authority. I was being boisterous, as 12 year olds are inclined to be, messing around with some of my fellow inmates. Our carer, a girl in her late teens or early twenties at best, stepped in to control matters, but we weren't going to give in easily. The carer shouted, we ignored her, that is, until a sharp slap caught me across the cheek causing instant order. To be fair, I probably deserved it. Perhaps our carer's inexperience was a contributory factor, and I know that many would find her actions inexcusable. The biggest blow was to my pride.

During a weekend visit home I related the story to my mother, who immediately contacted the home and complained. Upon my return I was summoned to see matron. The carer sat silently alongside her as she lectured me on the evils of lying and making false allegations. I insisted that I was telling the truth, but it soon became clear that whatever I said would make not one jot of difference. I apologised and thanked them for their understanding, as matron instructed me to do, and returned to my dormitory.

What I learned from that incident is that people in authority are not always as reliable and trustworthy as they make themselves out to be. It left me with distrust and, quite frankly, a distaste for all authority figures that remains with me to this day.

It may seem that those years in Germany were all a bit Oliver Twist and bowls of gruel but, let me assure you, they had their good side too. The German social care system was exceptional then, especially for children. The city maintained a number of holiday homes for socially disadvantaged children, and I was twice sent to the island of Sylt, near the Danish border, for a four week holiday in one of those homes, as well a having a couple of short breaks during the summer holidays in homes nearer the city. The long breaks were part of the health and social care programme, and included weekly health checks, the short breaks were designed to give stressed parents a break.

In 1966 we were finally allocated a small flat. A converted attic on the top floor of an apartment block in the suburb of Winterhude, it had two rooms, a kitchen and, for the first time, we had a toilet of our own. There was no bathroom as such, but at last the hostel was behind us. The living room doubled as my mother's bedroom, while I was allowed to arrange the other room to suit me. Foldable bed settees rather than beds were quite normal in small flats. The bedding fitted neatly into a compartment beneath the seat, and the whole thing folded flat when it was time for bed. Compared to what I had been used to this was luxury.

It meant a longer journey to school each day, but that was preferable to changing schools. As I was now well above six feet tall I was regularly challenged by the conductor on the trams I used to travel to school each day. They simply couldn't believe that I was entitled to travel for half fare, and I constantly had to prove my age. I must have been the only person in the city who had to carry his passport to travel on public transport!

Being further away from the school also meant less chance to socialise with my classmates, not that I was a particularly social animal anyway. There weren't many children where we lived, so I became even more of a loner. I was used to amusing myself, so it wasn't that important.

One day I saw an advertisement in a magazine for an electric guitar. It was white, and I was just getting into pop music. With my mother's blessing, I ordered it. I had found a job as delivery boy for a local grocery shop, which meant I could afford the ten monthly payments.

I couldn't afford lessons too, so when Aunt Frieda heard about the guitar she dismissed the whole thing as a dreadful waste of money. She said I would never learn to play properly without lessons. It was the greatest motivational speech she could have given me, and I spent many hours alone, practising chords and learning songs.

My grandfather, well step-grandfather actually, was an accomplished pianist and violinist, and had been a professional musician most of his life. He died when I was four, but I still remember him clearly. I'm told that when I was born he looked at my hands and announced to the family that I too would be a musician. I don't think I ever fully lived up to that prediction, but I hope that he wouldn't be too disappointed.

My height was becoming more of an issue as I progressed into teenage. Although younger than my classmates, I felt the usual pressure to fit in with the latest trends and fashions, but I was already at the upper limits of standard sizes. What I could afford was just that little bit too small and didn't look right, and so I felt even more excluded from anything resembling an 'in crowd', not that I ever felt really comfortable running with the herd.

The age difference also began to tell. I was taller than my classmates, albeit only just, and I looked the same age as they were, but the plain and simple truth is that I was different. My classmates were physically and emotionally just far enough ahead of me in their development that when they started to pair up as couples I felt even more excluded. They seemed so at ease with going on a date, and going to parties at which the lights would be dim and the dances slow. More than being just a loner, and I actually began to feel lonely.

I did try, so help me I did try, but my early approaches to girls were far from subtle, much less successful. Let's be honest here, they were ham fisted as hell, but then I was only thirteen while most of my classmates were fifteen.

I am nothing if not persistent and I kept on trying, even if it was only the girls' patience. It all came to a head one evening after a class outing, a classical music concert at a city centre venue. Once again I had earned a grade one brush off, when one of the girls let rip, telling me exactly what she thought of me. She pulled no punches, and although I was totally crushed and demoralised by her onslaught, it was one of the best things that ever happened to me.

A day or so later she approached me after school, and I thought I was about to get another helping of home truths. Instead, she apologised, and quietly explained what had caused her outburst. She changed my whole outlook on girls from that moment on. Her name was Sigrid. I shall never forget her, and shall be forever grateful to her.

She taught me that there was more to be gained from being friends rather than trying to be some sort of cool dude that I clearly wasn't and never would be. I know that this was a turning point in my life, one which has resulted in most of my closest friendships being with women. Yes, a man and a woman can be 'just good friends', and sex doesn't have to rear its ugly head to complicate matters. All it takes is a little appreciation and understanding of the individual, of who and what they are, rather than what they look like and whatever image they may be trying to convey.

I was fortunate to renew my acquaintance with Sigrid over 35 years later, and I reminded her of the incident. She had absolutely no recollection of it at all. It goes to prove that whatever we say to someone might not mean a lot to us at the time, but it may have a huge effect on them.

The change in attitude on my part led to new complications which arose when, as a more rounded and grown up 14-year-old, I went to a dance at a church hall. I saw a girl I really liked the look of and asked her to dance. She accepted and we did, several times. As it got later the music became slower, the dances closer, the room warmer and stuffier. We had to get some fresh air. I'm still not sure who suggested it first, but we were soon standing outside, leaning on a wall, watching the Alster river flow by as I slipped my arm around her waist.

"I mustn't be late tonight," she told me. "They close the door at midnight."

"Your parents," I asked?

"No, the nurses home," she said.

A cold hard hand gripped my heart and other assorted internal organs and squeezed, hard. "This must be what panic feels like," I thought.

She looked at me, and I knew she was expecting more than I knew how to do. I couldn't even bring myself to kiss her. All I could think of was that she was a seventeen year old student nurse, I was a fourteen year old schoolboy, and for both our sakes I couldn't tell her the truth.

It wasn't the only time that I found myself in a similar situation. In the bar on an overnight ferry I met a young man and two girls, aged about 18 or so. I was fifteen and wasn't about to let on either. My 6ft 5in stature did a first class job of camouflaging the truth, but once again I found that I was out of my depth when the music and dancing stopped.

The man had disappeared with the one girl, while I was getting along famously with the other. We took a walk on deck in the moonlight after which, like a proper little gentleman, I escorted her back to her cabin. I thanked her for a lovely evening, wished her a good night, made my excuses and went back to my own berth. The next morning her friend approached me to say that she had been quite concerned by my behaviour. Had she offended me, what was wrong? I assured her that nothing could be further from the truth, and made some feeble excuse about being tired, but I don't think she believed me.

When it came to the opposite sex I was a late starter in every way. The post concert bawling out had made me very cautious, almost painfully shy, with girls for many years afterwards.

It was during this time of rampaging hormones, sprouting hair and physiological change that I began to feel negatively about my height for the first time. I noticed that some girls would giggle as they looked across at me, and comments just loud enough for me to hear cut deeper than any knife ever could. This only ever happened where people knew me and knew how old I was, but I was blind to the significance of that fact.

I noticed magazine articles about very tall people who had operations to reduce their height, and read everything on the subject that I could find, which wasn't a great deal. The idea had its attractions, but the reality was clear: an operation to shorten my legs by removing a section of femur might require a series of similar operations on my arms, so that I would remain in proportion. It sounded extremely painful, and the pictures accompanying the articles didn't inspire a great deal of confidence in the possible results

Someone told me about a club for tall people that he had heard about. Apparently it could help with information on where to finds clothes, and to get discounts and the like. I eventually confirmed its existence, but only well after I had started the British Club. It's probably just as well I didn't have the German club as a blueprint. The fortunes of the Tall Persons Club GB & Ireland may well have been very different if I had.

My mother became increasingly concerned about my height. Even our GP thought it worth investigating, and I was referred to the Eppendorf Hospital for tests, lots and lots of tests. For several months I was tested, poked, prodded, measured and checked for more things than I can remember. The final diagnosis amounted to a well informed and highly scientific "Dunno."

My growth rate and everyone's concern reduced as I entered my sixteenth year, and I eventually reached something over 6ft 7in when I was sixteen. I finally topped out at my current 6ft 8in probably due to improved posture as my confidence grew in later years.

The only test of which I ever saw the result of was one of the IQ tests. It put me in the top 1% of the population, which suggests perhaps that my IQ was improved by my being in an environment requiring me to perform at a level two years ahead of my actual age; either that, or I was given the wrong envelope.

Having a decent IQ is not necessarily as good thing. Because I am usually able to deal with intellectual demands relatively easily and quickly I have not always been as tolerant as I should with people who find such things a little more difficult. Also, whilst I can apply myself to solving a complex theoretical problem, simple manual tasks can often leave me defeated and frustrated. Putting up a shelf will take three times longer than it would most people, it won't necessarily be straight, and whether it stays up has more to do with good fortune than my skill.

My self-confidence began to improve as my guitar playing skills improved. I was no virtuoso, that was for sure, but I could strum my way through a few popular songs from the charts.

In 1967 we went on a week long class trip to Detmold. Sigrid brought the acoustic guitar she had been given to celebrate her Confirmation. We took it along when we went on excursions, and soon I was the centre of attention, leading the singing of pop and folk songs as we walked. Suddenly I had positive status, and it felt good.

On the last night of the trip the girls sneaked out of their dormitories into ours. It was a just an ordinary 'get one over on the teachers' stunt, and they didn't stay long, but as they left some of them gave each of us a good night kiss. Only one gave me the briefest of pecks on the lips, but it was my first. She shall remain nameless, but not forgotten.

When we returned home Sigrid suggested that I have her guitar on loan, as I seemed to enjoy it so much. She was not as interested in playing it as I was. I had that guitar for months until her parents insisted that she ask for its return. It was so much better than the electric guitar, for which I didn't have an amplifier, and so couldn't hear clearly my many mistakes. At last I could hear properly what I was playing, and it aided my progress enormously.

My relationship with Frau Sass hit rock bottom in the autumn of 1967. We were in our final year, and I was looking forward to leaving school the following spring. They say that your school days are the best days of your life, and that you will look back on them with affection. Whoever said that was a bloody liar. I hated school and couldn't wait to leave.

German schools were very strong on *Klassenkameradshaft*, friendly social interaction with one's classmates, and Frau Sass wanted to know why I didn't become more involved.

"So are you complaining about your classmates," she asked?

"No, absolutely not," I said.

"Are you complaining about me then," she continued?

Everything in that moment was so wrong, and yet I couldn't help myself.

"Not necessarily," I said.

The classroom fell eerily silent.

In the moments that followed her face ran the full range of colours from white with a hint of pink via purple to vivid puce.

"Get your things and get out," she eventually managed to utter through clenched teeth. It was the last thing she ever said to me.

My mother was summoned to see the headmaster and my appalling misconduct was described to her in detail. Frau Sass demanded immediate expulsion, and a transfer to another school nearer my home. The headmaster agreed.

Buddhists say that when the student is ready the master will appear, and appear he did in the shape of Karl-Heinz Ebert, the class teacher of the year behind ours. He took us for history, so we had known one another for the past three years. He offered to take me into his year rather than see me expelled. Both Frau Sass and the headmaster strongly advised against it. They knew I was more trouble than I was worth, and did their level best to talk him out of it. He was undeterred, and so I joined his class the following week, where I was still both the youngest and tallest in class.

What a difference a teacher makes! I started to actually enjoy school for the first time in my life. He knew how to make learning interesting. Gone were the sessions of learning dry facts by rote, replaced by projects which required us to think for ourselves, to do research, to express our own opinions. What a revelation!

He acknowledged good work, never imposed his own opinions, but counselled caution when he thought it advisable. We were encouraged to be individuals.

My marks shot up, not because I was repeating work I had already done, but because I was enjoying myself, and wanted to please him.

PE continued to be the bane of my life, with Herr Laage taking over where Herr Kölzow had left off. The only time I ever received any positive acknowledgement from him was when I surprised him with a half decent time in the 50 meters breaststroke.

Swimming was one sport in which I could hold my own, even if I was never going to set any records. That said, I failed to gain one of the swimming awards we all aimed for. It was a multi-discipline test involving basic life saving. The first exercise required us complete 10m under water. Sounds easy, and most of my classmates found it so, but I kept coming up a meter or two short. I simply couldn't hold my breath for long enough to complete that short distance. It was not until many years later that I recognised this as the first sign of the health problems that would plague me later in life. These are, however, in no way linked to my height.

In almost any athletic or gymnastic pursuit I failed to perform as well as my peers. I would be out of breath long before any of them. Most could easily run a couple of laps of the football field, while I would be stopping for a breather before completing even one. None of this helped in my relationships with PE teachers until the retirement of Herr Laage and the arrival of Uwe Fortenbacher. I was still the tallest in class, but only just. Four of us had comfortably passed the six foot mark with me now less than half an inch clear of my nearest rival at just shy of 6ft 5in.

When Herr Fortenbacher walked into his first PE class with us his face lit up with the most enormous smile. He must have thought it was his birthday. Apart from being a teacher he was also trainer to a national league volleyball team. We must have been a dream come true, and at last I found a sport I could play on more or less equal terms. I still couldn't jump that well, but as we were the best part of a foot taller than most of our opponents it didn't seem to matter.

Things continued to get better. The annual school concert was due, and our music teacher asked me and two others to perform some songs together. On the big day I revelled in the feeling that I was being noticed not just for being the tall kid, but for doing something hardly anyone else could do. There was only one other boy in the school who played guitar, which he did better than I did, but he didn't sing, and that was the clincher.

After the concert, as I was leaving the assembly hall, some of the younger kids came running up and wanted to talk to me. Several of them even asked for my autograph – oh what joy! It may not be much in the overall scheme of things, but it all helped me on my way to a degree of self acceptance that I would not have thought possible before. The jokes became easier to tolerate and even ignore. I was actually happy.

Bullying was one of the consistent, but not overriding niggles throughout my school life. I was tall but neither strong nor coordinated. Taking down someone of my size was always going to be a feather in a bully's cap, and I soon learned that if I reported it to a teacher I would be met with an incredulous: "Oh come on, you are big enough to sort it out for yourself." Yet, if I struck out at the bully I was chastised for hitting someone so much smaller than I was. My solution to dealing with this particular Catch 22 was to keep out of situations in which bullying was likely to occur

My new class had its hard nut bully and sidekick, who quickly made my lowly status clear. I stayed out of their way as much as possible, but the sidekick continued to delight in taunting me at every opportunity, knowing that any resistance on my part would be easily dealt with by Mr 'Hard Nut' himself.

I was sitting quietly by myself in the lobby of our assembly hall one day, when the sidekick wandered over for some amusement. He stood taunting me about my height and kept poking me in the shoulder. I tried to walk away, as I always did.

"Just leave me alone," I said, as I got to my feet and stretched out my arm to push him aside.

A slight miscalculation in the height differential on my part led to my forearm not catching him across the chest, as I had intended, but firmly and squarely across the mouth instead. He was pole-axed. For the first time I actually saw fear I his eyes, as he turned and ran over to his master. I remained standing where I was, glowering in his direction. I knew this was going to lead to major trouble, and had no choice but to face it.

I watched as he showed the bully his mouth and lip, while gesturing frantically in my direction. The bully and I made eye contact, but I did not waiver. I still have no idea what overrode the basic instinct to run like hell, although I suspect the truth is based more in complete paralysis due to terror than in any kind of bravery. The bully looked away, and it was clear that he had no taste for a confrontation. Maybe it was my body language; perhaps he simply couldn't be bothered. I shall never know, but I was never again bullied at school.

This has led me to a simple conclusion: if you are being bullied, and you have exhausted all of the usual recommended avenues to a solution, then deck 'em, and deck 'em hard. You only need to do it once. If you get any flak for having done so, then so be it. You won't need to a second time.

I continued to flourish both academically and personally under Herr Ebert's guidance. He was the kind of teacher who valued the individual rather than to expect compliance with some mythical norm.

At the end of lessons one morning he asked me to stay behind. I thought I was in trouble when he asked me to step into the small side room off the main classroom and to sit down. He asked me how I was settling in to my new class, about my home life, he asked about me.

I have no idea how long we were there, but I do recall what he said as I prepared to head for home.

"Philip," he said, "You think differently to most people. But just because you think differently doesn't mean that you are right. It doesn't mean that you are wrong either, but it does mean that you are different. Many people will find that hard to deal with, and at times that will not be easy."

He continued: "Stop trying to hide your height. That also makes you different, but you cannot hide it. It is part of who and what you are. Be proud to be different, but learn to accept that not everyone will be comfortable with that difference. Remember too that if anyone judges you solely based on your height then they are not worthy of your time."

No-one had ever spoken to me like that before. Sure, I had been told to stand up straight, to not slouch and to be proud of my height, by lots of people, but this was different. The way he looked into my eyes as he spoke gave his words a meaning beyond words.

And so I entered my final year at school for the second time.

The highlight of the year was four weeks of work experience. Each of us had to find a position in the trade or profession we intended to take up when we left school. It was my ambition then to become an architect, and so I found a job with an industrial construction company, working on one of their larger sites. In Germany, becoming an architect required all candidates to serve a recognised three year apprenticeship in a building trade before beginning academic training as an architect, so it was the logical thing to do.

Three weeks into the scheme Herr Ebert visited all of his students at their place of work, to talk with their boss and to discuss their progress. I didn't know he was on site until one of the men shouted to me that the site foreman wanted me. I was busy driving the electric crane on top of the huge concrete mixing installation. It was a privileged position normally reserved for workers far more experienced than I was.

As I climbed out of the cab door and scrambled down the enormous pile of sand I spotted Herr Ebert standing with the site foreman. He had the biggest smile on his face I had ever seen. His pride was obvious. On work experience we were all expected to be given only the most menial of tasks. I was the stand out exception.

The company was so happy with my work they offered me a job whenever I wanted one, even during the holidays. I took full advantage of the offer, which boosted the coffers very nicely, thank you.

Back at school, Herr Ebert reported to the class on our respective work experience achievements. He made a point of how proud he had been to see me climb out of that crane, to know that I had honoured him and the school as much as I had myself in being trusted with such responsibility.

Coincidentally, both the bully and his side kick had also worked on building sites. Neither had been trusted with anything more exotic than a shovel and a broom. I was, of course, far too magnanimous to make anything of it; I didn't need to.

My height was becoming less of an issue, although I was still very conscious of it. Recognition for achievements was reducing the significance this obvious physical feature.

It is to my eternal regret that I was never able to tell Herr Ebert of the fantastically positive effect he had on my life. I visited Hamburg again in 1988, and tried to make contact, only to learn that he had passed away 18 months previously. I spoke with his widow on the telephone. She was asked whether I was sure that I had been in his class, as she did not recall my name from the list of leavers for that year.

I recounted the story of my proposed expulsion, and how he had intervened. She began to cry.

"You truly were in my husband's class," she said.

Mine was a story she had heard many times before. I was not the only disaster bound delinquent he had rescued from the brink. She told me how many of his former students had maintained contact and continued to visit him long after his retirement. He had been an inspiration in many a young life.

In 2006 I was fortunate to attend a class reunion, my first in 38 years, with the members of my original class. Frau Sass, now aged 85, was not present, due to failing health. I was recalling aspects of my rocky relationship with her to a former classmate when another chipped in from across the table.

"That woman caused me no end of trouble," he said. "She gave me a reference which said I was undisciplined and troublesome, and all because I had dared to kiss my girlfriend during a class outing."

Then others told of their own difficulties with her. It quickly became clear that I was not, as I had thought, the only one in class to not get along with her. The best that was said of her that evening was that she was ok, but no-one expressed any outright praise.

I then mentioned how Herr Ebert had been a positive effect on me, and it was like opening the floodgates. Even though he had only taught us for a few hours a week, many of my former classmates had happy memories and positive recollections of him.

"Now, that was a teacher," said one. "I wish I had been with him the whole time."

Time can play nasty tricks with memory, and I often wondered whether I had exaggerated the difficulties I had with Frau Sass, and over estimated the significance of Herr Ebert. I was wrong on both counts. She really does seem to have been Satan's gift to teaching, while he was the antithesis of everything she stood for.

Bless you, Herr Ebert, for the difference you made to more young lives than you ever knew.

Standing Taller

I have had contact with countless people who put their childhood and teenage difficulties down exclusively to their height, whether directly or indirectly. The attitudes they learned in childhood were then carried into adulthood, where they continued to affect that person's life. But things aren't always as they appear.

I was a loner who made few close friendships. I experienced isolation and prejudice, and was extremely self-conscious. But was it all down to my height? Almost certainly not.

I was effectively a German child in post war Britain. It is no surprise that some people viewed me as 'child of the enemy' and taught these attitudes to their children. Some of the children taunted me, calling me a Nazi. I don't blame them. The war was less than 20 years in the past. Most of the adults I had contact with would have lived through the war, whether on active service or as a resident of one of the cities bombed by German planes.

Thanks to my unreliable father we moved frequently, so I didn't learn to form close friendships in childhood. I spent most of my time with adults, and didn't really develop normal childhood social skills until much later. I was blessed, or cursed depending on how you view it, with above average intelligence, which set me apart from most of my peers. This was exacerbated by my love of reading and thus more extensive knowledge of subjects they cared little about. When I settled in Germany both my name and quickly acquired language skills could have easily concealed my British background, but I was proud of it and did nothing to hide it. Doubtless some people would have seen me as a child of one of the countries that had vanquished and now controlled part of their homeland. My mother was often ill, so I spent several spells in temporary care in children's homes, resulting in lack of continuity in other parts of my life, and again interrupted relationships with both my peers and with adults. Living in a hostel put me firmly at the bottom of the social ladder.

The above is probably enough of a recipe for lack of self-confidence and extreme self-consciousness, without my unusual height even entering the equation.

I do not think of it as having been an underprivileged childhood. I knew no different. To me it was normal. Yes, I was aware that most other kids had nicer homes and settled families, but that was them, and I was me. That's just the way it was, and I felt no resentment or ill will towards anyone.

Some tall people learn to feel negatively about their height because of the inappropriate behaviour of their own family. I have known too many cases in which what started out as good natured teasing eventually became so routine to the perpetrators that they failed to see the enormously negative effect it was having on the child. When confronted, the response was: "They know I don't really mean it. They don't mind."

Reality check, people: the youngster didn't know that you didn't mean it, and they did mind. In fact they hated it. It made them feel worth less than their siblings, different in a bad way, unattractive and, worse still – and I hate the word – freakish! I have known families continue this kind of treatment well into the child's adulthood, so much part of their normal behaviour had it become. Adulthood doesn't make it any easier to tolerate.

One family I knew had two daughters, one of whom had been affected by a height related medical syndrome. By the time we met she had undergone countless operations and medical procedures, finished school, gained professional qualifications and had a good job. At a family gathering to which I was invited along with several other Club members her mother introduced her to some friends and then introduced her sister: "…and this is our normal daughter."

It was one of those rare occasions on which I bit my tongue.

Parents can be a direct cause of a tall child's poor self image and lack of confidence. One mother, when out clothes shopping with and for her daughter, would moan constantly that her height made it so difficult to find clothes easily, that what she could find was expensive, and that life would be so much easier and cheaper if only her daughter weren't so damned tall! Now there's a mother I would have loved to grasp warmly by the throat and shaken vigorously until blue.

The negative feelings that mother created in her teenage daughter were still at work when the then 35 year old woman told me the story.

Yes, there are cases in which unusual height is a real cause of all sorts of difficulties for the tall individual. However, in my experience, those cases are almost always linked to a physiological cause for the height, such as one of the medical syndromes described in a later chapter. Fact is that the majority of tall people are so for genetic and environmental reasons, not because of some sinister underlying cause.

So you see, while my height has without question influenced who and what I am it is not, nor has it ever been, the sole determining factor. We are all complex individuals, the product of almost infinite variables which come together in unpredictable ways in the great scheme of things to make us who we are. We must guard against using height as an excuse just because it is so visible.

One of the great things about being different is that you tend to gravitate towards others who are also different, but in a different way. Whether that is by coincidence or just some indefinable attraction I don't really know. I mention this because where we lived there was only one other boy of a similar age to me. His name was Horst, and he and I seemed to get along just fine.

There is absolutely nothing strange about the name Horst, which is a common German given name. It was his hobby that was a tad unusual, a pastime he pursued in his cellar, which had been especially converted to accommodate his needs, and an activity that he wanted to take up professionally.

Horst was a dedicated and enthusiastic taxidermist. An otherwise perfectly sane and likeable 16 year old, he occupied his spare time by stuffing assorted materials into animal carcasses donated by local park wardens. Squirrels were his most frequent subjects, but a fair range of birds, rabbits and the odd fox also found themselves preserved for posterity, courtesy of Horst.

I helped him out a few times, and learned something of the taxidermist's art, but it never excited me quite as much as it did him. It was interesting, but the most positive result of knowing Horst was that he introduced me to Andreas.

Andreas was seventeen and had spent time living in India where his father had worked as an aircraft engineer with Lufthansa. As a result he spoke better English than most and was familiar with cricket. He had his own bat too, which he gave me as a present when he and his family moved away a few months later. I still have it, cracked now and beyond practical use, but I can't bring myself to throw it away, sentimental old fool that I am. We lost touch when he moved, but those few months were among the most enjoyable of my teenage years.

Andreas was a member of a local rowing club, and introduced me to the sport. We spent many summer weekends on the lakes, rivers and canals of Hamburg, and I was delighted to have found yet another sport at which I could hold my own. But all those miles of waterway spoiled me. No half mile stretch of river could hold the same appeal, and so my interest waned after I left Hamburg.

He also had a moped, a 50cc Zündapp with a pillion seat. Often we would go off on the moped to wherever the mood took us. We went no great distance, but then Hamburg is a big city, and as the outskirts of the city were changing rapidly as the city grew, there was always a lot to explore and investigate.

Only once during our all too brief friendship did my height become relevant. We were on our way home after one such outing. It was getting dark, a fine drizzle had begun to fall, and we were starting to feel the cold. I huddled up on the pillion as Andreas guided us expertly though the traffic. At a set of lights I felt the need to adjust my trousers, which were damp and sticking uncomfortably to my legs. I put my feet on the floor and stood up to make the necessary adjustments, when the lights changed. Andreas casually put the moped in gear and took off from between my legs, leaving me standing there in the middle of the traffic, much to the amusement of the other drivers. He had travelled a good 50 meters or so before he realised that the little Zündapp was performing far better than it had all day, and turned to see me still standing there, feet apart, at the lights, doing a fair impersonation of a bollard.

He made a quick U turn and came back to fetch me. By the time he got to me we were both so helpless with laughter that neither of us could do anything other than lean on the bike while the traffic continued to pass around us. We made it to the kerb where it took another couple of minutes for us to regain our composure sufficiently to continue our journey.

By the time the summer holidays came I was completely settled in my new class under Herr Ebert, and looking forward to a brighter happier future.

I knew what I wanted to do when I left school, and an apprenticeship was mine for the asking.

For the previous three years I had spent the summer holidays with my sister in England, and was looking forward to doing so again. Her husband, Tom, had left the army, and they had settled in his home town of Hereford.

A couple of days after my arrival Helen took me aside and broke the news. My mother was still not enjoying the best of health and she was finding life ever more difficult and stressful. She had asked Helen to confiscate my return ticket, and to keep me in England. It had all been arranged, and I was to live with her and the family for the foreseeable future. She told me that she wasn't happy about the way this had been sprung on me, and that it was ultimately my decision. She didn't think it fair that I hadn't been told, let alone given a choice.

It came as a complete bombshell. I had no idea that my mother had planned all of this without ever mentioning it to me, or consulting me. I felt deceived, betrayed even. My relationship with her was never the same again.

I made the decision more or less immediately. If she didn't want me then there was no point in going back. I handed over my ticket. Helen granted me that dignity for which I shall always respect her.

It was many years later, long after she too had returned to Britain, that my mother told me how the Social Services in Germany had wanted to take me in to long term care, because they were concerned for my well-being. It wasn't as though I was in great need of looking after. Because of my mother's poor health I had learned to cook and keep house, and was perfectly capable of taking care of myself and her if necessary, but I was only 15 after all.

As the summer holidays drew to a close I enrolled at the local technical college, Helen and Tom became my legal guardians, and I prepared to get my life back on track.

It never happened. Somehow the drive had gone. I was studying for several 'O' levels, but architects' training is very different in England, and the desire to pursue that ambition waned. I was lost, feeling unwanted, unloved, and very alone. My sister did everything she could, and I was very much part of the family, but something inside me had gone, and to this day I can't tell you what it was.

I did become more socially active, getting involved with the nearby youth club and, by default, the local church pantomime. It was another small step for Phil the performer. The first pantomime saw me cast as a minor romantic hero, who played his guitar and sang to the princess in *Aladdin*. She still went off with him in the end though; women! While rehearsing for the show I became very close to one of the girls in the cast. Things went along swimmingly, until I was unceremoniously dumped when she realised that I was eighteen months younger than she was.

The following year I was asked to take part in the pantomime again. Our director, Peter Lind-Jackson, was a curate at the church. I was not a churchgoer, but his attitude that people leading a meaningful and productive life was more important than whether or not they attended church endeared him to me and many other parishioners. At the casting he revealed his plans to make our production of *Humpty Dumpty* truly unique. Not for him the loveable portly little character we all know so well. Instead, Humpty was to be the villain, and everything the audience would not expect him to be. Yes, I was cast as Humpty Dumpty! I drew on every bit of acting skill and hideous green and red face make up to be the most evil, despicable and hateful Humpty there ever was, but the kids loved me; and I loved performing.

I didn't enjoy college that much so, when my sister told me how much of a financial strain the family was under, it was an easy decision to leave college and find a job. I briefly considered a career in the army, but was advised strongly against it by, of all people, the army recruitment officer. By-passing the usual 'we can teach you how to kill foreigners in lots of exotic places and interesting ways' stuff, he suggested I complete my studies, take a few 'A' levels, and then join the army. According to him, I would attend University on an army scholarship and then go to Sandhurst. When I mentioned that my parents were both German he did an about turn. It would make me too much of a security risk, he told me, and I would never progress beyond the rank of Captain. He was sure that I would find such an obstacle to progress frustrating and should, for my own sake, forget about the armed forces.

In August 1969 I started work at the local poultry processing plant, fondly known as 'The Chicko'. I was the lowest of the low, a factory floor worker, doing mindlessly repetitive tasks in exchange for a not overly large wage packet and a cheap chicken on Fridays. Oh, how my life had changed, from having potentially a glittering military career to standing knee deep in blood, guts, and miscellaneous detritus. Spot the difference?

The complex group dynamic within a factory will always lead to cliques and gangs forming, and I knew it was inevitable that my height would attract attention. It was a foregone conclusion that I would end up with some sort of height related nickname. I decided that rather than wait to see which of the predictable choices I would be lumbered with I would pre-empt them and choose my own. I grabbed a marker pen and labelled my protective apron first with my clock number, as we all did, and added in large letters below it 'Tich'. It was the name of a character I recalled from an old comic as well as the name of a member of the sixties group Dave Dee, Dozy, Beaky, Mick & Tich. Coincidentally, the first single I ever bought had been *Bend It* by that same group.

It worked; the name stuck and people seemed to like the fact that I was ready to take the micky out of myself. Funny how these things can linger in the mind though. Many years later, long after I had left the factory I was in a Chinese take-away with my wife, Carol, when a girl looked across and shouted "Hi Tich, how you doing?" Carol burst out laughing. She didn't know about that nickname, which no-one had used since those days at "The Chicko".

I was subject to a brief bout of bullying again, courtesy of the 6ft 4in charge-hand of a neighbouring section, who I think saw my 6ft 8in stature, as it was by then, as my attempt to usurp his role as dominant male. After a few verbal run-ins he threatened to give me a good beating outside the factory gates after work. I responded with: "Fine, just as long as you realise the amount of damage I can do to your fists with my face." Everybody laughed, he grunted and walked off. For some reason he had to work overtime that evening. The confrontation never took place.

Many years later we met again when he was with his wife and then grown up daughter. I reminded him of the incident, but he had no recollection of it, nor even of me. In a way, I felt slightly offended that I should be so forgettable. His wife however said: "Yes, that sounds like him. I soon put a stop to that when we got together." The 6ft 4in, 15 stone bully was tamed by a 5ft 2in, 8stone woman, a case of 'Love shall tame the savage beast' or something like that.

After a couple of months at the factory my supervisor took me aside and told me that a new quality control laboratory was about to come into service. Would I be interested in a job there instead? It meant working on microbiological and chemical samples of the processed meats, the water supply, factory environment and even from members of staff in the new cooked meats department. It was a salaried position, and I would be expected to attend the local college on day release and full pay for further training.

"You are wasted here," he said. "You're not like this lot. You can do better."

I transferred to the laboratory not long afterwards.

My guitar playing had been progressing nicely. It was still a mainly solitary pursuit, although I did occasionally play when among friends. One of our regular haunts was a pub which had live music every Friday, Saturday and Sunday. It was just an organist, a drummer and a singer/guitarist who doubled as a sort of compere, playing the standards while people danced, but it was a pleasant enough night out. I was still a relatively shy seventeen year old who hadn't yet graduated to Discos. As you may have guessed, I have never been challenged in a pub about my age.

One evening, while I was at that pub with some mates from the factory, the compere announced that a guest singer would be appearing. I was happy about that, as it would make a nice change from the same old stuff week in and week out. When the time for his break came, the compere began his introduction of the much anticipated guest. "Ladies and gentlemen," he said, "Will you please welcome Phil," and pointed to me. I had been well and truly set up.

My friends laughed, I was both stunned and terrified. I was handed a guitar and took my place behind the microphone. My kneecaps were physically jiggling out of control, and I could barely stand. I had always thought the idea of knees knocking in terror was a cliché, but there I was, living proof that it was uncomfortably true.

I gave it my best, and played three songs to decent applause. As I left the stage an attractive young woman stepped into my path. I had seen her there before, but knew she was way out of my league.

"I did enjoy that song you did," she said. "It's one of my favourites."

I mumbled a thank you of sorts. Then she reached out, placed her hand on my arm looked me straight in the eyes and said: "Will you dance with me later? I simply adore tall men."

Who said that being tall isn't the most fantastic thing that could happen to a guy? Wow! My posture improved more in that one second than at any other time in my life. She was gorgeous, and she wanted to dance with me!

I became a regular guest artist at that pub, my repertoire expanded, my appearances became longer and more popular. Even at that lowly level musicians attract a lot of attention form the opposite sex, and it was not long before I became a proper fully grown up man. What am I talking about? Oh, work it out for yourselves. What do you want - a diagram?

I started doing gigs at other venues, and before long was making almost as much from a couple of gigs a week as I did from my full time job. My height was no longer my defining feature. Instead of being the tall guy I became the singer who happened to be tall. In fact my height became secondary in defining who I was. I had a career in food technology and microbiology as well as being a part time professional musician and entertainer. I bought a motorbike and a year later moved up to my first car - a Mini van! I had a girlfriend; I was independent and free to make my own way, to make my own choices. The fact that I was unusually tall mattered not one jot. Not, that is, until I started the Tall Persons Club many years later, at which point my height effectively became the focus of my life. You could almost say that being tall became my profession.

Clothing was the only bug-bear. I didn't discover any of the specialist clothing suppliers until I was in my mid twenties. I couldn't get trousers or jeans to fit, and most shirts, coats and jackets were less well fitting than I would have liked. It's my legs that are disproportionately long and mainly responsible for my unusual height, but my upper body can be clothed reasonably well with a little determination and perseverance.

I cannot honestly say that my height was in any way significant in my life from this point on. I couldn't change it, so I stopped worrying about it. Yes, it was commented on and joked about, but I had learned a few answers to the usual jokes. Once I got into conversation with people it was my personality rather than my height that determined their perception of me.

That said, my height has been the cause of a few incidents, some of which still make me smile. I needed a coffee break on my way home from a trip to London, and stopped at a small pub near Chepstow. I was standing at the bar, enjoying my caffeine fix, when a man sidled up to me and enquired about my height. Nothing unusual in that, but he was determined to know exactly how tall I was, to the last fraction of an inch. I confirmed my exact height to him several times, before he gave me a big smile, thanked me profusely and vigorously shook my hand. He made his way back to where his companions were sitting, shouted "I win,", and raked a large pile of silver from the table. I wouldn't have minded, but he didn't even offer to buy me a drink!

Some years later, I worked at the Ideal Home Exhibition for a shower installation company. I was standing quietly next to one of the exhibits when two women stopped to take a closer look. They paid no attention to me as they twiddled knobs and examined fixtures.

I gave them a few moments, then said: "It's nice, isn't it?"

One of the women shrieked, jumped back a couple of steps, and clutched her hand to her chest. "Oh my god, I'm sorry," she said. "I thought you were a mannequin."

It is the only time in my life that I have been mistaken for a shop window dummy.

Sometimes the comments can be incredibly personal and potentially hurtful. I had stopped at a pub after work to have a coffee before heading for home. I used the place regularly and was known to the bar-staff and landlord. A group of young men came in and the leader of the pack decided to demonstrate his status by cracking a joke at my expense. I came back with a suitable response, and his mates all had a good laugh at how I had got the better of him. We started talking and he apologised, saying that I must have heard them all before. The conversation quickly moved to matters non-tall, and a lively discussion ensued about I can't remember what.

Suddenly the man looked at me and: "You know what? You're really quite intelligent, aren't you?"

The conversation died an instant death. You could have heard a pin drop. I just smiled, while his friends looked absolutely horrified. He realised what he had said, how it sounded, and began to apologise profusely, stuttering and stammering as he tried to recover from his gaffe.

It's not uncommon for people to assume that just because someone does not meet their expectations of what is physically 'normal' their mental abilities must also be different. Wheelchairs users will know this as the 'Does He Take Sugar' syndrome, in which people will talk to whoever is pushing the chair rather than the person in it.

Upon meeting Carol and me for the first time, many a person has made a height related comment to me before turning to Carol to say something like: "You must have terrible trouble getting clothes for him. How does he manage in a bed?"

Carol usually responds with: "Why don't you ask him?"

But that's not all they want to know. Some people are intrigued by how we manage, "…you know, 'it'…", and will ask us outright. Carol has her stock answers, none of which I can repeat here without putting a statutory warning on the cover. Let's just say that the good Lord knew what he was doing when he put the working parts in the middle, as it halves the height difference at a stroke. For the people who want to know whether I am all I proportion – and yes, they really do ask - I reply: "Thank Goodness I'm not. I wouldn't want to be 8ft 3in."

With the passing years, of course, the fascination with our reproductive habits has lessened as we attained the age beyond which the very idea of us indulging in such things became nausea inducing; according to most teenagers, about 35.

And that's another thing: why do people feel it's alright to say to someone, "Gosh, you're tall, aren't you?" (as if we didn't already know) when they wouldn't dream of saying, "Good grief, aren't you fat?" Political correctness, it would seem, has not yet reached the world of the tall person.

That said, my height has also had very positive effects. While working for a small Leeds based jewellery manufacturer, the sales manager and I were staying in an hotel on a sales trip. One evening, over dinner, the subject of my height came up.

"It's one of your greatest assets," he told me. "We must have interviewed 60 people when we came to Hereford. We had already seen about twenty people by the time you walked in. You got the job the instant you walked through the door. As soon as I saw you I knew I was going hire you. You were so confident and self-assured; great posture and you looked the part. Yours was the longest interview of the day. After we saw you, we got rid of most of the other candidates in five to ten minutes each. It was a waste of time seeing them actually."

He went on to tell me how one of the candidates claimed to have 20 years selling experience. When asked which markets he had worked in he answered: "Oh no, it wasn't a market, it was a proper shop."

Somehow I wish he hadn't told me that. I would have preferred to think I had won the job against stiff competition.

On reflection, I have often I have heard variations on that theme.

"You don't actually look as tall as you are, because you carry yourself so well."

"When you first walk in, the reaction is 'bloody hell', and within seconds it's 'wow'. You just look the business."

I don't mention this only to illustrate that the way a tall person presents themselves makes all the difference as to how they are perceived. I hope there's a lesson in this for those who have not yet reached the stage of being comfortable with who and what they are.

I like being different, and being noticed. When I enter a room full of people I don't know, someone will always come and talk to me. Yes, it usually starts off with a comment about my height, but the subject quickly changes. I can honestly say that I would hate to be any shorter than I am.

This is me, and I like me just the way I am, warts and all.

By the time I was 20, I had become bored with the work in the laboratory. It had become routine, and I felt myself descending into a rut. I wanted something different, something more challenging. My girlfriend and I split up, as much as anything because she was ready to settle into a certain future of wedded bliss and all that entails; I, on the other hand, most definitely wasn't.

My new girlfriend was almost four years older than I was, and had three children. My sister and her husband disapproved strongly and so, in one of those curious twists that life sometimes throws our way, I moved in with my new girlfriend and her family. I must have done something right in our time together because Keith, her son, and I are still in regular contact to this day.

I tried running my own business without a great deal of success, took various jobs just to pay the bills, and eventually drifted into selling as a career. I had always enjoyed a little wheeling and dealing, so selling had already been in the back of my mind as a second option to architecture. I joined General Foods, the makers of Maxwell House coffee, as a trainee representative. Very soon my boss began to extol the virtues of promotion, moves to other parts of the country, and generally mapped out my career for me. It didn't feel as good as perhaps it should have.

I liked Hereford. After six years I had put down roots, and I didn't want to move. It was the longest I had lived anywhere and I liked the feeling of having a place to call home for the first time in my life. Even today, when returning from a trip, I can feel myself relax as I come over the brow of the hill to see the city nestling in the valley below.

Hereford is a funny old place. I have met many people who washed up here by accident and ended up settling. Among others, our GP came to Hereford to complete six months of general practice as part of his training. He wanted to become a consultant paediatrician at a major London teaching hospital. After a few months he noticed that he was calmer, his wife was calmer, even his children seemed more settled, so he decided to extend his contract by six months. That was 37 years ago; he retired earlier this year. His is not an isolated story, and part of the reason why Hereford is known to many as 'The Graveyard of Ambition'.

I left General Foods, despite persistent efforts to change my mind by my bosses, who were convinced that I had what it took to reach the upper echelons of management. More short lived jobs followed, including the one with the jewellery company.

My mother got married again in 1976, to a delightful Scotsman called George. He and I got on wonderfully well, but my mother's happiness was to be short lived, as George died just eight months later. At around the same time my girlfriend and I split up, and I was single again.

Eventually I landed a job selling chemical products in the automotive industry. It was commission only, and my customers ranged from small one man outfits to large dealerships with several outlets. The company was owned and run by Dave Rayson, who had himself begun as a salesman in the industry, before starting his own company. A tremendous teacher, I learned a great deal from him about selling, marketing and man management, skills that would serve me well many times later in life. The company regularly brought out new innovative products and ways to market them. The selling environment was constantly changing, and it kept my interest for longer than any other job I had done.

Dave was another who acknowledged the positive side of my height.

"Looking the way you do, they won't always remember the company you are with, but they will always remember you," he told me.

Periods of earning good money were interspersed with less lucrative times, when routine set in again. The launch of a new product or marketing programme would always motivate me anew, but never for very long. Dave Rayson described it as my 'get by mentality'. I would always make enough money to meet my commitments, but never work so much that I didn't have time to spend doing the things I enjoyed doing most. If the truth be told, for much of my thirteen years with that company I don't suppose I really worked more than 25 hours a week. I knew that if I needed to, I could make £800-£1000 in a week to pay some bills, and then take it easy for a couple of weeks. That may not sound like a huge amount today, but in the mid 1980's it was serious money.

The boredom caused by routine was responsible for me briefly leaving the chemical company, and working in direct sales, for the shower installation company I mentioned earlier. That lasted a couple of years, after which I returned to my former company and sales area.

I was still gigging regularly, and making good money from it, although the money was less important than the pleasure it gave me. Music might easily have played a much larger part in my life, were it not that I value it as my main recreation and relaxation. I could have become a full-time musician several times, especially when I was offered the chance to tour the Continent with a band and to make solo appearances as part of the same tour; but it just didn't feel right. A couple of times over the years I got into the routine of doing so many gigs that I stopped playing for pleasure. The gigs became more like work than fun, so I simply stopped doing them for a while, until the desire to play in public again returned.

I eventually became involved with a programme on my local BBC radio station, writing, recording and producing jingles and novelty songs for the presenter. I also appeared on the programme many times, playing live, and sometimes as an honorary member of the production and presenting team. It wasn't my first encounter with radio, as I had worked on the local Hospital Radio station for a few months as well as becoming involved with the CB radio craze of the early 80s. BBC Hereford and Worcester was later hugely influential in the launch and growth of the TPC.

I didn't realise then how the various skills I had acquired and was continuing to acquire in different areas of my life would ultimately combine to help make the Tall Persons Club the influential organisation it was to become.

My thirst for knowledge generally made learning huge amounts of new information a pleasure rather than a chore. Performing both live and in radio studios stood me in good stead when I made media appearances. Selling advertising for the Club's publications came easily, as I had worked in sales for most of my working life. Without my German language skills communication with several other European clubs would have been difficult. The European committee meetings and events were also easier to cope with, and more enjoyable, because I spoke the same language as most of those taking part. I could go on, which I would normally do, but I won't.

From my early twenties onwards, the only time that my height made a real difference to my life was when I met Carol. She was always attracted to tall men, although her track record with boyfriends doesn't always bear that out. I don't even clearly remember our first meeting although, courtesy of my height, she does.

It was March 1977, I lived in a rather splendid flat which good fortune had brought my way, and I was single. In the course of the weekend I developed a strange rash on all of my joints. It was sore and very hot to the touch, made my joints stiff, and the large raised red blotches gave me cause for concern. On the Sunday morning the discomfort was so bad that I went to the casualty department of our local hospital. A doctor peered at the rash but was unable to give a definite diagnosis. He suggested an injection of antibiotics, and left me in the cubicle while he went to instruct a nurse accordingly. I stood waiting in the cubicle after dressing, with my head showing above the curtain. The nurse in charge saw me and thought I was messing about, standing on either the bed or on a chair. She strode over to put me firmly in my place, yanked back the curtain, and came face to chest with yours truly. Taken aback, she just said "Oh," and closed the curtain again. Shortly afterwards another nurse gave me an injection in my backside, and I went home.

A few weekends later I was at home reading when my flatmate, John, returned from a day out with some friends. I knew two of them, but not the young woman they had with them. They all settled down, and I figured someone ought to offer hospitality and got up to make a coffee for everyone. As I did so the young woman looked across and said: "I know you. You were in casualty a while back and I gave you an injection in the backside for a weird rash."

To this day I maintain she was attracted by the smile on my cheeks.

Carol, for it was she, and I got talking, and when John and the others headed off to the pub for the evening Carol chose to stay behind. We sat and talked until she went back to the nurses' home in the small hours.

We became friends but, because she was in a relationship at the time, we never dated. For the next five years fate conspired to ensure that whenever one of us was not in a relationship the other was. We remained the proverbial 'just good friends'. Whenever one of us had a break up, and we both had a few of those, we would turn to the other for solace and comfort. A partner had to accept that we were friends, and if they didn't like it, that was just too bad. Our friendship brought a premature end to relationships for both of us.

In 1981 Carol split from her then boyfriend. It was an acrimonious split, and she decided it was time to leave Hereford and to start again in another city. She applied for and got a job at the Kent & Canterbury Hospital, and made arrangements to move to Canterbury, where her parents also lived. The night of her going-away party I realised how much I was going to miss her, and told her so.

"I really don't want you to go," I told her.

"So what are you going to do about it," she asked?

In that moment I could think of only one solution.

"Will you marry me," I asked?

50

"Yeah, alright then," she said, and the rest is history.

We were so excited by this out-of-the-blue change in our relationship that we began phoning our friends at 2.15 in the morning.

"About time; talk to you tomorrow," was the most surprised reaction from anyone! It seems that all of our friends were expecting it sooner or later. Even Carol's parents took the news in their stride when we told them.

"Since Carol left home there has been only one man we have heard about consistently, and that's you," her father told me. "We thought you probably would get together in the end."

I like to think that it isn't only my height that attracted Carol, but either way I am glad that it did. We have been together for over twenty-five years, over twenty of them married, had our share of ups and downs, and come through them all. I am happy to be with her, and would be lost without her. She has backed me in many a madcap scheme or idea, including the day I called a TV show to tell my story about what it means to be taller than most. What followed that TV appearance would have sent many a woman screaming to the divorce courts. She took it in her stride, and has become every bit as much part of the Tall Persons Club as I or any other member.

Carol still moved to Canterbury as planned, and we began almost a year of travelling to see one another at weekends. It was more often than not easier for me to travel to Kent, but at least once a month she would arrange her days off to allow her to travel to Hereford. By the end of 1982 we figured that if we were going to make our relationship work long term it would be easier if we both lived in the same place.

She moved back to Hereford in time for Christmas and so we began our life together.

The Times they are a Changing

By 1984 my income had grown sufficiently for us to buy our first house together, the one that would become Tall Club headquarters a few years later.

Carol was unable to find employment in the local hospitals, and so had registered with a local nursing agency. She worked consistently, from doing occasional hospital shifts to a variety of private assignments, which occasionally took her away from home for weeks at a time. The latter has provided her with a wealth of anecdotes which would easily fill a book. But that is a book she will have to write for herself.

In 1987 our friend Barbara from Trinidad came to visit. We had played host to her son, Peter, for several months while he was at college. A former actress, she had returned to Trinidad after the death of her husband. Every couple of years or so she would return to the UK to take part in a play, and then visit us for a couple of weeks after the play ended its run. She used our place as a base from which to visit family and her friends from her days at the Bristol Old Vic. We quickly became accustomed to the voices on the phone asking for Barbara being ones we already knew well from countless TV shows.

She invited us to Trinidad as her way of saying thank you for the hospitality we had shown Peter. Carol went for seven weeks. I joined her for the last three weeks of her holiday, and we got married in the Red House in Port of Spain the day before we returned.

Trinidad is an amazing place. Being such a small country, things work very differently there. In order to comply with residency qualification I had to extend my stay by two days, which meant that I would not be returning to the UK until the day after my visa expired. To me, this was a potential problem, but not to Barbara.

She picked up the telephone and dialled.

"Hello, Jimmy," she said, and began a lively conversation which proved that they knew each other well. After a while she explained my situation, seemed to find some kind of solution, agreed to meet up for lunch very soon, and hung up.

"That's sorted," she said. "If you are stopped by immigration at the airport just tell them that Jimmy Williams *(name changed due to my faulty memory)* says it's alright."

"And that will impress them," I asked?

"It should do," said Barbara. "He's the Minister for Immigration."

Now I was impressed.

"Oh yes," she continued, "we go back many years. He asked me to marry him several times, but I always turned him down."

Yes, things do work very differently in Trinidad.

My experiences there would fill several chapters, but they will have to wait until another time.

I am the first to admit that I had trouble settling into married life. I felt as though in gaining a wife I had lost my friend. It took a while but Carol's tenacity made sure that it all worked out in the end. Details are irrelevant – it's not a time I am either proud of or want to remember, so let's leave it at that.

The following year I made my first visit to Germany in almost 20 years. I went to the town of Kleve, near the Dutch border to play in a chess congress. I was a member of a club in Worcester, which is twinned with Kleve, and the congress was part of their twinning celebrations. The events lasted four days, and when our contingent returned to England I set off on my own to visit my former home, Hamburg.

I had another reason to make the trip. Some years prior, while helping my mother to move to a new flat, I had come across a document among her papers with the name and address of a Werner Heinricy. When I asked who he was she told me he was my uncle. I never forgot the details. The address was only an hour or so from Kleve and close to my route to Hamburg, so it was too good an opportunity to miss.

I found the house easily. It was a strange feeling to see my surname, which is after all far from the most common name in the world, on someone else's door. I rang the bell, and a man answered. He was about 15 years older than me, perhaps 5ft 8in and of medium build.

"Are you Werner Heinricy," I asked.

He confirmed that he was.

"You have a brother called Bernhard?"

He looked at me rather oddly. "Go on," he said.

"He was born in 1908 in Frankfurt-am-Main, and his wife was called Adelheid?"

He took a small step backwards. "Who are you," he asked?

"Bernhard was my father," I told him, "which makes you my uncle."

He paused for a moment, and then said: "I think you had better come in."

We sat together in the living room while his partner prepared some coffee and biscuits. He asked me to tell him the whole story again, which I did. He asked my year of birth, which seemed to trouble him even more. Then he dropped the bombshell: "Bernhard was my father," he said, "but he died in the war."

I suddenly understood why he seemed so cautious with me.

"I have no photographs of him," he told me. "All I have is this."

He produced a sheaf of cartoon drawings from a folder and laid them on the table. The artist was clearly very talented. He had been in the same regiment as Bernhard, and produced several caricatures of his comrades for their amusement. I pointed to the top one. "That's my father," I said. It was an excellent likeness.

The colour drained from Werner's face. "That's my father," he said, "but how is this possible?"

It transpired that his family had told him his father had died in the war. All he knew was that he had got into trouble with the law prior to going on active service, shortly after Werner was born. He had no memory of him and, in common with many boys of his generation, had been raised by his grandparents.

We spent a couple of hours together, and I left with a promise to send him copies of the few photographs I had of our father. It feels odd referring to him as 'our' father, but that is what he was.

On my return to the UK I told my mother of my discovery. She stared at the floor as she told me she had known the truth all along. She hadn't expected me to remember the name and address I had seen, and thought her explanation would have brought an end to the matter. It seems my father – sorry, our father – had tried to contact Werner many times and even invited him to the UK for a visit, but his letters had been intercepted by the family. It was a source of great sadness to him that he would never again see his firstborn.

Werner and I did not develop a close brotherly relationship, although I did visit him and Jutta, his new partner, twice more during the next few years. During those evenings we became aware of how many little quirks and mannerisms we have in common. Coincidence - who knows?

I noticed that Werner was a very heavy drinker, while I hardly drink at all. By that time, courtesy of the Family Records Office, I had discovered that our father had died in 1974 from a condition related to his alcoholism. I told Werner of this, and recalled what little I remembered of his drunken rages. I expressed my concern about his own consumption. He responded, saying that he really didn't drink that much and that I shouldn't concern myself.

A few months later I received a call from Jutta. "I don't know what you said to him," she told me, "but he has cut down his drinking to a fraction of what it was. I was so worried, and I cannot thank you enough."

My contact with Werner has dwindled to very occasional telephone calls, but I like to think that we both benefited from meeting a brother neither of us knew we had.

During the latter part of 1989 my interest in my former home and in my roots once again came to the fore, as I watched the news broadcasts from the GDR. Civil unrest was destabilising the German Democratic Republic, where most of my family still lived, separated from the free world by the iron curtain that had split families for almost two generations.

Then, that fateful day in early November, I watched transfixed as the images of thousands of people streaming through the border were beamed around the world.

I cried.

In that moment I also felt the most incredible joy. I recalled how my mother had wept when in 1961 pictures of the Berlin Wall being built filled the newspapers. It was clear that a great part of me was still German, despite my British birth and upbringing. I had spent barely six years of my life in Germany, and yet that part of me was far stronger than I had ever realised. Yes, I had spent by far the greatest part of my life in the UK, had built a life here, but I could not deny my heritage, my family's history, my roots.

As Christmas approached, I was becoming more and more restless. I knew that I couldn't just continue to sit and watch what was happening. I had to be there. The day after Boxing Day, while Carol had gone shopping for cheap cards and wrapping paper ready for next year, I went into town and bought two tickets.

When she got back home I said: "You'd better pack a bag. We're leaving tomorrow evening."

"Where are we going," she asked?

"Dover," I said.

Carol was confused: "What for?"

"To catch the ferry" I said.

"What ferry?"

"We're going to Germany for New Year."

I do love to spring a surprise on her from time to time. This time she had one for me too: "But my passport's expired!"

Oops!

A few frantic phone calls and a quick trip to the Newport passport office the following morning solved the problem, and we left on schedule.

After an overnight stop in Germany, I decided we should visit Hamburg on the way. We had just over a day to spare, and I wanted to show Carol where I grew up.

Whilst there, we also dropped in on Berthold. It was a complete surprise to him and Margaret, his wife, when we turned up unannounced. Well, I suppose it would be. After all, I hadn't seen him for twenty-five years. I would have visited the previous year, but I had only recently tracked down his address.

Margaret and Carol gave up the fight to stay awake just after midnight, leaving Berthold and me to sit and talk We had a lot of catching up to do, and did just that with the aid of copious quantities of *Jachtkaffee*, 'Yachtsman's Coffee'. It's a lethal brew of strong filter coffee, a spoonful of cocoa and a very liberal dash of rum. An enthusiastic sailor, who owned a small but well equipped sailing yacht for many years, Berthold knew how to make it just so. Because I hardly drink at all I have rarely been really plastered. On those rare occasions in the past 20 years or so when I have been it's usually been with Berthold and his *Jachtkaffee*.

Unfortunately, I had a falling out with his son a few years ago, over the kind of trivia that should never have been an issue. Sadly it has resulted, families being what families are, in our contact being severely disrupted, and I really miss him. He is now well into his eighties, and I hope that we can resolve things before it's too late.

The next day Carol and I headed for the border. Although officially open, the controls were still strict and it took about 45 minutes to complete the formalities. I had often told Carol of the reality of Germany's separation, and described the border fence with its death strip, the watchtowers and gun placements that I had first seen as a fourteen year old on a class trip. I still clearly remember standing on small hill not far from Wolfsburg, protected by the West German border patrol, and looking across the border to where an elderly woman was toiling in the garden of a lone cottage. She was no more than a few hundred metres away, and yet while I was free to go where and whenever I wanted to, she was not. Some of my classmates called out to her. She did not respond. She didn't dare. East German border guards were keeping a watchful eye on us and on her from their elevated position in the nearby watchtower, their machine guns more obviously on show than they needed to be.

At the border crossing the border fence passed through a pine forest. A huge ugly slash of light sand, multiple barbed wire fences and watchtowers ran straight through the lush green of the forest. The trees had simply been removed to allow clear visibility and a clear shot. The border guards were teenaged conscripts, dressed in Russian style army uniforms, clutching machine guns. I was struck by how uncertain they looked, completely lacking in confidence, bewildered even. Although carrying out the same duties as before, they were in a new unfamiliar situation. The people crossing the border were not just happy, they were elated. No longer were they the enemy, to be treated with suspicion and disdain. This was freedom, something they had never experienced under the repressive socialist regime. Only the senior officer moved with any authority at all.

The formalities completed, we set off on the motorway that linked the West with Berlin. Carol was silent for several minutes, then she turned to me and said: "That was horrible."

"What was," I asked?

"That border," she said. "It was just kind of there, in the middle of a forest."

"I did try to tell you what it was like, but you didn't believe me, did you?"

"Well, no," she said. "I thought you were exaggerating. But it's still nothing like you described it – it's far worse. And those border guards, with their guns and those Russian style uniforms - God, they're some mean looking bastards."

As we drove mile after mile on the poorly maintained road, we saw huge home made welcome banners hanging from the motorway bridges. Traffic was very light; imagine a minor British motorway at half past three in the morning. We saw families just standing on the grass verges beside the motorway, smiling broadly and waving to everyone who passed. Just two months earlier they could have been arrested and detained indefinitely for such actions.

The motorway was built to avoid any settlements and to be within sight of as few houses as possible. People were forcibly moved to new locations and their homes destroyed, to make sure that they wouldn't see any of the corrupting influences of the decadent West, and that included their fancy cars. Junctions were few and far between. About an hour or so into the journey we came to a service area. It was shut.

Eventually we reached the crossing point into West Berlin, a large compound surrounded by a high chain link fence with the main border strip disappearing off into the distance in both directions. I slowly guided the car through the chicanes of bollards and barbed wire to a small hut next to a heavy barrier. The guard was more relaxed than the ones we had already encountered. He checked out papers and waved us through.

We drove up a quiet slip road, and within a few hundred metres joined a busy inner city dual carriageway. As we joined the road we became part of the hustle and bustle of a major cosmopolitan city. All around us the bright lights, advertising billboards and modern buildings told us that we had once again joined the free world.

"Wow," said Carol, "It's like driving out of a black and white movie into a full technicolour one."

Near the city centre we left our car among several dozen others on the edge of a large park. It wasn't actually a car park, but these were exceptional times and no-one seemed unduly bothered. It was early evening, the temperature was just below freezing and after a bite to eat we headed for the wall.

At Checkpoint Charlie the guards happily posed for photographs with whomever asked them to. A nearby museum was dedicated to the history of the wall, and to those who tried to escape, not always successfully.

Not far from Checkpoint Charlie stands the memorial to Peter Fechter, erected by the people of Berlin. He was one of the many who, in his desperation to escape the East, took the ultimate risk. Just seconds from freedom, he was shot by East German border guards and left to bleed to death. It was over an hour before they came to remove his body.

The wall was already looking quite tatty, courtesy of souvenir hunters getting their own piece of wall. I saw a hole, large enough to lean through, which I did. It was eerie, looking up and down the death strip from within. But there was something else. I stood aside to allow Carol the same view. As she withdrew from the hole I could see that she had experienced exactly what I had.

"That is so weird," she said. "Inside, there is not a sound; it is totally silent. Yet out here I can hear everything, the traffic, the people, everything."

She was right. I can't explain it, but the atmosphere within the death strip was of a different world.

Close by, I met a man from New Zealand. He had travelled to Berlin for the New Year celebrations and was happily hacking away at the wall with a hammer and chisel. I ask you, who in their right might travels from New Zealand with a hammer and chisel? I'm glad that he did. He allowed me to borrow them to get my own piece, and stood watching as I began to chip away at the concrete. It was supposed to be a touristy thing to do, to get a little piece of it, but suddenly I was consumed by the most incredible anger. This wall was the symbol of everything that had separated my family, that had prevented me from getting to know the people I had only heard about from my mother. With tears running down my face I began to smash the hammer into the wall again and again. The emotion was so strong that even as I write these words the tears are flowing feely once again.

When I stopped, with a few large pieces of the concrete lying at my feet, the man looked at me and said: "Wow! This really means something to you, doesn't it?"

I explained how most of my family still lived in the East, and he became positively excited. He ran along the wall, grabbing anyone he could find, shouting: "Hey, this guy has family over there. Come and have a photo taken."

A minute or so later I stood front and centre, surrounded by a dozen people from eight different countries, for photographs. My only regret is that we don't have a copy of those photographs.

At around ten o'clock Carol and I made our way towards the Brandenburg Gate. The crowds were gathering, and eventually grew to several hundred thousand. The top of the wall was quite wide and already filled with people, waving banners and flags. I shudder to think how they got the man in his wheelchair up there, but it was just that kind of night.

We found a place near the wall, next to a TV outside broadcast unit. A small gap in the crowd allowed people to walk back and forth. Often, when two people encountered one another, instead of the usual embarrassed shuffling from side to side before passing, they would simply stop, smile, hug and then go on their way without a word being spoken.

Fireworks illuminated the scene.

"At this rate they won't have any left for midnight," said Carol.

"Trust me," I told her, "you ain't seen nothing yet." I was right.

At one point the crowd started to close in on us, and Carol became concerned. "Don't worry," I said. "Just shout: *Vorsicht! Bin schwanger!*"

She did, and a space instantly cleared around her.

She smiled at me, somewhat bemused. "What did I say," she asked?

"It's ok," I said, "you just told everyone you're pregnant."

The TV crew behind us became active as a man in a leather jacket covered in flashing lights stepped on to an hydraulic lift, the kind they use to change streetlights. It was David Hasselhof, who was then a major singing star in Germany. He was elevated above the crowd, and performed his hit *I'm Looking for Freedom*, which had become something of an anthem of the time, to an enthusiastic audience.

A scaffold supporting a huge video projection screen was used by members of the crowd to climb all the way to the top of the Brandenburg Gate. A mighty cheer went up when they replaced the East German with the European flag. The scaffolding was also the cause of tragedy, when it collapsed under the weight of too many people climbing upon it. Both climbers and bystanders paid the price, with over 130 injured.

By half past one the cold had ensured our feet were insensitive to just about anything, including being stepped on. Jochen and Christina, with whom we had been chatting, joined us as we headed for the city centre. As we walked away from the wall another couple caught up with us. The man, full of high and alcoholic spirits, wore an enormous fur coat. His girlfriend's shoes would have been better suited to a catwalk.

"Ich bin Manfred," he slurred, and linked arms with Carol. It seemed the natural thing to do, and we followed suit, six of us, arm in arm and smiling broadly, walked together, leaving thousands of people to continue their celebrations. It was an extraordinary night; we were living history.

We found a bar on the main drag, the Kurfürstendamm, known locally as the Ku'damm, where we were glad to warm up again, and to eat and drink in comfort. A little after five in the morning we began the long journey home. It was pointless trying to find somewhere to stay in Berlin.

The speed limit in East Germany was 100km/h, and rigorously enforced. Quite how one of those tatty 1.6l Ladas, even with "Police" written on it, was going to apprehend a 2.8i Granada I have no idea but, on the other hand, it would never outrun a speeding bullet. Our time in Berlin had convinced us of police readiness to shoot people for not doing as they were told, so I drove impeccably until we reached the West.

Such were our energy levels, buoyed by the spectacle of which we had just been part, I made it all the way to Aachen, near the Dutch and Belgian borders. We checked into an hotel, where I collapsed on the bed and slept for a while. Sufficiently rested, we went in search of a restaurant. As we drove through the streets I pointed out to Carol where a few old buildings, churches mainly, had survived the War and were now surrounded by modern apartment and office blocks. I became aware that Carol had stopped responding, and looked across, expecting to see her asleep. Instead she was sitting there with her arms crossed and a disapproving look.

"What's the matter," I asked?

"You're speaking English with a German accent. Stop it," she said.

It was clear that my German language skills had returned with a vengeance. More evidence came in the restaurant. I dealt with the waiter in German but spoke English with Carol. When he presented us with our bill he could contain his curiosity no longer: "I have to ask which are you, German or English?"

It was neither the first nor the last time I have been asked whether I consider myself British or German. To be honest, I don't really know. I understand how the children of many immigrants must feel, but only in part, because my background is not evident from the colour of my skin.

My language skills and understanding of the respective cultures would allow me to live happily in either country, without anyone being overtly aware of my dual nationality background. It's almost impossible to explain why I feel equally at home in either country, yet truly at home in neither. I'd never really given it a great deal of thought, but the dichotomy did come into sharp focus at an open house and barbeque organised by a Tall Club member.

One young woman was attending her first TPC event, and had brought along her mother, for a bit of moral support. The young woman quickly joined in with the crowd, while her mother stood quietly to one side. I wandered across and introduced myself. It was clear from her accent that she was German, although she had obviously lived in the UK for a long time. It transpired that she had escaped from the former GDR during the 1960s, and eventually settled in Britain, where she had married and raised her daughter.

I asked whether she still had contact with her family. She told me that she visited occasionally, but that they no longer treated her as close family: "They say that I am more English now, because I have lived in England for so long. But here in England people still think of me as German, because of my accent. I don't feel I belong anywhere any more."

"I know exactly what you mean," I said.

With a derisory snort, she said: "You can't possibly understand; no-one does."

I switched into German and gave her a two sentence précis of my background and heritage, about how my parents were German, I was born in

London but spent my formative years in Germany, how I had family in both countries, yet didn't really consider myself a native of either.

She wept as she said: "You really do understand. I'm so sorry."

After the New Year break I went back to work, but something was different. I couldn't put my finger on it, but I was completely lacking any motivation; I felt flat. The only thing I had any enthusiasm for was a song I was writing for a friend of mine.

George Cooper was our vet as well as a friend of long standing. We first met through the local folk club just weeks after he came to Hereford in the mid seventies. In addition to being a first class vet, he was a musician with the Hatband, a local comedy band, and a tireless worker for charity. Whenever he was involved in a money raising project, he would organise a concert, and I would be co-opted to appear, for no fee, of course. It happened so often that I became almost an honorary member of the band, ready to step in at short notice if a regular band member wasn't available. I didn't mind though. It worked both ways: Four cats examined, one given antibiotics, all given booster vaccinations for a fiver, and that only because "I'd better charge you something, to keep the partners happy."

His latest project was to raise money for our local Shopmobility scheme, providing electric mobility scooters for disabled shoppers. He had secured the services of a local band and a recording studio to produce a song which would be recorded and sold, with all proceeds adding to the fund. He asked me to write a song, and I came up with *Get Moving*. I needed him to visit to hear what I had produced in my little home studio, so I called him and waited.

It was a cold wet Wednesday. I had had an awful day at work, and was soaked and shivering by the time I got home. I switched on the answering machine and found a message from George. The apology for having failed to appear when promised was George at his long winded and humorous best. By the end of it I was howling with laughter. I have kept the tape with that message on it to this day.

It suddenly dawned on me: this is what life is about; good friends, good people, joy and laughter. Sod the grind and the corporate bullshit, hang the expectations of others. Life is too short to waste it chasing someone else's idea of what is or isn't right.

George called to see me that evening, loved the song, and took away all he needed for it to be professionally recorded.

The following morning I called the office, and spoke to the head of admin. Ted Bolton was known to most of us as Uncle Ted. I told him to be prepared, that I was bringing all my stuff back the following Monday.

"You're leaving us, dear boy," he asked?

"Sure am," I said.

"And what are you going to be doing next?"

"I have absolutely no idea," I said – and I didn't.

Carol said very little. As long as the bills were paid she never put pressure on me about anything. I had been with the company for over thirteen years, was making good money with no great effort, and should have been content to carry on in the same vein. But it was the right thing for me to do at the time. I think Carol knew that I hadn't been happy for some time and, if the truth be known, she was expecting something to give sooner rather than later. People were saying things like 'Mid Life Crisis' well within my earshot but I knew that wasn't it, as I had dealt with that a couple of years earlier. It had been easy to recognise by the badge: Suzuki GS750, and yes it was fun.

I didn't make the connection at the time, but clearly the trip to Germany and our experiences in Berlin had had a far more profound effect on me than I realised. Outstanding orders ensured that I had enough money in commission coming in to last a few months, so there was no need for rash decisions.

I had already arranged a trip to America in connection with a sideline I had been developing, and which had been profitable enough to merit the expense. Although it didn't work out as well as I had hoped, I made some contacts which led to my return later that year to play some gigs in and around Pittsburgh. That was another box ticked: I had always wanted to do some gigs in America and, although the fees didn't even cover expenses, I couldn't resist the opportunity. The venues were just local restaurants and bars, but I thoroughly enjoyed the experience.

Ambitions are good, but be careful how you express them. You may well, as I did, fulfil many of your ambitions, but not in quite the way you were hoping to.

On my list of ambitions were, among others, that I wanted to gig in America, to appear on television and radio, and to "have my name on one of those black spinny things". Back then CDs were still those new fangled modern thingies that were never going to catch on. I had always expected to fulfil those ambitions with my music, to maybe enjoy some small commercial success, but it didn't work out that way.

The gigs were fun, and took care of one ambition. The television and radio appearances did indeed occur, but in connection with the Tall Persons Club. As for getting my name on a black spinny thing: on my return from my first trip to the USA a small package was waiting for me. Inside was a copy of "Get Moving" recorded by local band *Life*, and written by me. There was my name on the label of a 45rpm single. It wasn't quite what I had hoped for, but I have to admit that it met exactly the terms of my ambition as I had expressed it.

When money started to run short I took another commission-only selling job to make ends meet. It still wasn't what I really wanted to do, but then again I didn't know what I wanted to do. That was resolved later that year, courtesy of a television chat show which was making a programme about height.

It was a perfectly ordinary December day in 1990, ordinary that is, apart from the fact that I had overslept, and was a little late leaving for work. I finished my cup of coffee, picked up my briefcase, and was about to head for the door when the commercial break in *The Time The Place* drew to a close, and they trailed a coming programme.

"Are you very tall, are you very short? Has this affected your life? Do you have a story to tell about what it is like to be either very tall or very short? If so, call The Time The Place".

I called, and vented my spleen about some of the things that irritated me about being exceptionally tall, as well as explaining why I actually enjoy being 6ft 8in. The researcher asked whether I would be available to appear on the programme a few days hence, and so it was that I came to be in London a few days before Christmas, ready to embark on my first television appearance. Thames Television was paying for my room at the Ibis Hotel near Euston station. Little did I realise at the time that I would be back at the same hotel seven and a half years later, during the largest convention of tall people this country had ever hosted.

Waiting in hospitality before the programme, I noticed how all the tall people were at one end of the room while all the short people had congregated at the other. Both groups were sharing tips on where to buy the many things in which the user's or wearer's height was a factor. One of the men in the tall group, having just written down the names of two shops he hadn't known about, said: "Wouldn't it be great if there were some place you could call and get all this information?"

The seeds were sown!

As you can imagine, I raised quite a few points during the programme. Back in hospitality I got into conversation with Judith Levy, of the specialist retailer *High and Mighty*. I told her I wished that no tall teenager would have to go through what I went through without knowing that there was some support from people who understood. I proposed an organisation for tall people. She liked the idea and suggested we meet again.

The seeds were sprouting nicely!

Judith and I met again the following March, this time at the *High & Mighty* head office in Hungerford. She was most supportive, saying that co-operation between us could lead to them gaining a greater understanding of their market, and they would be happy to support a club with advertising.

The seeds had firmly taken root.

I suspect my long suffering wife thought that this was just another of my madcap ideas, which I would research thoroughly, but which would ultimately come to nothing. Unfortunately for her, I had been doing some bits and pieces with my local BBC radio station, BBC Hereford and Worcester, and knew the right producer to approach. Mary Johns, all 5ft nothing of her, was intrigued by the concept of a club for tall people, and interviewed me for the mid-morning show. Six people called in, wanting to know more. I made contact with them, and discussed the idea further, and it became apparent that this sucker just might fly. One thing I was certain of: the majority of people wanted information rather than social activity. All agreed it would be nice, especially for teenagers, but essentially it was 'Information before Intoxication'.

It would take a really nasty frost to kill these seeds.

A few days later I received a telephone call, which I at first thought was a wind up. Unbeknown to me, Mary Johns had passed our interview up the line within the BBC, and now the Johnny Walker programme wanted me to come down to Broadcasting House to be interviewed on Radio 5. Well, why not? I'd already done local radio, so what were a couple of million more listeners? I was slightly nervous, but the atmosphere was relaxed and enjoyable, and the interview a success. How much of a success only really became clear in the course of the following weeks.

As I was leaving the studio a researcher told me: "That was amazing – as soon as you started chatting, the switchboard lit up like a Christmas tree! We weren't ready for that kind of response."

She also handed me a piece of paper with a telephone number on it. A man from Holland had heard the show and called in to say that he was 7ft 3in, and head of the Dutch Tall Club; would I please call him? It was my first contact with Rob Bruintjes, or anyone from any Tall Club for that matter.

From talking with Rob I knew I was on the right track: Information, and lobbying. Rob told me of some of the Dutch Club's successes, which only further served to confirm what I already knew, that a British Tall Club was needed, and wanted.

As a result of my Radio 5 debut a news agency asked to interview Carol and me about how we cope with the 17in height difference and about this club I was proposing for an article in *Take a Break* - hey, a lot of people read this stuff! The article appeared without even a mention of the club. Oh, well.

Letters and forwarded notes from the BBC trickled in consistently, and it looked like the word was on the streets, that someone somewhere has started a tall club. The mailing list was approaching three figures. Those seeds were ripening nicely.

Terry Wogan was on TV three times a week with his early evening chat show, so imagine my surprise when Seana, one of the researchers called to invite me to appear. I knew the Wogan format well. Generally it consisted of a top line guest, a B list celeb, followed by someone slightly odd or quirky to make the others look good. I knew which one they had me down for. Had it been twelve months later, I would have relished the challenge, but I knew my limitations, and declined. I explained my reasons to Seana. She told me that her contract with the show was about to expire, but that she was moving to a daytime magazine show which would be far more suitable, and could she call me when she started her new job? She called me in mid July, and everything was arranged until that final glitsch.

"When did you start the club", she asked.

"I haven't yet".

"Oh! In that case we can't really do anything with this. When were you thinking of starting the club?"

"When were you thinking of transmitting?"

"August 1st"

"Sounds good enough to me"

Seana became excited at the idea of launching the club on *Garden Party*, a now defunct magazine show which was transmitted live from Glasgow Botanical Gardens; they flew me there for the day. What a pose: "I'm just flying up to Glasgow for the day to do some TV".

I sometimes wonder whether there really is some celestial computer gamer in charge of the ultimate role playing adventure game called "Planet Earth". It certainly seems that way when I look back at how my life developed.

If I had to write a profile for the ideal person to start and successfully build a club for tall people in the UK, it might look something like this:

Wanted – energetic and highly motivated individual, comfortable with appearing in public and in all media; good spoken and written communication skills are essential. Must be a good listener with reasonable counselling skills; the ability to accurately absorb large amounts of specialist technical information is important; good administrative and organisational abilities are a distinct advantage, the ability to delegate beneficial. Good knowledge of written and spoken German would be a distinct advantage, as is the ability to sell to businesses of all sizes and at all levels.

The ideal candidate will be able to act as PR person, journalist, cabaret performer, salesperson, administrator, buyer, event organiser, counsellor, radio and TV presenter, translator, diplomat, and general dogsbody. A good sense of humour is vital as the remuneration package is marginally above bugger all.

Now, does that remind you of anyone? Alright, I admit it: I am lousy at delegating, but I never said I was perfect.

Looking back over my pre Tall Club life I would never have imagined that such varied and disparate skills and abilities could ever combine to find a useful and productive outlet

It just shows you what I know!

We're Off!

August 2nd, 1991. The Tall Persons Club GB officially existed, and was up and running.

I had decided against setting a minimum height requirement, a philosophy which continues to this day. People know for themselves whether they are tall or not, and whether the information the Club provides would benefit them. I also felt that, as the population continues to increase in average height, it would be necessary to revise height requirement every couple of decades, to ensure that it truly remained a club for tall people. This would have presented a dilemma: when a height requirement was raised, what would happen to the members who had met the original requirement but failed the new one? Would they be unceremoniously booted out? If they remained, how could we justify refusing membership to those who were the same height, but had not joined in time?

A few members of the American organisation later took issue with me on our no minimum height policy. They felt that we could not be considered a Tall Club if we had no minimum height requirement. I pointed out that, even without a minimum, our average heights for men and women exceed theirs by a full two inches; they dropped the subject.

The first subscription cheque had arrived three days earlier, from Judith in Bristol, who had heard a preliminary interview and taken a leap of faith. We had our first official member. I gave her membership number 102 (Carol and I are 101), because I didn't want anyone to think that we were the tiny new organisation that, in reality, we were. The mailing list already had over a hundred names on it, thanks to the advance publicity interviews, but we still had a long way to go.

8.30am. I was sitting quietly with a cup of coffee, still on a high from the previous day, when I had officially launched the Club on the BBC television programme *Garden Party* in Glasgow. It had been a great day out. I had, for the first time, met someone taller than me. Chris Greener was at the time, and had been for many years, Britain's tallest man at 7ft 6¼in. Well, if you are going to meet someone taller then you might as well do it properly.

Meeting Chris, I realised for the first time how someone of 5ft 10in feels when they meet me; it was a real eye opener. He had been part of another attempt to start a Tall Club in the seventies. John Dunn, the 6ft 7in BBC Radio 2 presenter had also been actively involved. The group met a few times in London, before it eventually petered out and disappeared into oblivion. Chris admitted to me several years later that he thought my attempt would go the same way. He took part in the programme anyway because it was a nice day out, and the BBC was paying for it.

He was glad he was wrong, and enjoyed being part of the Club. What pleased me most is that he sent in a cheque for his subscription, just like any other member, although I will admit that I didn't have the heart to cash it. At events he was treated just like any other member. "Newbies" would sometimes be a little awed by his presence, but soon overcame it. To everyone else he was just Chris. Sometimes he would jokingly say: "I'm a star. You've got to be nice to me."

The response was usually along the lines of: "On yer' bike Greener. It's your round."

Chris made his living in the media and through personal appearances. He was often seen on television and in feature films and used every opportunity he could to promote the Club. I recall an invitation to appear on one programme because Chris had agreed to appear only if they invited someone from the Club as well.

The late Paula Yates had a slot on Channel 4 called *On the Bed with Paula*, in which she interviewed a celebrity while they lay together on a huge, garishly decorated, bed. The interview that was eventually transmitted was the fourth or fifth take and had met with the director's approval only after he had said words to the effect of: "Will you please shut up about the bloody Tall Persons Club. This is an interview about you, not them!"

Chris's initial belief that the Club would be just another flash in the pan was shared by most of our friends and, if the truth be known, my wife. They were used to me coming up with all sorts of hair brained schemes, most of which ultimately amounted to little more than temporary amusement and diversion.

The telephone rang. It was a journalist who had seen the programme, and would I be prepared to give an interview, and pose for some photographs. Naturally I agreed, and a time was set for him to visit. I settled back to my coffee and the letterbox rattled, and rattled again, and again, and again. I found over 70 letters lying on the mat. Good start, I thought.

The phone rang again; another journalist. I had barely hung up when it rang again, and again, and again. Newspapers, radio programmes, television shows, freelance journalists, magazines, news agencies, everyone wanted to know more about this new Club. For a while we became a media flavour of the month.

Among the calls were many from people who wanted to join, and had tracked me down by calling the BBC for my number.

It set the pattern for that day, and for most of the next few weeks. I didn't make it to work that day, or for most of the following week actually. I was amazed by the level of interest, but figured it would subside in a few days, once the novelty had worn off. For now, life meant the telephone starting to ring before 8.00am, and continuing throughout the day, often until almost midnight.

Subscriptions were set at £9 for a full membership, with concessions at £5 per year. The materials I sent out to new members were basic in the extreme, and I felt that at that level I could provide at least some value for money. All those original members received was a short letter from me, a copy of the last newsletter I had sent out to those on the mailing list, and a Supplier Directory. It sounds better than it was, because the truth is that it was all printed on an elderly dot matrix printer, then collated and bound by hand into a flexible plastic spine. Impressive it was not, but it was a start.

That little printer served me well, until it finally gave up the ghost about six months later. Often I had to let it run overnight, just to keep up with demand. Printing 1200 pages takes time. The print head would become so hot that it warmed up the whole room. By the time of its demise the directory was being professionally printed, but it still had to cope with more work than it was ever designed to do. Bubble jet and inkjet printers were still new and horrendously expensive then, so I replaced it with another, which gave several years of loyal service, printing renewal forms, and address labels. To save money, I used to refill the print ribbon cartridge with endorsing ink. I avoided spending the Club's money on anything I didn't absolutely have to. Scrooge would have been proud of me.

My plan was for the Club to be simply an information provider, somewhere tall people could find out about suppliers of clothing, footwear, long beds and the like. I was confident that I could handle the day to day running of the Club in my spare time, while continuing to work as a commission only salesman.

I knew by this time that the majority of Tall Clubs around the world were essentially just social organisations. Providing information was a purely secondary, almost accidental function, for most of them. Several of the clubs in the United States even declared themselves to be "Tall Singles" clubs, in other words, dating agencies. Many others excluded members who had dared to marry someone who was not tall, and did not meet their height requirements. Even those that welcomed the average height partners of tall members as associate members excluded children, because most social functions involved the consumption of alcohol. Thus no-one under the age of 21 could even join an American Tall Club. Lip service was given to supporting tall teenagers, but few clubs did anything beyond talk about it.

The American umbrella organisation styles itself, rather grandly, "Tall Clubs International" (TCI). It embraces a few clubs in Canada too, which is how on its website it justifies calling itself "...truly an international organisation". It has minimum height requirements of 6ft 2in for men and 5ft 10in for women, unchanged for almost seventy years. Its very first Chapter, as they called the member clubs, was the California Tip Toppers, founded by Kae Sumner in 1938. She was working for the Disney Studios at the time. Her last major assignment had been, of all things, the film *Snow White and the Seven Dwarves*. The Tip Toppers claimed theirs to be the first Tall Club in the world. Whilst it is certainly the oldest still existing club in the world, it is most definitely not the first.

The first Tall Club in the world was the Six-foot-high Club in Edinburgh, Scotland, which was founded in 1826. That was the name as it appears in the journal of Sir Walter Scott, although other sources refer to it as the Six Feet High Club, or some variation thereof. One of its regular meeting places, Hunter's Tryst in Oxgangs Road, operates as a restaurant. Whether it is the actual building used, or the name originally referred just to the local area, I have not been able to ascertain. The Club encouraged and promoted athletic pursuits at outdoor venues where they indulged in running and throwing disciplines. Its membership criteria are obvious from its title, although it bestowed honorary membership on significant citizens. Back then, the average man was only around 5ft 4in, so a 6ft man was quite exceptional. The author Sir Walter Scott proudly notes in his journal that he served as the club's Umpire in 1829. The poet James Hogg was also a member as was, albeit much later, the writer Robert Louis Stevenson.

Since we pointed this out to the California Tip Toppers they have changed their claim to being "...the first modern Tall Club in the world", and I can't argue with that.

TCI, as part of its mission statement proclaims one of its functions to be to "...select a new Miss Tall International®, the official public representative and goodwill ambassador for TCI". It does this by means of a pageant held at the annual Convention. Henceforth I shall refer to her as Miss TI. The full name is a trademark of TCI, and I can't be bothered to keep looking for that little ® thingy to use.

In Europe too, most clubs were, and still are, primarily social affairs. In all but a few countries the structure was one of local groups forming and joining a national umbrella organisation. The national organisations cooperate informally in a European Council, the Europarat, chaired by a president elected for a two year term. It holds one meeting a year, at the European Tall Clubs Convention, the Europatreffen. The German club, being the largest and oldest in Europe, had rather dominated the European Tall Club scene, so all proceedings were conducted in German.

The notable exception was the Dutch Club, the leader of which had contacted me after hearing an interview on the Johnnie Walker Show on Radio 5 a few months earlier. As a national organisation they campaigned widely with political and commercial bodies, and actively highlighted the needs of all those who are tall, whatever their age.

We only knew about the Dutch Club at that stage, so I decided to stick with my original plan: one national club, with local groups forming and meeting, according to members' wishes.

From the letters I received it quickly became clear that some members did want social events. Some were happy to receive whatever information we could provide, while others hoped that the Club would become an active political campaigning force.

I found myself spending more time on the telephone simply talking with people. Someone would call for more information about the Club, and then begin to talk about their own experiences as a tall person, or as the parent of a tall child. Some of the stories I heard were almost beyond belief.

A mother was almost in tears as she told me about her twelve year old daughter. For weeks she had worked with her classmates on a fashion show, and was looking forward to the big day when she too would take to the catwalk. Instead, her teacher told her that she could not possibly be in the show as she was far too tall. Not content with that, she told the girl to stop wearing such high heels, as they made her "...look ridiculous." Talk about kick 'em when they're down!

I wish this story were exceptional, but it isn't.

This is exactly the kind of attitude and behaviour which leads to so many tall youngsters feeling self-conscious in social situations, and even inhibits normal social development. These patterns, once set in childhood and teenage, may endure into adulthood. I have met many tall people, highly intelligent individuals, who did not achieve their potential precisely because of conditioning like this. They underachieved, not because they weren't motivated or capable, but because they had been conditioned to fail by the very people who should have been their inspiration.

I became a counsellor, a confidante, a sounding board, a mentor. Some members would simply phone for a chat, or to tell me that they had seen something about the Club in a local paper somewhere. Press agencies put stories about the Club on their services, from where it was picked up by newspapers and publications as far away as Australia and New Zealand, the USA and Japan. I even gave interviews over the telephone for radio stations in Australia and Japan. The whole thing was growing beyond my wildest expectations.

After just ten weeks the Club already had well over 200 paid up members, and we were sending out information packs at the rate of over 100 a week. I was finding it increasingly difficult to meet the demands of the Club and to still earn a living.

The never silent telephone was beginning to wear on us too. We had resorted to turning off the ringer and not answering the phone after 9.00pm. Even then we couldn't escape the regular clunk of the machine as it took yet another message. Often three beeps would signal a full 45 minute tape and we'd to insert a fresh one. One evening we had enough of the phone, and went out to eat. I snapped a fresh cassette into the machine and we went in search of peace and quiet. It was 5.30pm. When we returned at 11.30pm the machine had taken 47 messages, and while we stared at the machine in disbelief it took yet another.

Carol too answered many calls from prospective members, and was an informal counsellor to many a caller. Tall women in particular seemed to assume that she too would be tall, and felt safe with Carol's understanding and reassuring manner. They poured out their hearts to her, sharing intimate thoughts that they would not even tell their closest friends. As a consequence she understands the tall woman's lot in general probably better than most tall women do.

One negative can outweigh a hundred positives, and so it was for me too. Media interest continued, and never a week went by that I didn't head off somewhere to give yet another interview or to appear on a show. In addition I was collecting and setting the information for the first printed directory, selling advertising, and confirming entries with listed suppliers. I had just completed the first newsletter to be printed professionally, for which I had also sold enough advertising to cover its production and postage costs, when it happened: a member from Loughton in Essex sent back everything and demanded a refund. The accompanying letter was less than complimentary. I was crushed.

Normally I would have taken it in my stride. As a salesman one becomes accustomed to rejection. But I was tired; actually, I was exhausted. I had been working 16 hours a day to stay on top of the demands of the Club, and only managing to work for a few hours here and there to pay my bills. Something had to give, and this was the proverbial straw that broke this camel's back.

I called Carol into the dining room, which had become the Club's office, and showed her the letter. She was well aware of the pressure I had been under.

"I've had enough," I told her. "I can't do this any more. I've been busting a gut and for what – this? I'll write to everyone and see whether someone is willing to take it over, otherwise I'll just have to let it go."

Carol stood to her full 5ft 3in and a bit and looked me straight in the eye, at least as straight in the eye as you can when there is a seventeen inch height difference. I knew that look, and could already feel my resolve wavering.

She reached across to where a pile of letters waiting to be filed lay on the desk, picked up a few of them, and thrust them in my direction.

"Read these," she said. "You can't let these people down. They are depending on you."

I looked at the top letter. The writer was Jonathan, from Cornwall. It was typewritten, and said only that he was 17, 6ft 7in tall, and would like some more information about the Club. There was a P.S., which said simply: "Thank you for starting the Club. It's nice to know I am no longer alone."

End of discussion.

"We can manage on what I earn," said Carol. "You run the Club. We'll find a way."

The Tall Persons Club became my life. I lived, ate, slept, breathed Tall Club 24/7. It was an organic being, with a life of its own. I tried to be like a parent, guiding it along the path that seemed to suit it best, although at times it was more like trying to control a bunch of over excited five year olds at a birthday party.

The only time I took away from Club business on a regular basis was a local music night. As long as I wasn't committed to Tall Club business I would be there.

The Black Swan in Much Dewchurch is a beautiful 14th century coaching inn, complete with priesthole, and still privately owned and run. It even has a buckshot mark in one its walls, rumoured to be from an assassination attempt on Oliver Cromwell, but I think far more likely the result of a trigger-happy farmer who had overdone the local scrumpy. Most Thursdays local musicians gather for a singaround. The standard ranges from beginner to those who could have been professional, the music from trad folk to modern classics and self-penned material. It's all very informal; someone sings a song or plays a tune, then someone else has a go. Sometimes others join in, sometimes not. It's simply an enjoyable night for both the music and the company.

The Black Swan was my bolthole, somewhere I could relax and forget about the demands of the Tall Club. Of course there was some good natured teasing if I had appeared on TV or in the papers that week, but I think the locals were secretly quite pleased to have a very minor celebrity in their midst, although they would never admit to it.

My old DOS based computer was no longer adequate for the Club's needs. I replaced it with a 286PC with a whole 4MB of memory. The old computer used only floppy discs, so to have 40MB of hard disc space was fantastic, and all for just £700! My, how times change.

Were it not for the relentless forward march of technology and software, that old 286 could still be handling the Club's administration today. As it was, after a couple of years it had to be replaced. When it comes to the basics, there is nothing XP can do that Windows 3.0 and the old 286 couldn't handle. It's a sad fact that new technology is now forced upon us not because we need it, but because it's there.

I was still learning about medical conditions that were relevant to height. Diane Rust of the Marfan Association contacted me. I had never heard of the condition, and she sent me some information. The Child Growth Foundation also got in touch, and I learned about other height related syndromes, such as acromegaly, XYY syndrome, Klinefelter syndrome and Sotos syndrome.

Information on ergonomics, British Standards, height restriction and reduction, trivia about tall people past and present, and more besides, arrived in a steady stream. Harry Galloway was the source of much of this information. He had joined the Club in the first couple of weeks. His support, both practical and moral, was invaluable. I often turned to him for help when I needed specific information. As a librarian, he knew exactly where to look, which reference works could prove useful, and how to locate organisations which might also be able to help. Hardly a week went by without the arrival of a manila C4 envelope, sealed with Harry's trademark invisible sticky tape. He provided at least a third of the information that made up the Club's first Supplier Directory.

Sadly, Harry died in 1996, but some months before he sent twenty pounds, ".... to be used in a way that will benefit the Club". I bought a plaque, and instituted the Harry Galloway Member of the Year Award. Charles Frost was its first ever recipient, and I am glad that Harry was there to see it. It is people like him who help to build and sustain organisations such as ours, and who are too often forgotten in the shadow of those who stand in the limelight.

By the end of 1991, the slim newsletter of the early days became a 20, sometimes 24, page magazine called *6ft+*, so named by Carol's father.

When I wasn't dealing with the day to day demands of the Club I was reading. I received huge amounts material, much of it highly technical. Often written with professionals, usually doctors, in mind, it was full of the kind of Latin no-one learns in school. Light bedtime reading it was most certainly not. I needed to understand the articles, because I then had to condense the information for the magazine, so that it could be easily understood by everyone. It was worse than being back at school.

Members too submitted many articles over the years. Often they were not of a standard that I could simply publish them. Instead I had have to use my very best editing skills to rewrite the article into a readable form, whilst retaining the character and content of the original. It was important that the contributor recognised the published article as their own work. The boost to a member's confidence from seeing their article in print was underlined by the many letters of thanks I received from those whose work I published.

Still I wasn't sure how the Club would develop. I knew that it meant different things to different people, and that it was impossible to choose one course in preference to another. It was equally impossible to be all things to all members.

Requests for social events had increased, and I knew that the first would have to be organised by me, in order to get things off to a flying start. A few members were already acting as local co-ordinators, contact points for local media and, hopefully, a focus for local social events. Unfortunately, the British psyche being what it is, people are reluctant to turn up to a place they may not know, to meet others they have never met, and so the social scene was still a non starter.

Billy Connolly tells a story that sums it up perfectly: Two Welshmen, two Scotsmen and two Englishmen are stranded on a desert island. After twelve months the Welshmen are getting along fine, having started a choir. The Scotsmen have started a whisky distillery. The two Englishmen are still waiting to be formally introduced.

I got to work arranging the first ever social event of the Tall Persons Club at the Manor Hotel in Datchet. The plan was for an afternoon business session, followed by music and dancing in the evening. I could not have known then that the buffet I ordered for the evening's festivities would be far from adequate.

November 1991 was more hectic than ever. An appearance on TV AM had generated over 1500 additional letters in a couple of weeks. While I was sitting on the couch in the London studio talking to Kathy, the host, back home the postman was making yet another delivery. We lived in a small terraced house, and the TV could be seen from the front door. That day the postman had an item that had to be signed for. As Carol was doing the necessary, the postman looked over her shoulder.

"Is that your old man on telly," he asked.

"Yes," said Carol.

"Oh sod it," said he. "I'm taking next week off!"

I have to say at this point that our local postal service was wonderful. They took the sudden surge of mail in their stride. Our postman would sometimes call at our house first, before even starting his round, which could be at half past six in the morning.

"If you think I'm going to carry this lot around the walk, forget it," he would say with a wry smile, and deposit another large bundle of mail into Carol's arms. It was all in the best of fun. I think he quite liked having a minor celebrity on his walk.

Although strictly speaking it was against the rules, they also ensured that common sense prevailed. The mail wasn't always addressed correctly. The house number, sometime even the street, would be wrong, but if the envelope said anything resembling Tall Persons Club, and there were plenty of variations on that theme too, then it was delivered through our door. Some letters even arrived, albeit that they may have taken an extra day or two, via Hertford, with a hand written scrawl on the envelope suggesting: "Try Hereford."

The best was the letter containing a cheque for membership which was delivered by first class post less than twenty-four hours after it was posted. It was addressed: "The Tall Persons Club, Hereford somewhere, please help Post Office."

I am not sure who deserves the greater admiration, the post office for getting it to us, or the sender for his faith in enclosing a cheque when he wasn't even sure of the address.

The media loved us to the point that we even made it as a question on *The Newsquiz* on Radio 4.

"Which club is aspiring to new heights," asked chairman Barry Took, and the panellists got to work, with Ian Hislop at his satirical best.

When I called the programme the following day to ask if we could have a tape recording of it, the researcher was very cagey.

"Ian Hislop was a bit unkind about you," she said.

"I am a Radio 4 listener," I told her, "and this is the Newsquiz. If they had simply answered the question and moved on, then I would have been offended. I take the fact that I merited that amount of insults as a compliment."

She laughed, and the tape arrived two days later.

Then I had a call from Kevin Pilley. A former staff writer for *Punch* but, now a freelance journalist, he had a commission from the *Mail on Sunday*'s colour supplement, *You* magazine, to write an article about this strange guy in Hereford who had started a Club for tall people. He arrived together with Richard, a photographer, and we got to work.

The article was straight forward stuff, but Richard wanted some out of the ordinary photographs. An ideal location was a local bridge on a small back road which has a sign warning of a mere 6ft of headroom. We have used that bridge many times since for similar shots. He also wanted a shot of me in a bath. Our bathroom at home was too small, which is how I came to be lying in a bath in my underpants in an unheated bathroom showroom on a local industrial estate in the middle of November. His assistant sprinkled water over my legs to make it look as though I really was having a bath. It was cold, very, very cold, and I was shivering badly by the time we were done. The things I did for the Club!

Kevin took us out for a nice meal that evening. Once a year or so, he would call me to update the information that he already had and then rework it into another article for yet another publication. Over the years he must have done a dozen articles about the Club for various newspapers and magazines.

I joked with him once that we were going to rename the Tall Persons Club.

He thought I was serious. "What's the new name going to be," he asked.

"The Kevin Pilley Pension Fund," I said.

A few days later I set off for Germany, via Holland, to attend my first ever Tall Club event.

The German Club has two major three day gatherings each year, one in the North, the *Nordtreffen*, and one in the South, the *Südtreffen*. A welcome evening on Friday is followed by outings and a Gala Ball on Saturday, with a final farewell gathering on Sunday morning. *Nordtreffen* was held in Bremen that year. The Gala Ball would attract around three hundred members, mostly from Germany, but including some from clubs in Holland, Switzerland, Austria, Poland, the former East Germany (this was pre-reunification, although the border was open) and Sweden.

My first stop was the home of Wiert Jan Huttema, of the Dutch club, where I also met Rob Bruintjes, the club's chairman. Rob is a gregarious character who speaks three languages. At 7ft 3in, he was at the time the tallest man in Holland, and very well known in the world of Tall Clubs. They had arranged a visit to Ronal Project, an office furniture manufacturer, the following day. Afterwards we met up with a man who was trying to start a club in France. He and I travelled together in my car while Rob and Wiert went in a Mercedes they had been loaned by the Mercedes press office in Holland. I was amazed, but Rob just smiled.

"We publish car reviews in our magazine," he told me. "The car manufacturers know that our club gets a lot of publicity. As long as a major newspaper doesn't want the car it is only standing around doing nothing, so they let us have it."

I made a mental note.

Before we departed Rob said: "By the way, you don't speak German, ok?"

"But I do," I protested.

"No you don't," said Rob. "I want to make sure that everyone will remember you."

He gave me a huge grin, and I figured that whatever he was up to, he knew what he was doing.

Four hours later I arrived in Bremen and soon found the venue for the Welcome Evening. Rob spotted me as I walked in with my French travelling companion, and I joined him at his table.

Word had got around the German club that someone in England had started a club there too, and a few people came over to talk to me. Practising almost forgotten school English, they did their best to make me feel welcome.

It's tough pretending that you don't understand a language when people around you are telling jokes and funny stories. I did my best to look uncertain until someone translated what had been said for me, and then laughed politely.

A man asked: "So you speak no German at all?"

"A little bit," I said, and made the appropriate sign with thumb and forefinger.

I feigned concentration for a moment and then said: "*Ein Bier bitte*," in the worst possible accent I could muster.

The Germans winced, and nodded knowingly. Clearly here was another one of those darned Brits who didn't learn foreign languages, and expected the rest of the world to learn English.

Rob shook visibly as he tried not to laugh, and gave me a wink and surreptitious thumbs up.

Thomas, a member of the Bremen club had offered to put us all up for the night. Back at his flat, while he and Kirstin, his girlfriend, were in the kitchen getting drinks for everyone, I told Rob that I couldn't keep up the deception for much longer. He had been chortling to himself all evening as I played my role to perfection. Thomas and Kirstin had already worked out that something was going on, but had no idea what. Our hosts rejoined us. The atmosphere was a little strained, as everyone did their best to make sure that I didn't feel excluded.

Rob and I began a conversation about the joke we were playing on everyone, all of it in German.

If I had whacked Kirstin between the eyes with a mallet, she could not have looked more stunned.

"You're speaking German," she exclaimed, "but you said you don't speak German."

"No, I didn't." I said, and pointed at Rob. "He said I don't speak German."

The atmosphere relaxed instantly, and we had a great evening, with me resuming my act in public the following day

Rob had told me to dress smart casual for the gala event. When I walked into the room to see a large part of the crowd dressed in formal evening wear I did feel a little self-conscious. My act continued, albeit that I didn't have to try too hard. Also at our table was Uwe Seyler, of the German club, who speaks excellent English. A well known regular at Tall Club events around the world, he is also member of TCI. We chatted happily while the evening went on around us.

All formal events have speeches, and as Rob was joint European President at the time he was invited to say a few words. He explained how a club had recently started in Britain, and that it had attracted over 350 members in just three months. Then Rob invited me to join him, to introduce myself, and to say a few words.

"Whatever Phil says I will translate for you," he told the audience.

It had got around that I didn't speak German, so half the audience mentally switched off, while the rest paid polite attention.

I took the microphone, and began: "Good evening ladies and gentlemen. It gives me great pleasure to be here at the *Nordtreffen* in Bremen."

I handed the microphone to Rob, who translated into German and then returned it to me.

"I would like to apologise for the way I am dressed. I didn't realise that we were supposed to come dressed as penguins."

Rob translated again, and the audience had a little chuckle.

I took the mic: "*Ich möchte mich auch bei Rob und Wiert bedanken.*"

The room fell silent as Rob translated what I had said into English this time: "I would also like to thank Rob and Wiert."

The audience burst out laughing. Those who had switched off suddenly woke up and wanted to know why everyone was laughing. I switched back into English again, and Rob translated into German.

The audience was now well and truly confused, unsure whether they had heard right, and checked the strength of their beer.

I took the mic for the last time, and completed my little speech entirely in German, admitting to my background, and left the floor to hearty applause.

The TPC had well and truly made its mark, and they wouldn't forget me in a hurry.

Just how much of an impact Rob's and my little stunt had became clear a few years later, at the European Convention in Prague.

I was waiting to be served at the food and drinks counter, when a man from the German club joined me and spoke to me in English. I responded in English, and we talked for a few minutes. A waiter who had served me earlier in the evening arrived to take my order. I speak no Czech, and had already established that he spoke German but no English, so I gave him my order in German.

My companion was so shocked that his voice became a little louder as he exclaimed: "Oh! You speak German!"

A German voice piped up from several feet behind me: "Yes he does, and he conned us good and proper in Bremen."

I am glad that I attended that first gathering in Bremen alone. It helped me to understand what some members felt when they came to our first meeting in Datchet. Above all, it underlined one important fact for me: I like being tall; I am happy being tall.

Never before had I been in a room full of people where no-one gave me a second glance, or stood at a bar and not had someone start a conversation with some comment about my height. To some it is wonderful to melt into the throng, to not be noticed, to just be one of the crowd.

I hated it!

It was as though someone had stripped away a huge part of my identity. I felt I had become invisible and, after years of being noticed, to suddenly be ignored was not easy to accept. Even today I cannot completely shake off that discomfort. I am so used to being the tallest person in a room that when I am not it simply doesn't feel right.

December was relatively quiet. I thought things were slowing down at last; wrong! Throughout the life of the Club December has been a quiet month. Regardless of the publicity we may or may not have had, new members are thin on the ground. I suppose the run up to Christmas makes people more guarded about their finances. Enquiry packs still go out in good volume, but financially it was always a lean time for the TPC.

Kevin Pilley's article appeared in the Mail on Sunday Supplement a week before the event I had organised in Datchet. He had arranged it that way, and made sure that the event itself was prominently featured, so that we would get extra publicity to follow on from it. That was not all we got.

I had about 40 bookings for the event on January 11th, 1992, and was confident that everything was under control. I never learn! Immediately after publication the phone went berserk. People phoned the magazine and the hotel for my contact details. I didn't know that the hotel manager was telling people to simply turn upon the day as well.

On the Wednesday he called me and apologised.

"I'm having to tell people not to come now," he said. "The hotel is fully booked, and I have had so many calls that I know we will exceed room capacity".

"Have you got another function on the same day," I asked.

"No," he replied. "It's all guests who have booked in for your party. I've kept a bedroom for you, just in case."

It was just as well he had. A group from the German club arrived on Friday, as did Rob and Wiert. A couple of journalists were eager to cover what was a unique event, so I had to travel down earlier than originally planned.

Uwe Seyler led the German contingent. They had travelled together in his car, a stretched Cadillac limousine. In 1992 such vehicles were virtually unknown on our roads, so that caused quite a stir in itself.

Carol drove down to join me on Saturday morning together with our friend Allison, who had offered to help with what looked like it was going to be a busy day.

At three in the afternoon we opened the doors to the function room to begin the business session, which was attended by about 40 or 50 members. I was surprised at the distance some members had travelled to be there. Many had travelled for two to three hours. Kate Edwards had flown in from Aberdeen.

I took my seat at a small table at one end of the room, and got the session underway by reporting on what had happened since the launch to bring us to that point. The first printed Supplier Directory had been recently sent out, as had a 20 page magazine. I pointed out that it was impossible to maintain that standard of service at the current level of subscription, and announced an increase to £15 per year, starting in February. Not one person objected, much to my relief. I then opened the floor to find out what members wanted from the Club.

After a short break for coffee I gave details of the Club's finances. We then reached the most critical moment in the Club's history to that point.

"As far as I am concerned, this is your Club," I told everyone. "If there is a group of you willing to form a committee to take over the running of the Club, I am perfectly happy to sign everything over to you right now."

I pointed to all of the bank books, cheque books, and administrative materials lying on the table in front of me. The necessary forms to transfer everything were also there. I was ready to hand over everything there and then, and to get back to my own life again. Someone asked what would happen if the members present couldn't decide. I said I would keep it going a little while longer until they had formed some kind of management committee.

Pete Diamant stuck his hand in the air, and announced very loudly: "Personally, I think Phil has done a great job, and we ought to let him get on with it."

The round of applause and generous cheers left no-one in any doubt.

Someone shouted: "Well that's that then. I'm off to the bar for a drink."

That met with another, even more enthusiastic, cheer, followed by the sound of feet stampeding for the door. Within seconds the room was all but empty, leaving me sitting at my table, Carol and Allison at theirs and three or four members who looked as bewildered as I felt.

Ever wondered how I ended up running the Club for the best part of ten years? Well, now you know. But still I was not prepared for what happened when we opened the doors again that evening for the social part of the event.

People were queuing. Some had travelled 100 miles or more on spec, just to come and meet a group of tall people for the first time in their lives. Carol and Allison did sterling work manning the desk, welcoming the visitors, most of whom joined on the spot. The only time during the next three hours that they managed to raise their heads was to see who else was thrusting money at them. We passed the 500 member mark that night.

I had figured on around 70 people tops for the evening, and had catered accordingly. A buffet for 70 people does not go far when 130 people descend upon it. The hotel manager constantly asked people to move into the bar to chat as, with a room limit of 90, a fire officer would have taken a very dim view of regulations being not just broken, but positively smashed to smithereens.

Three things struck me above all else that evening.

First, hardly anyone danced. The number of people dancing never made it into double figures. They were all too busy chatting.

Second, hardly anyone sat down. It was such a novelty for most, to be able to have a conversation while standing, that they took full advantage. Usually, of course, tall people take the full brunt of the music above the heads of the crowd. This time they were the crowd. No bending down to hear what people were saying. This unfortunately also led to my most embarrassing moment of the evening.

"Hi Carol," I said to a beautiful 6ft 3in woman, who was wearing three inch heels. "Didn't you bring the old man?"

She smiled, and nodded to her left, where her 5ft 7in husband stood, lost in the crowd, unable to join in the conversation going on above him. Talk about sticking your foot in it! My toes still curl whenever I remember that moment.

Another member was clutching the small of her back.

"My back is killing me," she said. "I haven't stood as straight as this for as long as this in my entire life."

"There's plenty of chairs," said my wife Carol.

"I know," she replied, "but the buggers won't sit down!"

Finally, there were no obvious age barriers. Eighteen year olds chatted happily with those in their seventies. Generation gaps weren't just bridged, they disappeared.

The hotel manager appeared again.

"I've got Sky News on the phone," he said. "Have you got someone available for an interview in the studio? They're sending a car in half an hour."

I looked at Pete Diamant: "Can you handle that? I want to stay here, just in case I'm needed."

Pete regularly called me for a chat, and had already given some press interviews for us, so I was confident that he could do it. Although it was the first time we had actually met, I felt I already knew him reasonably well.

It's probably the only time I ever saw total panic in his eyes. I didn't know then that he had been making full use of the bar. He appeared on the programme, looking a little less relaxed than I had hoped, but still gave an excellent impression of someone who is stone cold sober.

The evening also produced some unexpected reactions. Dave Firman, a confident 6ft 6in man who is not easily phased, came to within a whisker of not becoming the active member he later did

"When I walked into the room I knew there was a step in there somewhere, because I couldn't see the opposite wall," he later told me. "I paid my money, and started to shuffle across the floor, watching my feet, looking for the step. Half way across I stopped and looked up. I realised that there was no step. The people were all as tall as me, many were taller. Even the women were looking me square in the eye. Suddenly I felt incredibly claustrophobic, and vulnerable, and it freaked me out. I walked straight out of the room, and went across to the bar. I needed a stiff drink to steady my nerves. I was on the verge of going home when I suddenly thought: 'Hang on. You came here to meet other tall people. What the hell did you expect?' I went back in, and am glad that I did. I would have missed out on meeting some fantastic people, and some fun times, if I had gone home."

As the evening drew to a close I noticed something else that has remained part of the Club to this day. People hugged as they said goodbye. Not just one of those polite 'A' frame hugs, but genuine, warm, affectionate hugs that lasted longer than one would have expected from people who had met for the first time that evening.

That's one of the downsides of being tall: people are reluctant to hug you. As children we are seen as older than we are, and therefore not in need of the hugs and cuddles that other children of the same age get. In adulthood the tall person is often seen as strong and capable, and not in need of that kind of affection and affirmation. Hugging when there is a significant difference in height is not always comfortable, and so the tall person misses out. That said, I still remember the first hug I gave 6ft 2in Lin Gardner. It was only the second or third time we had met, and when I hugged her I felt her body stiffen. I immediately let go and apologised for having been over familiar. "No, it's not that," she said, "It's just that it's the first time someone has hugged me and it's gone dark!"

Come to any TPC event, and you will see hugs being shared freely, with real affection, and not only when meeting or parting, but just because it feels good – and that includes the guys; long may it continue.

The following morning brought yet more TV cameras, more interviews, and a telephone call from a radio station in Leeds, asking whether they could talk to a local member. I thought immediately of a seventeen year old young man who had joined just three weeks after the launch. He had written to me a couple times, and I knew from the way he wrote that he would be the ideal candidate. I called him.

Charles Frost, for it was he, became part of TPC lore. He admitted to me years later that he was awestruck that I, the "Tall Guru", star of *Mirror*, *Mail* and TVAM should be calling him. It was an attitude I encountered many times over the years, and not one I ever felt comfortable with. As far as I was concerned, I was like any other member, and just happened to be running the office.

Charles became a regular contributor to the magazine, and his articles were enjoyed by many. Some were light-hearted nonsense, others more serious. Directly and indirectly, both generated a steady flow of readers' letters. His contributions as the Club's self-appointed Roving Reporter, Fudgy the Wonder Sheep, brought many a smile to many a face. We still wonder whatever happened to Marvin the Floridian alligator and his lovely wife Shirley, and we never found out whether Mabel the cow's walk-on part in *Emmerdale* led to a mooing role.

He also wrote a series of articles which has become known as '*The Unseen Abuse* series'. In these he charted his personal development from shy teenager to independent adult. His frankness struck a chord with many members; he was an inspiration.

We didn't actually meet face to face until almost a year later. It was another year, and a few encounters more before Charles became a regular weekend, sometimes week long, visitor to our home. We would sit into the small hours talking and philosophising, and I did my best to offer advice and wisdom, although at times I felt a right fraud doing so. During these visits Charles also got to see me in my early morning, incoherent, pre-coffee state, and awe was quickly replaced by healthy dose of reality.

During one such late night session I told him that one day he would have the same conversation again, but that he would be on the other end of it. He shook his head in disbelief: "That's a long way off," he said.

"You'll be surprised," I told him. "It will happen much sooner than you think.

At the next annual event that Charles attended, a young man approached me during the Gala Ball. He asked whether the writer of the Unseen Abuse Series was present, and could he meet him. Later, back in the hotel bar, I effected the introduction, and left them to talk. They immediately fell into deep and earnest conversation. Over an hour later the young man got up, smiled and left the bar. Charles got up from his stool and walked across to where I was sitting. I knew from the look on his face what had happened. I got up and moved towards him. Not a word was said; we just hugged.

A little later, as we sat together armed with fresh drinks, Charles turned to me and smiled.

"That was so weird," he said. "As we were talking I suddenly realised that I had had this conversation before, but last time I was on the other end of it. I couldn't help but smile, because I could hear your voice saying 'Told you so'."

As we help others to grow, so we too grow.

I no longer think of Charles as a member. He has become a close friend to Carol and me, and continues to be a regular visitor. In his professional life too, he continues to lead and inspire others.

The social side of the Club has never been and, I hope, never will be the main reason for its existence. Only about 15-20% of the membership ever takes part in a social event, but its importance should not be underestimated.

The confidence some members gain from interacting with other tall people carries over into the other areas of their lives, both professional and personal.

At one member's fiftieth birthday party I was approached by the birthday girl's sister. She told me: "My sister's life began when she joined the Club. She used to hate going out because of the attention. Now she just doesn't care."

That member became well known for riding a Honda 350 motorbike called Flo to events, and referred to herself as a Hell's Auntie – too old to be a Hell's Angel, too young to be a Hell's Granny.

Most members are happy to be saving money on clothing, and finding suppliers of the less common items such as beds, bikes and baths. Others support that fact that the Club regularly highlights the needs of not just tall people, but of all people. They were aware that, with standards already woefully out of date, an increasingly large proportion of the population will suffer from ailments and, in some cases, even eventual disabilities that are caused directly or indirectly by those outdated standards.

There are also those members who simply like the fact that the Club exists.

"I'm glad to be part of the Club, knowing that it is working to make sure that future generations of tall people will not have to endure what I did when I was young," wrote one member.

Another wrote: "Just knowing you are out there has given me new confidence. I only wish you had been around when I was a girl." The writer was 57 years old.

There were hundreds of similar letters over the years, and I feel proud and privileged to have been the catalyst that allowed such changes to happen.

Media appearances started to become more subject specific, rather than the general interest theme that had started us on our way. General design, ergonomics, bullying, medical implications, public transport seating, tall schoolchildren, all were highlighted in a wide range of programmes and publications. Then there were the shop openings, exhibitions, conferences and seminars, all of which became part of the day to day routine. Carol and I were even invited to the launch of the 1994 Guinness Book of Records at Canary Wharf, where we met Sandy Allen, then the world's tallest woman, for the first time. A great lady with a wicked sense of humour, she smoked like a trooper.

One advantage of these occasions was that I got to see many a celebrity differently from their public image. Among others, Robert Kilroy-Silk and James Whale were two whose incredible professionalism was masked by their on screen persona. It is why I am not overawed in the presence of celebrity. Having met so many, I have learned that they are merely ordinary people doing a very public job.

Actually, that isn't quite true. In 1997 Carol and I together with TPC member Val Sims (now Johnson – she married a tall club member from California) attended a performance by Victor Borge at the Barbican in London. He was already well into his eighties, and yet still did a two hour show with the energy and verve that would have put most fifty year olds to shame. I was lucky enough to meet him as he left that night, and to get his autograph. He was such a gentleman, and our encounter rendered me completely speechless for half and hour afterwards – a record, I can assure you.

And so to Foreign Climes

Europatreffen, the European Convention, had begun as the *Bundestreffen*, the German club's annual event. It was attended by so many members from other countries that it was renamed in 1968, and occasionally hosted by another country's club. Traditionally the event was held in the week of Ascension Day, which is a public holiday in Germany. It had grown to become a week long series of events, with the main programme running from Thursday to Sunday. The *Europarat* meeting was always held on the Thursday, and the Gala Ball on Saturday evening. In 1992 it was scheduled to take place in Vienna, and so I got to work.

Pete Diamant came up trumps, thanks to someone he knew at Ford UK. I still don't know how he managed to arrange five Ford Granadas for us to travel in. They even modified one of them for Chris Greener to drive. A Sky News team came to see us off. In addition Pete even squeezed £250 out of his employers for petrol, in exchange for which we displayed their banners in the rear window of each car.

Vienna is a very long way, and we should have flown. But it was our first European Convention, and I knew no better. I was accustomed to travelling long distances on Continental roads, but some of our group found it incredibly wearing.

I continued to drive to most of the European events, but the rest of our contingent generally chose a quicker and more convenient way. For me these events were always a great excuse to get a car on test from one of the manufacturers or importers. I had learned from Rob and Wiert that it was possible and took full advantage. Over the years I had several cars from Honda, Renault, VW, Vauxhall, Kia, Daewoo and Rover. Sadly, I never managed to blag a Roller.

We arrived mid afternoon in Vienna, and I went straight to the *Europarat* meeting, while everyone else went to check in at our hotel. I was a little late, and took a seat at the back of the room, behind the observers who were there to watch the proceedings, and to contribute when permitted to do so by the chairman, Rob's co-president, Hero Janssen. There had been a tie in the last election and they had agreed to serve a year each.

Rob spotted me, interrupted the discussion, and invited me to a seat at the main table. The discussion centred on venues for future Conventions. A German member felt strongly that the tradition of the past thirty years, alternate years always in Germany, should be maintained. It was actually a tradition they had intended to establish, but which was never quite adhered to. Another felt that with so many countries now having active clubs it was time to let that idea go. The first speaker maintained that, as Germany had the largest club, it should continue as before.

Rob argued that soon it might not be that way. The British Club was not even a year old and already had over 1000 members. We had passed the 1000 member mark in April of that year. Future venues were chosen, and the tradition was officially dead.

Discussion then turned to what assistance might be given to other countries, to help them to get Tall Clubs started.

Uwe Seyler was in the audience, and raised his hand.

"I don't think we should get involved," he said. "Let's face it, we tried to get a club started in Britain a couple of times in the past, but back then we didn't know there was a Phil Heinricy, who shakes such things out of his left sleeve."

The audience gave a generous round of applause, and that was the end of that one.

Ours was officially the fastest growing club ever. Admittedly, we had the advantage of copious media not available in the fifties when the German club started. Also, we launched nationally rather than with scattered local groups. However, it took the German club 10 years to reach the 1000 member milestone.

Somehow the discussion got on to social versus practical aspects of Tall Clubs, and I think someone asked whether the German club was going to publish a Supplier Directory, rather than just a simple list of shops. At that time only the Dutch and British Clubs published such directories, complete with an additional section full of hints and tips, practical advice and information. I stressed the importance of the practical work that Tall Clubs should be doing, saying that the majority of our members never attended social events. As I described the amount and type of publicity we were generating there were nods of approval in the audience, and a few long faces around the table. The meeting eventually ground to a halt, and I headed for the table where coffee was being served.

A small group from the Cologne Club in Germany approached me. They were not happy that I was playing down the relevance of social events, and began to give me a hard time.

"That's the trouble with you English," said the man who had advocated maintaining the alternate year hosting tradition. "You always think you know best, that everything should be done your way. You English are so..."

"Hold it right there," I said, "I'm German."

That stopped him in his tracks.

"No you're not," he said, "you're English."

I looked him in the eye: "My mother was born in Boizenburg, my father in Frankfurt, and I grew up in Hamburg. I'm German."

He made some harrumphing noises, then he and his friends left me to my coffee.

"Having a spot of bother?"

It was Toby Brown, a TCI member who had brought a group of about twenty fellow members over from America. I met up with him many times over the years. It was he who introduced me to the joys and the beauty of his home town, Chicago, when I later attended an event hosted by the local Tall Club. Thanks to Toby I had a wonderful time. He introduced me to lots of people and made sure that I didn't feel left out.

Toby was a regular visitor to European events, and was the best ambassador TCI could have wished for. They should have dumped Miss TI, and given the job to him. They could have stuck him in a dress, if it made them feel better, even though the beard would have clashed with the tiara.

We chatted a while, and he diplomatically suggested that I might be rather outspoken at times, and that this would ruffle some feathers in the world of Tall Clubs.

Toby was right, of course. Until the emergence of the TPC, Rob had been the only campaigner for more emphasis on the practical work Tall Clubs should be doing. Because he represented a small country, and was something of a lone voice in the wilderness, it had been easy to shout him down. With my arrival, those days were over. Rob knew it, and loved it. Quietly, and always out of earshot of their Club's leadership, many people voiced their support and encouragement, which helped to keep us both going.

The programme of events organised by the Austrian Club was exceptional. It included a visit to Schloss Rosenburg, a mountaintop castle with spectacular views over the valley below. We were greeted by the castle's owner, welcomed with a fanfare from trumpeters in period dress and treated to a falconry display, the like of which I don't expect ever to see bettered.

The display took place in one of the castle courtyards in which I expect jousting tournaments would once have been held. Stone steps around three sides provided seating for the crowd of several hundred. The fourth side was just a four foot wall beyond which lay a sheer drop of several hundred feet and breathtaking views of the surrounding landscape.

Buzzards, falcons and eagles delighted the crowd, swooping out over the valley, before returning in a high arc over the castle walls to their handlers. I had never seen vultures as part of a falconry display before, so I was surprised when two were brought into the arena.

Vultures are a bit like the grumpy uncle who turns up at a family party determined not to have a good time. They showed absolutely no interest in demonstrating their flying skills. The handlers solved the problem by picking them up and hurling them over the precipice. After plummeting earthwards for several seconds they grudgingly spread their wings and flew back up over the castle and into the arena. By way of protest they were not going to fly any further than they absolutely had to and landed at the first opportunity, which was usually in the middle of the spectators. It was obvious where they had landed from the shrieks and screams and sudden gaps that appeared in the crowd. They stomped and waddled their way back to their handlers for a small reward, only to be thrown over the wall again. After a few flights, they received a well earned treat, and went back to doing what vultures do best: sit and stare.

That year's convention still holds the record for the highest number of participants, with over 850 people attending the Gala Ball at the Palais Ferstl on the Saturday evening

Dressed in our finery, we made our way across the city centre towards the venue. Some members of our group were still tired from the previous day, and took taxis instead. As we crossed one of the squares, I spotted some horse drawn carriages, waiting for tourists to take the city tour. It was too good an opportunity to miss. We quickly reached agreement with the drivers, and continued our journey in four open top carriages.

As we arrived, over 500 people already stood waiting for the doors to open. The crowd, which completely filled the narrow road, parted as our carriages carefully made their way through the throng. There were some discontented mutterings as people moved aside ahead of the horses, when someone shouted: "It's the Brits!"

Uwe Seyler was already waiting with some friends. He shouted "Hey, Phil," and began to clap. As his solitary clapping grew into full scale applause from the crowd, I just couldn't help myself. I stood up, and took a bow, spreading my arms in acknowledgement.

People waved and cheered. The Brits had well and truly arrived on the European Tall Club scene.

A little later I saw Rob Bruintjes, and asked him: "What did you think of that?"

"It was terrible," he replied, "really bad."

His stern expression had me worried. I hadn't wanted to upset or offend anyone, so I asked: "Why? What was wrong with it?"

He grinned: "Because I didn't think of it first."

I still find it impossible to believe that we were the only people to arrive in that manner, but we were.

Carol was worried. In the middle of a crowd of tall people, she couldn't see a yard in front of her. Wearing heels and a full length dress meant the steps leading up to the entrance were going to be difficult enough to negotiate without the crowd surging up behind her.

As we stood with Uwe and Rob the doors opened and the crowd moved forward. Carol immediately lost her balance and panicked. Uwe and Rob reached down, grabbed an elbow each and bodily carried her up the steps with her feet dangling in mid air. They put her down once they reached the huge foyer, and Carol relaxed once more.

To describe Palais Ferstl as grand and opulent does it no justice. It is, without doubt, the grandest venue in which I ever attended a Tall Club event.

Even the Connaught Rooms in London, where our own *Europatreffen* Gala Ball was held in 1998, doesn't come close.

Upon our return to Hereford we found the mail stacking up nicely. It was by now a mix of enquiries, bookings for our first annual event in Stockport, questions from members, readers' letter for the magazine, supplier and general information.

Unfortunately, we also started to get enquiries for membership from 'Tall Hawks', the tall person's equivalent of the Chubby Chaser. If a telephone call started with the question "Is it true that you don't have a minimum height requirement," I immediately became suspicious. Men of perhaps 5ft 8in asked to join the Club in order to meet a tall woman. They referred to themselves as Admirers of Tall Women, or the term that I really dislike, Amazon Admirers.

These men were easy to weed out. I would ask whether they had problems buying clothes in the High Street, whether there were any cars they physically could not drive and whether they could fit into seats on public transport. Once we had established that none of these were issues for them I asked: "So what do you want to join the Tall Club for?" Most would apologise before hanging up to bother us no more.

One Tall Hawk who did manage to sneak into the American Club, courtesy of meeting the minimum height requirement by a fraction of an inch, received an unceremonious comeuppance. The object of his desires was a striking woman of 6ft 7in. She lived almost a thousand miles away, and he would regularly travel to spend the weekend with her. The relationship came to a shuddering halt when she told him that it wasn't advisable for him to make the trip that weekend as she was getting married.

Our dining room was heaving at the seams. I had acquired a very large and higher than usual desk from a local shop that was closing. Built especially for two people to work at, it suited my needs just fine. Our stationery supplier had found us an inexpensive second hand photocopier. In addition there were boxes of stationery, magazines, directories, envelopes and box files full of information on more things than I care to remember, as well as a large filing cabinet. The phone still rang at all hours, seven days a week. We were running out of space and sanity, and needed to regain control of our lives.

In the middle of this mayhem, Carol and I were also hosting foreign students, who attended short language courses at a local school. The French students stayed for two or three weeks. Others, most from either the USA or Japan, were on short cultural visits and only stayed a few days. They were meant to stay with average English families so that they could practice their spoken English, and learn more about English culture, but some of them ended up with us! The small fee we received was welcome, and most of the students were a pleasure to have around. Some suggested with a smile that average families do not usually have television crews as regular visitors, but they were prepared to put up with it.

One of the students arrived back from his lessons to find Chris Greener, then Britain's tallest man, in our front room. Chris had been making a public appearance in nearby Tewkesbury, and came to spend the night with us rather than drive back to Kent. The next day we had a call from the language school's boss.

"Did you have a man of 2.30m staying with you last night," he enquired?

We confirmed that we did.

"I thought you might, he said. "Antoine told us all about it, but no-one believed him. Knowing you, I thought it was probably true."

Another, whose English was quite poor, spent a long time one morning working out exactly what he needed to tell us, with the aid of a dictionary and phrase book. He then walked up to Carol, grasped her by the shoulders, looked at her earnestly and said: "Carol! Listen very carefully, I shall say this only once."

We never did find out what he wanted to tell us.

Shino, a wonderful young Japanese lady, is still a regular visitor and calls us her English mum and dad. I even get a Fathers' Day card from her every year!

In those early days some of the students were even roped in to help stuff envelopes for the Tall Club. Our little house had become more office than home.

Allison, our helper at Datchet, told me about her friend Sue, who was starting her own secretarial services business. Her suite of offices was larger than she needed, and she had a spare room which suited my needs perfectly.

We agreed a rent which was affordable for the Club, and which would help her while she built her customer base. She opened her doors on 1st August 1992, and the Tall Persons Club moved in a month later.

There was a telephone line already in that office, which I had transferred to our home. Our home telephone was transferred to the new office, because it was already too well known as the Club's number. It was also cheaper to give our friends a new number rather than to everyone associated with the Club.

When Sue wasn't busy she helped me out, just to have something to do. If I was away for a day or two, I rerouted the telephone to her, so that there would be a real person on the end of the phone, rather than a machine. She became so much part of the Club's daily life that she joined us for the Gala Ball at our annual celebrations in Grantham, in 1997. Sandra, who had started working with Sue on a part-time basis, and eventually became her business partner, was also there.

Sue's business was so successful that some years later she moved to larger premises. The Club moved to a temporary office, as we then had only a few months to go before I handed over to a new leadership.

The TPC now had its overall direction and balance. Major social events provided eye-catching pictures which appealed to television and newspapers. The items which accompanied the pictures highlighted our message, which in turn gave chat shows and magazine programmes a theme for an item on a show. Radio stations, especially local broadcasters, requested interviews. It's not easy to fill a three hour programme every day, so chatty and entertaining interviewees are always in demand. I became known as the 'Tall Activist', but the message was always tempered with humour. As I said in many interviews: "We are serious about what we do, but we try not to take ourselves too seriously."

All this provided the Club with free advertising by the bucket-load, which in turn generated new members, whose subscriptions helped to finance the services we were providing. Subscriptions were kept in check by selling advertising to companies that were happy to pay to reach such an accurately targeted market. The club also did a fair a\mount of unpaid work, providing information, advice and assistance to a wide variety of organisations and individuals.

Members still expressed concern that the Club was too social, and didn't arrange enough social events; was too serious, and not serious enough; not politically active enough, and making too much of practical and financial issues; not doing enough for teenagers, and concentrating too much on the young; not doing enough for older members, and directing far too many articles in the magazine at the more senior members.

I guess I've made my point: whatever I did, someone didn't like it or disagreed with it, while others believed that a book might be read by the gentle glow emanating from my backside.

I believed then, as I still do today, that I had the balance as near to right as I was going to get it. Almost 1500 members in the first year must prove something. If family members were counted separately, the figure was closer to 2000.

A network of local co-ordinators was in place, and local social events, although sporadic at best outside of London, did happen.

Our first annual took place at Bredbury Hall, in Stockport on the first weekend of August 1992. It was a two night affair, running from Friday to Sunday. In 1994 I moved the event to the August Bank Holiday weekend, so that it could become a three day weekend. Costs were similar, as most major hotels were quiet over the Bank Holiday, and willing to give us rooms for a fraction of their usual rates. The Club's media profile also ensured that they were well aware of the value of the publicity a Tall Club event would attract to their hotel. News tends to be in short supply on a bank holiday, so the media were also more interested than usual.

During that first annual dinner and dance Nic Holc-Thomson joined me at our table. Also known as Gnic the Gnome, he was 5ft 7in while his partner Cathy was 6ft 3in. The Club has always welcomed the average height partners of members, because they too live with the rigours of being taller than average on a daily basis. When a tall person is subjected to one of the tired old jokes it is more often the partner who takes umbrage. The partners needed us and each other too.

Nic's request was simple enough: "Would you go over and say "Hello" to those girls over there," he asked. "They would love to meet you."

"Well, tell them to come over, and have a natter," I told him.

"They don't like to," he said.

"Why on earth not," I asked.

His reply took me aback: "Because you are Phil."

That was exactly the image I didn't want to have. I didn't want to be remote and unapproachable.

One or two more prominent members expressed their disappointment at not having been invited to sit at the 'Top Table'. There was actually no such thing. It was merely taken to be so because Carol and I were sitting there.

I was so determined that the Club should always be seen as a group of equals, run by members for members, that I never allowed a top table at an event. I once told a dining room manager who asked me where I would like the top table to be placed: "There will never be one of those at any TPC event as long as it is within my control. If I ever walk into a TPC event and see a top table I shall walk straight out, and go and eat elsewhere."

I meant it then, and I mean it still.

Each year Carol and I would wait while most people took their seats before entering the dining room. If possible, we would choose a table at which some first timers were seated. We did everything we could to avoid accusations of being cliquey. It didn't always work, but we did our best.

I shall spare you a blow by blow account of the weekend. Let's just say that we filled two hotels, attracted plenty of media coverage and shocked the heck out of William Roach, Coronation Street's Ken Barlow, during a Granada Studio tour. During the gala dinner I received a TPC First Birthday cake, Carol was presented by a group of members with a bright yellow sweatshirt with SWMBO (She Who Must Be Obeyed) emblazoned across it, and Mark Grey proposed to Julie Felton in front of everyone.

It was just an average Tall Club weekend really.

Mary Noakes is another member who has since become first and foremost our friend. I first met Mary at Datchet. She had been attending an exhibition in London that weekend, and decided to drop in on her way back to her home in Devon. She was curious to see what this new club was all about. I met Mary several more times during that first year, including at Europatreffen in Vienna.

By the time the Stockport weekend came around my nerves were well and truly frayed. It was at the time the biggest event I had ever organised, and

I was anxious for it to succeed. Mary noticed immediately that I was running myself ragged, and stepped in. She delegated all the bits of fetching and carrying that are part of any major event, found members prepared to have their photographs taken for the press, organised groups on and off busses, and generally kept me sane. If I started stressing about something she would sit me down somewhere, stick a cup of coffee in front of me, and take care of whatever it was that needed doing.

She acted as an unofficial meet and greet contact, welcoming new arrivals, making introductions, and putting everyone at their ease. Her training as a Norland nanny stood her in good stead, and by the end of the weekend she was 'Auntie Mary' to one and all. Even today she is rarely referred to any other way. She now lives and works in Spain, but people still ask us: "How's Auntie Mary?"

It took me several days to come down from the high of that weekend. Just how much of an emotional impact it had on me only became clear on the Wednesday after our return home. I had been into town to run a few errands and was on my way home. Waiting in traffic at a set of lights I suddenly burst into tears. I wasn't sobbing or crying as such, but the tears just streamed down my face. And yet I was happy and content. The tension of the weeks leading up to the event, and the high of, well, everything really, was released as I came down from that emotional high with an almighty bump. I don't know whether anyone saw me sitting there, with a huge smile on my face as the tears streamed down my cheeks, and quite frankly, I don't care.

I told Carol about it when I got home. It was an odd reaction to have had, or so I thought, but I later discovered I was not the only one to have felt that way.

Letters arrived, thanking us for a wonderful weekend. I smiled as I read the first one that said: "I don't know what happened, but when I got home I sat down and bawled my eyes out."

There were many more letters and telephone calls in which that same admission was made, by both men and women. When I recounted the story to a long time member and friend years later, he smiled sheepishly as he admitted that he too had shared that experience after his first TPC weekend.

Such displays of emotion were not limited to social events. I recall standing in the middle of a shop in Holland with a 23 year old 7ft tall member who had tears streaming down his face despite the fact that he was grinning from ear to ear. It was a specialist shop which stocked a bewildering array of clothing for the tall man. To them a 40" inside leg was a normal stock item, and he couldn't believe what he was seeing. "I don't know what to do," he said, "I've never had a choice before." Like so many tall people, he was used to buying whatever fitted, regardless of whether he liked it or not. Another member, thanks to our Supplier Directory, discovered a specialist supplier, where he spent so long in the changing rooms trying to reach a decision that the assistant came to check whether he was alright.

The first round of membership renewals served to stabilise the Club's precarious finances. Each edition of the magazine, and there were six a year at that time, cost over £1000 to produce and post. It was a pace that was impossible to maintain, both in terms of the work required to put each one together, and the costs.

I collated the magazine using a Desktop Publishing programme. Doing the layout, setting advertising, transferring hand written articles into computer files, editing each one, writing additional material and proof-reading and correcting the whole thing took care of at least a week, more often nearer two. Address labels were printed on the trusty Epson, applied to each envelope by hand, magazines were enveloped and the envelopes sealed by hand. The whole lot had to be pre-sorted according to postcodes, in order to guarantee the discounts we received under the contract we had with the Post Office. Each issue necessitated at least three visits to the printer so, in total, it took at least a week to ten days just to print and despatch each edition, never mind just producing it in the first place.

Within a couple of years I reduced publication to four editions a year. It was still a demanding pace, but at least one that I could cope with.

The first year renewals ran at about 55%. I was a little concerned about that at first, but after a chat with Rob, and one or two other people I knew who had been involved with running other kinds of club, I discovered that it was totally in line with expectations.

A lot of people had joined just to get the Supplier Directory. Now that they had it, they saw no reason to continue their membership. Many of them rejoined every three years or so to get the latest edition of the directory and lapsed a year later. Renewal rates increased year on year. The longer someone had been a member, the more likely they were to renew. Renewal rates for those who had been members for four years or more were around 85%. The remaining 15% accounted for those who had shuffled off this mortal coil, had emigrated or were working abroad (although some who did still renewed), and those whose circumstances had changed dramatically, and for whom membership had thus become a much lower priority.

Later that year the only major event organised by members in Scotland also took place. I travelled to Perth for the weekend to join the festivities, which included a visit to the smallest whisky distillery. For the final dinner and dance I even wore the kilt, the full Royal Stewart complete with all accessories. To my surprise it was one of the most comfortable garments I have ever worn. Some say you should only wear the kilt if you have a Scottish family connection. My mother had married a Scotsman, and that was good enough for me.

In January 1993 I did my level best to ignore my fortieth birthday. I suspected that an attempt would be made to surprise me with a party, and expressed my concerns to Carol over a meal out together on New Year's Eve. She asked who I thought would try such a thing, and I mentioned Mary Noakes and Pete Diamant, among others.

"Darling," she said, as she smiled at me innocently, "if they were up to something, don't you think I would know about it? Let's face it, they couldn't organise anything without me knowing about it, could they?"

My fears allayed, I relaxed. Big mistake!

A little over a week later Pippa Boulton and Paul Escott came to visit. It was Saturday, and Pippa asked me about an old coaching inn about twenty miles away. The Skirrid is Wales' oldest inn, and I had told her so much about it that she insisted on a visit. It was, in fact, part of a dastardly plan, and I walked right into it. We returned late afternoon, and she and Paul left to continue their respective journeys, or so I thought.

Carol and I joined some friends to celebrate my birthday with a meal at a local pub. I knew the landlord, a superb chef, who had owned one of our favourite restaurants, before selling it to buy the pub. As we stood before the dining room door he smiled and said: "I hope you like the way we've done out the room."

It was the first time I smelt a rat. Too late!

The door opened, and I was pushed through to face 120 guests, about 90 of whom were TPC members. People had travelled from all over the country to be there. Uwe Seyler and my cousin Stefan had even come from Germany to join us. Talk about hook, line and sinker!

When I confronted Carol and accused her of lying to me she denied it: "I just said that they couldn't organise anything without me knowing about it. I never said I didn't know about it."

That woman I thought I knew so well has been living with a salesman for too long.

Pippa and Paul's visit had been a 'Phil sitting' exercise, to keep me out of Hereford, lest I run into some of the guests, who had taken over most of a local hotel.

The years that followed were, by my standards, relatively routine. Even the numerous media appearances were just part of the job. I expect you have heard the theory of 'Six Degrees of Separation', that everyone in this world is linked to one another by a chain of no more than six people. Thanks to the media, a lot of chains linking me to famous people are quite short. My big claim to fame in that respect is my link to Elvis Presley. During one TV show I met actor Leslie Nielsen, who worked with Priscilla Presley on the "Naked Gun" films, and she was married to Elvis. I usually put it another way: I have shaken the hand of the man who kissed the lips that kissed Elvis Presley.

Over the years I have been interviewed by Richard Madeley and Judy Finnegan, Anne Diamond and Nick Owen, James Whale, Jonathan Ross, and Johnnie Walker, among others, so I am similarly linked to anyone they have interviewed, which is one heck of a list. I could have met the legendary country singer Johnny Cash, when he and I were guests on the same show. I saw him as he went to the green room for some hospitality, while I nipped out for a smoke.

I even have a link to Al Capone, which still makes me smile. Sitting at the counter in a Florida diner I got chatting to the man next to me. He was 94 years old, had a handshake that could crush walnuts, the most wonderfully wicked smile and a twinkle in his eye. He told me of his days as a bootlegger during Prohibition, which is how he met Capone.

"All the time I was a bootlegger, I only got arrested once," he grinned, "and that was for spitting on the sidewalk."

His elderly woman companion became exasperated with him. She was ready to leave and continue their journey, while he was happy to stay and chat. As we parted company, he smiled and said: "That's my daughter. Just 'cos she's 72, she thinks she can boss her old man around."

I made my first appearance on German television in 1993, during *Europatreffen* in Munich. The welcome evening had attracted attention from the local television news, and a reporter and camera crew were in attendance. The German organisers and the club's president had given their interviews, when someone told the reporter that the British contingent was led by someone who could speak the language. He came over and spoke with me for a few minutes, to make sure that I really could. The German leadership looked on anxiously. My reputation for being outspoken, and not always as diplomatic as I could be, was well established. When the reporter invited me over to where the camera was set up, anxiety became panic. As I took my seat opposite the reporter Christian Schmidt, a prominent German committee member, sat down next to me. "I'll join you," he said, "in case you need any help."

I assured him that I would be fine. The reporter concurred, signalling Christian that he should leave. He did, but remained close by, listening to every word. The interview began, and I explained how the British Club was more concerned with the practical aspects of height, that we published a Supplier Directory, and provided a wide range of medical information to our members. I then explained how we found social events, such as the one we were attending, to be a lot of fun, and that we hoped to learn from the German Club how to make our own events as vibrant and enjoyable as the one taking place in this beautiful city.

I could see a smile spread across Christian's face as I spoke.

Interview over, I got up to rejoin our group. Christian said: "Well, Phil, you certainly know how to play the game, don't you?."

"There is much that I will say in private that I will not say on camera," I told him.

I don't want to be stereotypical here, but Christian was definitely not like a lot of Germans. He was more laid back, easy going and charming. At

6ft 10in and well built, he was the kind of man who could make knicker-elastic twang just by entering a room.

The whole event was memorable for me for two reasons. First, a visit to the Berchtesgaden Salt Mines, where I got to ride down a wooden slide on a leather apron, traverse an underground lake on a raft and ride astride a narrow gauge underground railway train, just as the workers once did before the mine became a tourist attraction. Second, somehow or other I ended up agreeing to the TPC hosting the European Convention in 1998. I thought I was on safe ground, that by then someone else would have taken over running the Club. Wrong!

It was also the last year that Carol and I took part in the whole of the main programme of the convention. The Club had taken over our lives to such a degree that we felt it important to set aside whatever time we could to spend together. In Prague, the following year, we gave the outings a miss and went exploring on our own. A year later we left our members to enjoy Amsterdam, and made the four hour drive to Hamburg instead.

I visited Munich again a couple of years later, due to another of those odd language connections. While working in the Tall Club office one day I received a telephone call from a researcher from "Welt der Wunder", a German TV programme produced in Munich. She asked whether I could put her in touch with someone knowledgeable within the German club whom they could invite on to a programme they were making about height. I noticed that she was struggling a little with her English and asked whether she would prefer to speak German. She assured me that she could manage, but I switched into German anyway. She was both amazed and relieved, not having expected to encounter an Englishman who not only spoke German, but did so with a Hamburg accent. After chatting for ten minutes or so she told me not to bother with an introduction to a German club member, and asked whether I would be prepared to fly to Munich for the day to take part in the programme. Well, what would you have said?

It was during that programme that I met one of Europe's leading ergonomics experts, a man who had worked extensively for the European Community on the subject. His name was Professor Doctor Doctor Hans Jürgens. Yes, the Germans love their titles, and when a German has more than one doctorate he uses them all. Meeting him turned out to have been fortuitous when I was called upon to act as an expert witness in an industrial tribunal a couple of years later. What I learned from him in the course of the few hours we spent in each other's company came in useful at the hearing.

Our 1993 anniversary in Birmingham was the last to be held on our actual anniversary. As we were preparing to leave on Sunday I received a call inviting me on to BBC WM, for their lunchtime show with presenter Malcolm Boyden. Four guests, including me, sat round the table with him, while the producer and her assistant worked at a nearby table. In the neighbouring control room an engineer attended to the technical stuff, including playing the music. Our interview began with the usual questions, but then Malcolm referred to "…the Tall Mens' Club". I put him right, saying that it was the Tall Persons Club.

"So you have women as members as well then," he asked.

I confirmed that we did.

He continued: "So tell me, Phil, how many women have you got in the Club?"

"Oh come now, Malcolm," I said. "You can't expect me to answer a question like that! What would my wife say?"

Everyone except Malcolm burst out laughing. I smiled at him. It took a second or two before it dawned on him how the question might be understood, then he too completely lost it. It felt like a good 20 seconds before he regained his composure sufficiently to continue.

Our 1994 anniversary event was scheduled to take place in London, which I knew would appeal to members from TCI.

Within TCI almost every chapter hosts a major gathering, usually on a particular weekend each year. These usually include at least one themed party, with Toga Parties and Luaus among the firm favourites. Held on the first weekend in February, the Chicago weekend is the first of the year. Its timing is perfect for shaking off the post Christmas and New Year malaise, which also makes it the most popular of the year. It has been known to attract even greater numbers than the national Convention. Well organised, with plenty of optional extras, it's a great weekend and so, encouraged by Toby Brown, I made the trip across the water.

I was the first TPC member to attend the weekend, and promptly proved an English stereotype. A woman asked whether I was the English guy, and I confirmed that I was.

"I thought so, "she said. "I said to my husband at breakfast that it was you, but he didn't believe me. Then you picked up your coffee cup, and your little finger came out, so we knew. And anyway, no American man would ever wear a shirt like that!"

Another American woman levelled the stereotype score. While waiting to be served at the carvery one evening she told me how she wanted to visit Europe. She then stopped me in my tracks. It doesn't happen often, but she succeeded with this little gem: "I've always wanted to go to Paris," she said. "Tell me, where exactly in England is Paris, France?"

It took me a couple of seconds to comprehend what she had said, and to realise that she was serious!

"Paris is in France," I said eventually.

"Yes, I know," she said, "but where in England is that?"

"France isn't in England," I told her. "It's a different country..."

She still looked uncertain.

"... just like the USA and Canada are different countries."

"Oh," she exclaimed, "I never knew that."

I was not the only person to wince. As she left, the man next to me said: "It's incredible. There really are people like her. No wonder the world thinks Americans are stupid."

I made several more visits to TCI events, as with our own European Convention approaching far more quickly than I had anticipated I wanted to encourage as many American visitors as possible.

A 15 strong contingent of TPC members made the trip to New York City and State for Pre- and Main Convention in 1996, where we were encouraged to promote our events at every opportunity.

I was welcomed not only as a participant but also as someone who had a contribution to make. My reputation for generating publicity preceded me, thanks to several TCI members who had been at our 1994 anniversary celebrations. Media attention was so great that the hotel equipped me with a pager. It was easier than trying to find me with each call. While chatting with our visitors I was called away several times for yet another interview.

Returning to them with a Sunday Times journalist in tow really impressed them. This led to an invitation to assist in the convention's media workshop. I was even permitted to sit in on the national board's business meeting as an observer, though not allowed to comment or contribute. The best part of a day was spent discussing mostly trivia in great detail, but not actually achieving very much; a typical committee meeting, really.

Unfortunately this convention proved to be the notable exception rather than the rule.

During that week I also confirmed my ability to occasionally make a complete and utter twit of myself. Main Convention took place at a resort hotel in the Catskill Mountains, in upstate New York. At breakfast on the first morning I looked at the copious meal placed before me and remarked, more to myself than with any expectation of a response: "What, no bacon?"

"No," said the waiter, rather more abruptly than necessary, I thought.

It was only later that day, as I made my way into the local town of Monticello that it dawned on me why so many of the local hotel signs were written in Hebrew as well.

TCI Convention in Clearwater Beach in 1997 was the total opposite of the previous year. During the final dinner and dance of Convention all member clubs attending promote their respective weekend events. I was told that I couldn't promote *Europatreffen* in London, because "...this is a TCI event and yours isn't." I had to virtually beg for the two minutes they eventually allowed me.

I became increasingly aware with each visit to the USA of the number of TCI members who would seek me out to ask about our Supplier Directory, how we encouraged teenagers to join, our lobbying of politicians as well as commercial and educational bodies. They were aware of Marfan syndrome, but knew nothing of the many other syndromes which can lead to unexpected height. They had heard about these things from fellow members who had travelled to our events in the UK, and seen for themselves how much more pro-active we were. Our own Matthew Langmaid was a regular visitor at TCI conventions and a tireless advocate for the TPC and its work. It was obvious that they wanted the same kind of service from their own club and chapters, and that getting it wasn't going to be easy. TCI had been plodding along happily since 1938 as a social organisation for adults aged over 21, and meeting such additional demands wasn't considered a major priority.

A few chapters did manage to start teenage sections, but I got the feeling that it was in spite of rather than because of the leadership in some cases.

The was a strong feeling of 'We should be doing what you're doing' from rank and file TCI members, but a sense of 'We were founded as a social organisation, and we support the US Marfan Foundation, but we can't be doing with all that other stuff', from the national board.

The staunchest supporter of the TPC in North America was Ryan Anthony, who published an independent regular review of the TCI chapters' newsletters under the banner of *Talltown Observer*. It was a labour of love which lasted over fifteen years., and in which he featured *6ft+* in its own section, *Notes from across the Pond*. In his editorials and articles he was often outspoken in his criticism of how TCI was run, often referring to the organisation as *Toga Clad Inebriates*. He admired what we were achieving in the UK, and wished that they would do more to emulate us.

Around the same time another organisation for tall people sprang up in the US. Under the banner of National Institute for Tall People Carlisle Bean sought to provide the practical information that the TPC had become known for in the UK. He was swamped with requests for information and looked set to emulate our success, providing the practical assistance to complement TCI's social activities. Unfortunately, he had a career as an architect to support his family, and help wasn't forthcoming. The organisation disappeared with ne'er a whimper, more's the pity.

A Lot of a Doo

By the mid-nineties the Tall Persons Club was well established and was often asked for assistance by people who were highly respected in their field. One such occasion was a call from a consultant endocrinologist at a major London teaching hospital. He had been invited to give a presentation at a medical conference in some exotic location. His presentation was to include specific information about medical and genetic conditions which cause an individual to become taller than expected.

We talked for over an hour, during which time I gave him a précis of the main symptoms of each condition, and explained some of the physiological and psychological implications. Some of these were not mentioned in medical literature on the subject, but I had confirmed them through discussion with a wide range of people, who had been affected either directly or indirectly by the condition. As an endocrinologist he was, of course, already familiar with some aspects of some syndromes, and we exchanged experiences and knowledge.

After a while it suddenly struck me as odd that he should be calling me for this information.

"I'm curious," I said. "Why have you called me, when you could have got this information from colleagues in other hospitals?"

His reply surprised me. He told me that each of those specialists was only really familiar with the condition in which they specialised. Each would give him reams of detailed technical information which he would then have to make comprehensible to an audience that was expecting salient information presented in an easily understood way. By calling me, he got the information he wanted in a way that was easy to understand and convey. Also, doctors only see patients in the context of a consultation, while my relationship gave me greater insight into the psychological aspects of each condition.

"Because you have all the information in one place, no-one has greater breadth and depth of knowledge of the subject than you," he told me. "As far as I am concerned, you are this country's leading expert on height."

Another doctor told me that I probably know more about the subject of height than most doctors, as they tend to be either general practitioners or specialise in one or two conditions at most. I proved that statement right on more than one occasion.

On the other hand I also came under fire from one or two specialists who took issue with me over the opinions I expressed. They were not comfortable with the idea that a layman was questioning their wisdom and expertise.

One doctor, a leading specialist in his field, called to remonstrate with me over advice I had given a family who had a son with Marfan syndrome. He had recommended height restriction by means of accelerating puberty. The parents called me for my opinion and I counselled extreme caution. I had met the family several times, and knew that the boy was 15 years old and already well into puberty. I had my doubts whether the proposed hormone treatment would have the desired and promised effects. Timing of the treatment is crucial, and I wasn't convinced that the optimum timing hadn't already been missed.

The good doctor and I spent the best part of an hour on the telephone discussing our respective views. Although we didn't reach an agreement, he did concede that my recommendation to the family to ask lots of questions and to not go ahead unless they fully understood all of the possible implications was actually good advice.

By 1997 I was starting to consider my options for the day that I handed over the Club to a new leadership.

I have always believed that no-one should be left in charge of anything for more than five years, seven at most. After that time the person has brought all to the job that they are ever likely to. The initial enthusiasm and optimism will have waned, and they begin to take the line of least resistance. Whatever they are in charge of will stop developing and moving forward.

There was little more I could do to raise the Club's profile. We had appeared in every major national and regional newspaper several times, most major magazines, been on every major TV magazine show, and were still giving several interviews a year on local radio. We even made two appearances in Dublin on Ireland's prime time *Late Late Show* with Gay Byrne. The first lasted almost half an hour, the second a good fifteen minutes when David Conroy and his family organised the Club's first Irish weekend some five years later. Our anniversary celebrations were so established that each year we would have several media enquiries about the event before I had even sent out the press release. Even so, it was time to hand over the helm. But first I had to honour my commitment to the Club's biggest event to date.

Four years earlier, at the *Europarat* meeting in Munich, I had foolishly volunteered the TPC to host the 1998 *Europatreffen* in London. A superb team of people gathered around me, each of whom had particular skills or knowledge that perfectly complemented the team needed to organise and execute the biggest and most complex event the Club had ever undertaken.

Until this point, the Club had benefited from that most perfect of management structures: a committee of one. I used to say, only half in jest, that ours was a fully democratic organisation – we discussed everything fully, and then we did it my way. Even so, I was never autocratic or dictatorial in the way I ran the Club. If I had a particular idea or plan, I would run it past members with whom I had regular contact, and even ask those who just happened to call the office for some totally unconnected reason for their opinion. Many an idea of mine met its demise at that stage. It always became clear very quickly what would or would not work, and what would or would not be welcomed and supported by the membership. Now, for the first time, I had to work with a wide range of people and their opinions, and their personal likes and dislikes.

All things considered, it worked better than I initially hoped, and major bloodshed was avoided. I did, however, notice that politics began to play a role in Club life. How big a part became clear during the 1997 Europatreffen in Dresden.

The office of European President was largely a ceremonial one. Because no system of funding that was fair and equitable to all Clubs could be agreed upon. Most Presidents did nothing more than send out the minutes of the last meeting, and issue a formal invitation to the next. Rob Bruintjes had been the only one to actively encourage greater cohesion and cooperation. In theory that was exactly what he was supposed to be doing, and what everyone said they wanted the President to do. In reality, what they said and what they did were usually very different.

The subject was discussed again at the Europarat meeting, and it looked for a moment that an agreement might be reached, but no. Funding the office was left to a final decision at the next gathering in London. They did agree that the President be granted a free place at the Europatreffen Gala Ball, so that was progress of sorts. Because a candidate would be likely to have already paid for the programme in the year of his or her election, it was agreed that free attendance would first be granted the following year, and again in their outgoing year, when they were technically no longer in office.

It was an election year. Our Europatreffen team wanted me to run, as the Presidency would lend additional impact to our publicity efforts for the following year. I resisted, knowing that how I would want to carry out the duties would add considerably to my workload. Organising a week long series of events in addition to the routine workload of running the Club is not easy, no matter how good a team you have around you. The Presidency would only compound the problem and so I did not stand as a Candidate.

Uwe Seyler, Rob Bruintjes and one other delegate did. Uwe really wanted the job. He often travelled to events abroad, and knew that the office would add to his standing at those events. The vote was tied between Uwe and Rob. A second round of voting was requested, and someone asked whether new candidates could also stand. Normally, of course, a run-off should be only between the two tied candidates but this time the meeting allowed new candidates.

I knew the other delegates well enough to know that we were facing an endless series of ties. The only possible candidate likely to break that tie was me. Our event organising team had wanted me to stand together with another TPC member as joint candidates, so that the resulting workload might be shared. However, other decisions made earlier in the meeting had made that inadvisable. All proceedings had been conducted in German as usual, so I only had time to tell the team that I would explain later why I could not run for the office with my intended presidential partner.

I announced my readiness to stand as a Candidate to the meeting's Chairman. Rob Bruintjes smiled, and immediately withdrew his candidature, leaving Uwe and me to contest the election.

There was an objection from the German delegate and Club Chairman, Lothar Haan. As I worked full-time for the TPC, the only Tall Club official in the world to do so, he felt that my candidature was incompatible with the prevailing ethos of honorary service. My nett income from the TPC amounted to less than half the legal minimum wage, but as far as he was concerned I received a payment and that was all that mattered. The fact that Rob's wife was a paid administrator of the Dutch Club was perfectly acceptable to him, as she was not an official of the club.

Votes were cast, and I became European President. Christian Schmidt expressed surprise that my margin of victory had not been greater.

Uwe was upset: "You stole my job, buddy," he said angrily, and he wasn't joking. It placed a strain on our relationship for the duration of my term.

Back at our hotel that afternoon I was summoned, and I do mean summoned, by two of our Europatreffen team. Obviously they had a grievance, and having me come to them was meant to give them a tactical advantage. They both lay stretched out on the bed, their posture signalling total confidence and inevitable victory. In no uncertain terms they told me that I had better do something about establishing a joint European Presidency, or the whole team would withdraw from the event. I was sure that they did not have the support of the whole team, a suspicion confirmed much later, but for now I was being blackmailed.

My first instinct was to invite them to perform several unnatural acts upon themselves, or each other, whichever they preferred. I had the briefest thought of simply announcing cancellation of the event at the Gala Ball, and inviting anyone who wanted to know why to direct their questions to these two. Had I done so, I would have lost all credibility in the Tall Club community. Whether it was pride or integrity that stopped me I don't know; you decide. But I realised that this was politics rearing its ugly head; it was a seminal moment. I knew then that it was time to hand over the Club to a new leadership.

My presidency, although welcomed by most Clubs, was not, or so it seemed, as enthusiastically received by the leaders of most of the German affiliate Clubs. For the duration of my term I regularly met with obstruction and what I can only call constructive ignorance. I always met with warm welcomes and friendship both before and after my term, but only rarely during.

The first example occurred later that day at the Welcome Evening. Out of the blue the organisers told me that I would have to give the presentation for next year's event that evening. Traditionally the presentation is given at the biggest event of the year, the Gala Ball on the Saturday evening. That would not be possible this year they said. I explained that I had a video that I wanted to show as part of the presentation, but that it was back at the hotel. Too bad, I was told, I would just have to manage.

I refused point blank. As European President, I would be expected to make a short speech at the Gala Ball, and I could include the presentation then, I suggested. They weren't happy, but knew they couldn't prevent it.

The team had decided that for our presentation we should show a five minute Tourist Board video and distribute flyers and booking forms to everyone present. I dropped in at the venue during the afternoon to make sure that video facilities were on hand; they weren't. I negotiated with the AV contractors who were still on site to provide a large video screen. Some cash changed hands, and the deal was done. Unfortunately they positioned it right in front of the stage instead of at the side, as I has requested. The organisers were extremely annoyed, which I completely understand. I got the blame and told I was shamelessly impertinent. They eventually listened to my side of the story, we made our peace. When we arrived that evening the screen had been all but moved to Hungary and was just about visible to about half the audience, but I was not going to make an issue of it. We were guests after all.

I was so busy with the myriad trivia that these events involve, that I almost missed the hot buffet and I only just managed to secure some food. I had barely taken my first forkful when a welcome parade of all national Clubs began. The Chairman or President of each was invited forward, officially welcomed with a huge bouquet of flower and then stood in line with their peers to highlight the wide range of nationalities present.

I was still chewing when the TPC was called, and so signalled 'Auntie' Mary Noakes to take the accolade. She was already well known on the European scene and viewed as my right hand man, so to speak. She protested, but the buffet had closed and I was not about to let anything come between me and a very tasty goulash. There were a few raised eyebrows when she accepted the welcome in my place. All was well again an hour later, when I was introduced as the new European President.

"We thought you were insulting us," one man said, as I headed for the stage, "but it all makes sense now."

They do take all the ceremonial stuff so seriously.

I made my speech first in German, then in English, saying only that I thanked everyone for their trust, and hoped to prove myself worthy of the great honour that had been bestowed on me. The applause confirmed that I had been suitably humble and concise. I concluded with our presentation for *Europatreffen* 1998, in what was probably the shortest speech and presentation ever given.

That evening was the only opportunity to gather together all of the Europarat delegates for an EGM. We withdrew and I explained the proposal to appoint a joint or vice president to share the workload. All they had to say was either yes or no, but it still took fifteen minutes. They agreed that I could nominate a representative, but that no official title would be granted; meeting closed.

I took the news back to the rebels. They declared themselves satisfied that I had tried, and that was good enough for them; end of boycott. "You did what we asked," said one, graciously. "I now support you all the way."

I looked him square in the eye as I told him that if he ever tried another stunt like that, I would personally see to it that two parts of his anatomy were served up on a plate, decorated with skewers and other sharp pointy things.

Petty politics make me sick.

That convention in Dresden was not the most enjoyable for Carol and me. It did have one outstanding highlight, but one that was nothing to do with tall clubs in any way. *Europatreffen* was work for me and this one had already frayed my nerves very nicely by the time Carol and I set off to spend the Friday exploring on our own

Dresden is in the heart of some beautiful countryside and just a short drive away lies a picturesque town with a hilltop castle whose name is etched deep into the history books: Colditz. We checked out the small local shops around the market square of the quaint old town and had lunch, before making our way up to the castle.

It was a curious experience to walk along the same path we had seen in so many films and documentaries. We could have been on a film set, and yet we were constantly aware of the historical significance of our surroundings.

Less than a decade since the fall of the former GDR, the East was still a long way behind the West in economic terms; it showed in the castle.

Almost anywhere in Western Europe it would have been a major tourist attraction, fully restored, and bristling with tour guides and gift shops, but at that time Colditz Castle was just sort of there. I can't think how else to explain it. It all served to underline the huge gulf in attitudes between East and West in those early post-reunification years.

After the war the castle had been a hospital and nursing home. It had also housed psychiatric patients, a fact now glossed over even though the last residents had moved out barely a year before. Given the dilapidated state of the place I found it difficult to believe that anyone could have lived there as recently as that. The paintwork was peeling, the plaster crumbling and the stonework in desperate need of attention.

We, along with the few visitors who made their way up the steep path, were able to just wander in. Most of the castle interior was closed to visitors. Such was the condition of the place it was quite simply too dangerous to allow people to go where they pleased. Even so we were able to look into a few of the rooms, and to sit in that famous courtyard, trying to imagine what it might have been like for those brave souls who spent years incarcerated within those walls.

There were no facilities for visitors, not even toilets, and that was starting to become a problem. I had noticed a door in the famous arched passageway leading to the courtyard. A small wooden sign identified it as the office. My knock was answered by an ebullient gentleman in his fifties to whom I explained our predicament.

"Come on in," he said. My German language skills once again proved useful. The office was almost bare, except for a large office table – it wasn't even a desk – a couple of shelves and a small cupboard. A pot or two of paint might have helped to make it more inviting, but even here neglect was the order of the day. A neighbouring room housed the only working facilities in the place.

I asked about the castle, its past and possible future. I'm not sure whether he was pleased that someone was showing interest or he was just lonely, but he found a couple of chairs for us and set about washing up some cups while he boiled a kettle. We spent almost an hour with him, chatting and drinking copious amounts of coffee. It was more like visiting a friend than being mere visitors.

In the course of the last decade the Colditz city fathers have recognised the value of the site, and set about restoring the Castle to attract visitors and their money to the town. Today, part of the Castle serves as a youth hostel, while guided tours of those parts of the castle that have been made accessible are the norm.

I'm glad we saw Colditz Castle as and when we did. I have the feeling that somehow restoration and presentation for the benefit of tourists will have sanitised the experience.

Our time in Colditz, and the wonderful welcome we received there, served to balance what would have otherwise been a not very enjoyable convention weekend.

Back in the UK, I started to pass more of the administration over to Sue, our office landlady. Her business had grown, but was still at a level where any work was welcome. She agreed to work for the TPC at a lower rate, on condition that the work was done at her convenience, when she had no other work waiting.

I began to consider my future beyond the Club, and later that year bought a half share in a small private hire operation. It sounds more grand than it was. My friend Dave owned a taxi. He had been offered another, albeit elderly car with a licence in place, but couldn't afford it on his own. The business provided a small additional income, which reduced the financial strain on Carol and me.

Our European Convention year kicked off with personal business. Carol's 40th birthday could not be allowed to pass without due recognition, so amidst the preparations for convention I managed to arrange a surprise birthday party for her. Our friends, the rock band, even travelled over from Germany to provide the music. I then spirited her away for a weekend at Hampton Court Palace. Thanks to Club members Mick and Jo Jager, who told me about the Landmark Trust, I secured a former grace and favour apartment in Fish Court, in the heart of the palace. Henry VIII is Carol's favourite king, and being able to call his former palace home for four days and three nights was an experience to savour. We were even invited to join some of the security guards on their late night patrols around the palace by torchlight; an unforgettable experience.

A Lot of a Doo

Trying to put together a comprehensive programme for an event as large as *Europatreffen* within the then traditional budget constraints demanded by some Clubs is extremely challenging. For years organisers were pressured to keep the costs for the main programme to a limit that became laughably low. It is only in recent years that a more realistic attitude has been taken by both organisers and those attending. The main programme was expected to consist of the *Europarat* meeting, the Welcome Evening with entertainment and food, the Friday outing and evening event with food included at some point, the Gala Ball with live music and preferably a meal included, the Sunday morning Farewell Gathering and all this for £85, preferably less! Thanks to some hard negotiating, we did it.

We were in the final run-up to *Europatreffen London 1998* and I thought I had tangled with Lothar Haan, the German Club's chairman, for the last time; I should have known better. His professional background had made him a good administrator. Unfortunately, good administrators rarely make commercially aware businessmen, which became abundantly clear when our booking forms were distributed to all Clubs. When in 1996 we first announced the outline programme and price, the German Mark stood at DM2.27 against the GBP. By 1998, when bookings and payments were due it was DM2.77, a change of over 20%.

Herr Haan was outraged. Our prices were exorbitant! If we didn't reduce them he would tell all his members not to attend. I pointed out that it was the value of the German Mark that had fallen significantly, not the price that had changed, but it made no difference. Germany's club was the largest, and therefore all prices had to be acceptable to his members first and foremost. In actual terms that difference amounted to about £15-£17 per head, a fraction of the overall cost of attending, but a principle was at stake. Unless we reduced prices he would withdraw support.

Most German club members were of my generation, and I knew that they would follow the advice of their leadership – that is not a dig, that is a fact. I told the organising team, and we set about modifying the programme to reduce the price, knowing full well that we were damned if we did, and damned if we didn't.

Proof came at the Europarat when I opened the floor for general discussion. I came under attack from a party of Germans for not giving value for money. Delegates from other clubs took over the argument, pointing out that I could not be held responsible for the Pound Sterling's recent strength, and that they too had suffered at the hands of volatile exchange rates. It didn't pacify them one bit.

Thank Goodness I had separated the funding of Europatreffen 1998 from Club funds, by setting up a Company Limited by Guarantee to administer it. This also met with Herr Haan's disapproval. The legal documentation of the company specified that any potential surplus funds at the time of winding up would be donated to charity. He demanded that any surplus should be distributed back to those who had attended. Further demands were made in case any surplus was too small to be distributed economically; and so it went on with each and every aspect of the event.

As I recall (and my memory is far from infallible) he even made his feelings clear in the twice yearly German Club magazine. He didn't attend, nor did quite a few of the regulars, so the German contingent was well down.

In the end we lost a little over £1500 on the event. Had Herr Haan been a little less divorced from reality, we would have just about broken even, which is all we ever wanted to do. I'm sure he would have been delighted if the TPC had been financially wiped out, as long as the ethos of honorary service without profit was maintained. Perhaps part of the reason was that I, together with Rob, had become a thorn in the side of the German leadership, because we were loosening their iron grip on the European Tall Club scene.

Thank Goodness, the leadership changed soon afterwards, to be replaced by a more conciliatory and cooperative group of people.

Our event ran smoothly, thanks to the tremendous work done by the team. Delegation has never been my strong point, because I am only too well aware that the buck will always stop with me, regardless. Yet I only had to voice that something needed doing, and it was be taken care of. Each member of the team assumed far greater responsibility and workload than I could reasonably have asked. Simple thanks are wholly inadequate to express my gratitude to each and every one of them for what they did for the Club and for me personally and that even includes the two Dresden rebels.

The only moment of dissent between me and some members of the team occurred at the Thursday Welcome Evening. I had wanted to include that most English of traditions, Morris Dancing, but was voted down and vehemently castigated for daring to suggest such a naff idea. Although there was some support for the idea, the vote made it clear that I was to authorise no part of the event budget at all for anything so awful, so I didn't.

The room was packed when I took to the stage to make the opening announcements. I saw looks of dismay on the faces of several of the team as I continued: "Ladies and Gentlemen, I had wanted to include something quintessentially English in tonight's festivities, however our organisation team has refused to let me do so, and would not authorise the expenditure. Therefore, what you are about to see has not cost a single penny, but has instead been donated by the Tall Persons Club as a present to all of you here at Europatreffen 1998. Please give a warm welcome to the men of the Greenwich Morris Team."

I could feel the dirty looks and daggers boring into every part of my body. Had they not been metaphorical daggers I would have looked like an overgrown pincushion. I didn't dare mention that 'Auntie' Mary had been my co-conspriator, which is how we had managed to sneak them in unseen.

The doors opened, and in they came. The crowd loved it, especially when they pulled up several audience members to come and join them, among them 7ft 1in Matthew Langmaid from Wales. All entered into the spirit of the occasion, dancing with more enthusiasm than grace, flailing their hankies and jangling their bells. It was a complete success, and is still one of the most talked about events of the week, second only to the Gala Ball. Afterwards, even those who had fought tooth and nail against it admitted: "You were right, and we were wrong."

Media attention was plentiful that week too, and not just from the UK. Quite aside from the numerous interviews for the press, TV and radio in this country we attracted media interest from around the world, including the US, Canada, Germany and Japan, gave a live interview via a satellite link for one TV station in Canada and we made it as the "...and finally" item on *News at Ten*.

I was also invited to a small press conference at the International Press Association. The journalists were all very polite, and most receptive to what we were trying to achieve: to raise the profile of the needs of tall people, especially as populations world wide were becoming taller.

After about an hour of questions and lively conversation, an American journalist said: "So, in summary, the work you are doing now is not just for the benefit of tall people today, but for all people of the future."

I smiled. "Beautifully put," I said, "That sums it up perfectly. I wish I had said that."

He gave me a wry smile, and said: "You did, about five minutes ago!"

It is customary for the Gala Ball to include some kind of display of formation dancing, performance art or something of that nature. We were constantly asked what we had lined up. Only members of the team knew what it was going to be, and they weren't telling.

Uwe Seyler especially was determined to get some inside information. Time and again he tried to find out more, only to be told that it was secret for reasons of security. Rumours ran rife throughout the week, as people speculated on what it might be. The general opinion was that, while it was likely to be good, we were building it up far more than was justified.

Saturday evening came, and the team arrived early at the Connaught Rooms. Each member was equipped with a security pass and a walkie talkie, all except me for some reason.

"You're not having one," said Mary, "because you'll only worry and start to interfere. Now go away!"

I did as I was told. Whoever was in charge, it certainly wasn't me. Humph!

Everyone had been told to not be late, and warned that the doors to the function room would be locked at the start of the evening, and not reopened for at least half an hour. Speculation increased.

As people arrived, the team marshalled them into the bar. Only a few people were late, having not believed that the doors would be locked at the appointed time, but they were. At 19.50 everyone was shown into the main room. By 20.00 they were seated, and the huge dividing doors to the bar were closed. Stragglers were diverted by the team to a bar in another part of the complex.

I sat at our table, feeling useless. Everything had been taken out of my hands. I wasn't used to sitting back and letting others do the work, but I wasn't given a choice.

Mary Noakes took to the stage and welcomed everyone to the Gala Ball. Then she announced: "Tonight music will be provided by an eight piece dance band. First, however, they have brought along sixteen of their friends. Together they will Beat Retreat. Ladies and gentlemen, will you please welcome the Band of Her Majesty's Royal Marines, Britannia Royal Naval College Dartmouth!"

The dividing doors to the bar slid open. A drum roll broke the silence, followed by the opening strains of The Liberty Bell, better known as the theme from *Monty Python's Flying Circus*, as the band emerged from the bar and took to the floor. The audience produced a spontaneous Mexican Wave, except that no-one sat down again. The applause and the cheers were deafening. We had done it!

Uwe Seyler looked across, nodded, and gave me a smile and thumbs up. Even he was impressed.

A German news cameraman wanted to get a shot of the action close up, and knelt in the middle of the dance floor as the band approached. Mary ran over and dragged him to the edge of the floor.

"They would have gone round me," said the cameraman indignantly.

"They wouldn't," Mary told him. "They'd go straight over the top of you."

The look of disdainful disbelief was wiped from his face as he was unceremoniously barged out of the way by a very large Marine wielding a deadly trumpet.

"Oh," said the startled cameraman, and retreated to a safe distance.

The display ended with a rousing performance of Elgar's Pomp and Circumstance, with those who knew the words belting out Land of Hope and Glory at the top of their voices. Union flags had been placed on every table for all, and were waved by the crowd, regardless of nationality. I still get goose-bumps whenever I recall that evening.

Charles Frost complained to me later: "For Goodness' sake, I'm 6ft 11in, and I had to stand on a chair to see!"

Mary had secured the band for us, as she still had connections, having once been married to a Royal Marine officer. It wasn't cheap, but was worth every last penny. Because she had made the booking, protocol prescribed that she was Officer Commanding for the evening. Therefore, the display complete, the Drum Major approached Mary and saluted.

She stood to face him as he spoke: "That concludes Beat Retreat by the Band of Her Majesty's Royal Marines. Permission to withdraw?"

Mary gave a wicked smirk: "Actually, I'd rather you didn't."

His face registered total panic, as the Drum Sergeant behind him did a terrible job of trying to suppress his giggles; he was in on it.

In all his years, no-one had ever refused permission to withdraw. The Royal Marine manual covers every eventuality, what to do in any situation, whether on the battlefield or on ceremonial duty – except this one.

Mary turned to Carol: "What do you think, shall we let them go?"

Together they hammed it up for a few moments before Mary relented.

"Oh, alright then," she said, "off you go."

He saluted, and smartly got the heck out of there, in case she changed her mind.

After an excellent three course dinner, the band returned, and played for dancing until 2.00am. I have not seen the dance floor still packed at that time of the morning at any other Gala Ball.

Before leaving that night, the Drum Major complimented Mary and the team for the best organised and most smoothly executed event in which the band had ever taken part. High praise, indeed, from a military man.

A Danish delegate was equally complimentary, although in a less flattering way. "Thanks a bunch," she said. "We have to follow that in a couple of years." She expressed her doubts that our display would ever be bettered, so they weren't even going to try.

A few people teased us about the level of secrecy we had maintained. We had to explain that, although the threat of terrorism was not considered great, our band was still first and foremost a crack military unit in an enclosed space in Central London. Secrecy had been part of the booking conditions. The colour drained from many a face as the possible implications dawned.

The Dortmund Club gave its presentation of the programme for 1999, which they were hosting. It consisted largely of an interminable slide show, including several of buildings under construction that would not be completed until 2002. The speaker's voice was quiet and monotone, and not as enthusiastic as the excellent programme would have justified.

After almost twenty minutes of this, with the bar filled to capacity and most of the remaining audience losing the will to live, I had a quiet word. People wanted to dance, I told him, and in five minutes I would pull the plug. He was not happy, as he still had a fistful of presentation cards to get through. We spoke briefly later. He hadn't realised how long his presentation had gone on, but his disappointment at not being allowed to complete it was evident.

As the evening drew to a close I felt the need to be alone for a while. It was a pleasantly cool and dry night, and the hotel was only a fifteen minute walk away. Making my way towards the main road I saw four young men coming towards me. They looked at each other, and exchanged a few words. As they drew closer they parted, with two passing me on each side. Seconds later I heard a voice shout: "Tall people – we respect!"

I turned to see them smiling, with their right arms raised in a clenched first salute. I smiled back, and continued on my way.

It was a wonderful finishing touch to an incredible week.

The End of an Era

Back in Hereford I attended to my Presidential duties, and sent out the minutes of the *Europarat* meeting. One or two clubs wrote back to say they disagreed with the minutes, but were prepared to accept them, as only minor details were wrong. Another refused to accept the minutes as accurate in any way. I wrote, asking them to submit their proposed corrections, but all I got was another letter saying the minutes were wrong, and that was it. Try as I might, even after a telephone call, I could not get anyone to tell me even one thing that was incorrect, but still they insisted. It was never resolved, and the Club's delegate duly raised the protest as instructed at the next *Europarat* meeting. When asked to clarify their objection she could say only that she had been told to object, but was given no reason why. No prizes for guessing which Club it was.

I later tried to rally the troops, and encouraged all Clubs to lobby their MEP to improve ergonomic standards in the EU. One wrote back to say that as they weren't in the EU there was no point. A success with their national government would add impetus to our cause with the EU, I explained, but to no avail. Another wrote to say that they were far too busy with Club matters, and that it was up to me. I understood why Rob had found the job so frustrating. Everyone wants change and improvements, but no-one is willing to do a damned thing to get them.

I went back to concentrating on the TPC and our anniversary celebrations for later that year. Carol and I had made an exploratory visit to Glasgow the previous year to check out possible hotels.

I do love staying at nice hotels for nothing. Before making any booking I always insisted on staying at the hotel, in order to gauge its suitability for our purposes. I only ever paid for a room once, and even then it was at a reduced rate. Bed and breakfast in a four star Central London hotel, with a view of Tower Bridge, for £50 will do me very nicely, thank you. You see how I suffered for the TPC and its members?

The importance of those exploratory visits was underlined while planning our 1995 event in Newcastle. We had stayed at a Holiday Inn and at the Swallow Hotel in Gosforth Park, the one we eventually booked. On our way home we passed a Marriott Hotel, located right next to the Metro Centre, a huge shopping complex. I had heard that they had some interesting themed rooms, Hollywood, Elvis Presley and a sheik's tent among them. Perhaps I could allocate one to the first person to book, as a surprise. It seemed silly to not check it out while we were there, so we called in.

I asked for the conference and banqueting manager. She was a woman in her thirties, dressed in the Marriott uniform. I explained who we were and why we were there, and asked whether we might take a look around. We were dressed very casually, as we had a long journey ahead of us. She obviously thought we were time wasters, but showed us around anyway.

The height of flattery would be to describe her attitude as disinterested. She chomped away on her chewing gum the whole time, and any information had to be dragged out of her. Back in the foyer she bade us a curt farewell and left us standing there.

"Shall I get some prices," I asked Carol, knowing full well what the answer would be.

"I've seen enough," she said. "If she is an example of the kind of service we can expect for spending twenty grand in here, you can forget it!"

We think so much alike at times, it's spooky.

We had terrific local, and quite a bit of quality national, publicity for that event, I often wonder whether she saw any of it, and how she felt when she did.

Carol and I had two candidate hotels to check out in Glasgow. On the way I made an excuse that we needed to make an overnight stop at an hotel in the Lake District. Carol seemed a little unsure, as it is not like me to break a journey of a mere 300 miles. As we booked in I asked the receptionist: "What time's kick off."

"You mean the antiques weekend," she said?

Carol became most excited, as she loves antiques, porcelain and jewellery in particular. "You hear that, Phil," she said, "They're having an antiques weekend."

"I know," I said. "We're already booked in for it, and the guest speaker is Henry Sandon."

Carol put her hands on her hips and with badly feigned anger called me an awful lot of names. I don't remember any of them being 'sweetheart' or 'darling'. Still, it's good to know that I can still spring a surprise on her.

131

On our second evening in Glasgow, Carol and I experienced another of those strange chains of connection coincidences. We were joined by local member Dave Holladay, and his new girlfriend, Louise. She had recently returned from Milan, where she had been working in the fashion industry. Carol's work colleague had a niece who also worked in Milan.

"Strange girl," said Carol. "Bit of an eccentric. Got married in a black dress with feathers everywhere."

Louise shrieked, the barman almost dropped a glass, Dave and I thought she had sat on something sharp.

"I was at her wedding," she said, and Dave and I resigned ourselves to the ensuing girlie chat about wedding dresses and stuff.

In July 1998 Dave and I bought a stretched limousine to expand our little business. It was the first in the county, and caused quite a stir. The idea was born of a shopping trip I had organised the previous year to New York.

Dave had joined us, as did a journalist for the *Sunday Telegraph Magazine*. In total, ten of us went on a successful and enjoyable trip. On arrival in Newark I gathered everyone together outside the terminal to wait for our transport into Manhattan.

Two limousines pulled in front of the terminal building, and I discreetly signalled the drivers. One of the girls nudged me: "Look Phil, there's our transport."

I said: "It is. Get in."

She thought I was joking and didn't budge. The drivers had already opened the boot, and I handed one my bag. There were smiles and laughter all round as everyone clambered in, while an airport traffic marshal demanded loudly that we get a move on and clear the road.

I had told no-one that two limousines would work out cheaper than three taxis. The airport bus service, which stopped at Grand Central, was no cheaper, and would have left us eleven blocks from our hotel.

The limousine Dave and I bought was added to our little fleet, which had grown to three vehicles. The business was building slowly but surely, and I knew that I would have something to keep me busy after I handed over the Club.

Just a week or so later Carol joined our friend Alli on her hen night. They were having a wonderful time in a local nightclub when a few bars in to

Come on Eileen Carol's Achilles tendon snapped. It couldn't have happened at a worse time.

The tendon was surgically repaired, and her leg put in plaster. The foot was positioned pointing downwards, so getting around was difficult, even on crutches. Although she could make a cup of coffee for herself, she couldn't carry it anywhere. I had to help her with everything, and I do mean everything.

Every three weeks the plaster was removed, the foot repositioned to gradually lengthen the repaired tendon, and the plaster replaced. She was in plaster for a total of twelve weeks. There followed three weeks of recovery and exercise, to reclaim some of the resulting muscle wastage. It was a difficult time for both of us. Charles came to stay for a couple of weekends to help out, but it was crunch time.

I was running the TPC, organising the annual celebration in Glasgow, helping Dave with the private hire business and looking after Carol who couldn't be left on her own for long periods. Stress, anyone?

Attendance in Glasgow was disappointing, especially as I had been getting grief from some Scottish members for not having held the event in Scotland before. Less than ten Scots joined us, and one of those had travelled from his current home in Somerset. On the plus side, he met a fellow member from Edinburgh, and was married two years later. Carol did not join us for the weekend, as she was still plastered, and not in a good way.

The event went reasonably well but something was missing. The atmosphere was different to previous years.

It was after the Gala Ball, in the wee small hours of Monday morning. We were all together in the bar, winding down. One member stared morosely into his pint, shook his head, and said: "It's just not the same without Carol."

There was general agreement. A 'newbie' asked why it was so and was told: "Come to the next one; you'll see."

I sometimes forgot just how big a role Carol had created for herself in the Tall community, but there was always someone to remind me. As I walked into the hotel at an event in Chicago, I heard no welcome or enquiries after my well-being. Instead, I heard Tom Cashman bellow above the noise in the foyer: "Hey Phil, where's the little 'un?"

Someone asked who he was talking about, and I had to listen to several Americans tell stories about Carol for a few minutes before someone finally said hello to me.

In Germany she was known by many affectionately as "Kleine Wurst", or little sausage, thanks to her love of German bratwurst. Even those with whom I did not enjoy the most cordial of relationships treated her with kindness and respect.

The attention she received wasn't always positive. A few of the women of TCI could be particularly scathing when referring to "…those short women who steal our tall men."

One tried a little one on one dig: "I hear you have a problem with being short," she said.

"No," said Carol, "but apparently some of the American women do."

Sandi Marse, a statuesque 6ft 4in Floridian smiled. "You tell 'em, girl," she said, and gave Carol a big hug. That didn't go down too well either.

One of them even complained to me: "What is it with you tall guys? Why do you always marry short women?"

"I didn't," I told her. "I married a woman who is intelligent, has a kind heart, a loving and giving nature and a great personality. She just happened to come in a package that was 5ft 3in."

The Co-ordinators' Meeting at Glasgow took place, as always, on the Monday morning. It has since transmogrified into the AGM, but then it was still an opportunity for the co-ordinators and me to share ideas and thoughts about the Club. More importantly, it allowed them to share ideas with one another in a quiet and measured way that wasn't possible in the hectic atmosphere of the rest of the weekend. I would also brief them about any publicity that was coming up.

This time it was a little different. I asked for a clear run for five minutes, with no interruptions or questions. It was the first clue anyone had that something was afoot.

My belief that no-one should be left in charge of anything for more than five years, seven at most, was well known. No-one thought for one second that I would apply that maxim to myself.

I told them I was running out of steam, and could no longer maintain the pace of the past few years. The demands of that year's Europatreffen had been immense, even with the fantastic support I'd had. I was increasingly taking the line of least resistance instead of driving the Club forward as I had done. Sure, I could keep pottering along, but I would no longer be doing what I had promised to do. That wasn't fair on the members; nor was it good for the future of the Club. Carol's misfortune had been the final straw. I was breaking under the strain, and enough was enough. I wanted my life back.

I announced my intention to retire from leadership of the Club no later than 1st August 2000. That would be a nine year run, and much longer than I had ever planned to do. If they could decide on a suitable legal structure and assemble a team of people to take over the Club, I would sign over everything, lock stock and proverbial barrel. If not, I would shut the Club down.

The silence was broken only by the sound of jaws hitting the table.

I reminded everyone that I am not immortal. One day I would no longer be around to run the Club. It made sense to hand over while I was still fit and well, and could help a new leadership to settle in. I would remain available to advise and provide information, because I knew only too well how much there was to learn.

It suddenly hit home. "You mean it, don't you," someone asked?

No-one had believed that I would ever step aside, and their shock was evident.

I felt a weight lift from my shoulders. The decision had been made, and made clear. There could be no doubt that it was time for others to step forward, and to take over where I was soon to leave off. I could see a future in which I would no longer be at the beck and call of others, a time when Carol and I could plan our lives around what we wanted to do instead of around the demands of the Club.

Back in Hereford I felt a new sense of purpose. I knew that the light at the end of the tunnel wasn't a dirty great train coming the other way, that I was truly back in control of my life for the first time in years.

Does that sound resentful? It's not meant to. I loved every minute of my TPC life, even including the run-ins with certain other clubs' officials. The lessons I learned from those are not taught in school: to bureaucrats the process matters more than the result; trying to overcome dogma with logic is like shovelling treacle uphill with a fork.

If I thought I was in for a smooth run to the finish I was mistaken. I still had the next *Europatreffen* in Dortmund to go, and I was still European President until the election.

Secure in the knowledge that the free place at the Gala Ball for the European President had been confirmed by the *Europarat* in London, I set off for Dortmund. The Gala Ball was the only event I planned to attend, apart from fulfilling my obligations to the *Europarat*.

Traditionally a press call is held immediately prior to each sitting. I thought it my duty to be there, and arrived in plenty of time. I entered the room just as proceedings were about to get underway. The tables had been arranged in a large horseshoe shape. At the head sat three German Club members. They barely acknowledged me. I could already see how this was starting to unfold.

The press conference got underway, with the three or four journalists asking the usual questions. The hosts explained how Tall Clubs were social organisations, in which tall people could meet with others of similar height, to exchange information and to socialise. I might just as well not have been there, and yet I was sure that in previous years the incumbent had always participated actively in the press call.

After three or four questions and answers of a similar nature I couldn't help but chip in. The hosts looked daggers at me as I explained that not all Clubs were mainly social. Some, notably the Dutch and British Clubs, concerned themselves greatly with providing practical information not only about clothing, but also about ergonomics and the medical conditions which may result in unexpected height.

They actually started to look interested. "Who exactly are you," one of them wanted to know?

"I'm only the European President, don't worry about it," I said.

They looked a little confused and asked me to repeat what I had just said. I did, and they looked questioningly to the head of the table.

One of the hosts introduced me by name, saying that I was from the British Club.

"And European President," asked one of the journalists?

The host blustered a little, obviously uncomfortable at having been compromised, and did his best to explain the office away as just a ceremonial function for the meetings.

The journo and his colleagues now became more interested in me and what I had to say. I mentioned our Supplier Directory and then talked a little about ergonomics and the medical information we provide to our members.

"Doesn't the German Club do anything like this," asked one?

The hosts shuffled about in their seats, and said that of course they were aware of these conditions, and did their best to keep members informed.

The journalists asked a few more general questions and then took their leave. Judging by their manner I had badly undermined the hosts' credibility.

The meeting proper got underway, with me still in the same seat rather than at the head of the table. It made no odds to me. I'd had enough of the bull, and wanted out of there as quickly as possible.

The German delegate, as she had been instructed to do, objected to the previous meeting's minutes. As she was unable to give any concrete reason for the objection the minutes were accepted, and I moved through the agenda as quickly as possible, so that we could get to the election of my replacement.

I bluntly pointed out the obvious unease that existed between the German and British delegates, and suggested that neither should provide the next President. Instead I proposed the Swiss delegate. He was duly elected, and so the office passed into the safe and uncontroversial hands of a man who was resigned to the German Club, being the largest, always getting its own way in the end.

I got out of there as soon as I could. At last, I thought, the petty posturing and point scoring was over.

You are clearly more astute than I, because you already know that I was deluding myself.

I went to the venue for the Welcome Evening, fully prepared to pay the entrance fee. The reception desk was unmanned, so I waited by the door to the main room, hoping to attract someone's attention. After about 15 minutes of being totally ignored by anyone who could have facilitated my entry I gave up, and returned to my hotel.

The evening of the Gala Ball, I was told at the door by the organisers that no free place had been allowed for me. I reminded them that it had been agreed upon twice by the *Europarat*. After a few half hearted excuses they managed to come up with one that sounded almost credible: they hadn't been told in time, and there was no way to accommodate a free place at this late stage.

I had been attending to family business during the day, and was still in my casual clothes, my dinner suit safely stowed in the boot of the car. I had hoped to find somewhere private to change. It was academic now, as they weren't going to let me in, no matter what.

I stayed in the entrance area, waiting for our contingent. They needed to know what had happened so that someone else could officially represent the TPC if necessary. As I stood waiting, I was greeted by person after person as they entered the venue, and all of them wanted to know why I wasn't inside and dressed for the occasion. I told them, and several questioned the organisers about it. They became increasingly embarrassed.

To relent and let me in would have been as good as a defeat, and was therefore not an option. Eventually one of them said that I could go in after all, but I would have to pay.

We were on a huge exhibition complex on the edge of the city. There wasn't a restaurant in sight, and I was hungry. There was usually food at these events, and I just wanted to eat; I paid. I fetched my dinner suit, and changed in one of the unused exhibition halls in the building.

We do indeed live and learn. Whether food was served that evening or not, I'm not certain, but I sure didn't see any. If indeed food was not part of the deal that evening, it means that my individual attendance did not add to the expense of staging the event in any way. To pretend therefore that some great logistical exercise was required for me to be granted the free attendance I was due was, in fact, a load of horse manure. The organisers, whatever their reasons, dealt me a personal insult, and thereby also insulted both the TPC and the office of European President. It would be wholly improper for me to speculate whether the free place would have been granted to a German incumbent.

During the evening I encountered a member of the local club who had attended the event in London the previous year. He was nodding appreciatively as he watched the people enjoying themselves.

"It's a good event, don't you think" he said?

"Yes," I agreed, "these evenings always are. But I think we did a little better in London last year."

His face changed. "Oh no, this is much better," he said.

"But there is no food," I protested. "We included a sit down three course meal last year."

He remained unmoved.

Now, perhaps, it's my turn to allow a little pride to come to the fore. I prefer to think that I'm being realistic. We were on the edge of the city in a semi-deserted exhibition complex in a cavernous exhibition hall that certainly had plenty of room. A competent five piece semi-professional show band tried to fill a stage that could have accommodated a symphony orchestra. The show piece of the evening was a demonstration of folk dancing by a troupe of eight and nine year old children from a local dance school. No food was served, as far as I could tell.

In London we had been in a prime city centre location. The impressively decorated room didn't get too crowded, thanks to the large adjacent bar area. Our show piece was a full military band, and the dance music was provided by what were in essence professional musicians. We also served a three course sit down dinner.

I know which was rated more highly by most of those who were present at both. But I guess you can't win them all.

I will concede, without question, that the Gala Ball at the Palais Ferstl in Vienna was grander than ours, although I don't remember there being food at that one either.

That evening I also ran into Helga Schunk, the new Chairperson of the German Club. With her at the helm I knew that I would encounter much less of the obstructive nonsense that I had dealt with under her predecessor. We chatted briefly, and I told of the trouble I had encountered earlier. She gave a resigned shrug. "Let it go," she said, "it will be different in future."

I'm sure it was, but I never attended another *Europatreffen*, nor am I likely to.

The stresses of that two year period were more taxing than I realised. Even now, as I write about that time and the memories return, I can feel the old frustrations welling up inside. I hated listening to all the talk of working for the good of tall people, of providing help, support and information, knowing that talk was all it was. When they trotted out the official line of fellowship and cooperation among Tall Clubs it was all I could do to not laugh out loud.

I do not deal well with hypocrites.

At that same time the TPC was still generating a steady flow of good quality publicity for the cause of tall people. We continued to consult with and to provide information to learned institutions and politicians. The Supplier Directory and the medical information continued to be updated and republished as often as was practical.

Most other clubs provided information on Marfan syndrome and, in most cases, Acromegaly and Gigantism. But when I mentioned Sotos syndrome, Klinefelter syndrome or XYY syndrome to them I was met with blank stares. They had never even heard of them, much less knew what they were, despite the fact that a good number of their members had almost certainly been affected by one or other of them.

Credit where credit is due: their social calendars have always been more comprehensive and more successful than ours, so they are clearly meeting some of the wants and needs of their members. Without question, the TPC can learn something from them in that area.

That the German Club produced a new Supplier Directory for their members in the mid-nineties is, I believe, not a complete coincidence. The Dutch and British Clubs were attracting attention throughout Europe for their proactive rather than social ethos. My appearance on the popular German TV show *Welt der Wunder* would not have passed unnoticed either.

I did not intend for my account of that period to sound as though I am anti German. How could I be? I am one, but for an accident of birth. It is just a simple fact that, as the largest Club in Europe, it had totally dominated the scene for a long time, and become accustomed to getting its own way. To fight against that inertia creates the kind of repercussions I experienced, as people tried desperately to defend their comfort zone. The largest and potentially most influential Club in Europe had become fat and lazy, and was resting on its rather old and dusty laurels. The new kids on the block were having a noisy party which everyone could hear, right next door, and they didn't like it.

I only had just over a year to go before stepping down from leadership of the TPC. My taste for most of the international events had been well and truly soured. If the truth be told, I was more than ready to walk away from all Tall Clubs, other than the TPC. It wouldn't be long, but I still had work to do.

More heavyweight media was taking an interest. Documentary makers contacted us, and I had lengthy meetings with researchers. In all such ventures I tried to make sure that the Club received due credit for its contribution, whether by being featured even in a small way in the documentary, or being acknowledged in the credits. To maximise the potential market, one of the documentaries was to feature both British and Americans.

The film crew arranged with the hosts of TCI Convention that year, the Golden Triangle Tall Club of Pittsburgh, to tag along on one or two events. I made sure that I too attended Convention. The interview they filmed with me there ended up as a real "Blink and You'll Miss It" appearance.

I had been to Pittsburgh a few times before, and was familiar with the city and some of the surrounding area. It was too good an opportunity to miss. Two of my favourite places in the whole world are not far away. The first is McConnell's Mill, a deeply spiritual place for me and virtually unknown to all but the locals. The other, Frank Lloyd Wright's Fallingwater is world famous. I made the most of what would be my last Convention, and visited both.

Documentaries take a long time to complete, so I was no longer in charge by the time the programme maker introduced the Club to Michael Colwell. Michael is 5ft 2in, and wanted to set up an organisation like the TPC, but for those at the other end of the height range. He felt that by combining the two we could campaign for changes that would benefit both groups. I could see the logic in his argument, but felt that although the difficulties experienced by both tall and short people are similar, the differences were such that they would be better addressed by two separate organisations. I welcomed the possibility of joint campaigns and informal cooperation as appropriate, but didn't feel comfortable with the idea of a single organisation to serve both groups.

The programme makers asked whether Michael might address a meeting of the TPC to present his proposal, with cameras present. The new board asked my opinion. I advised extreme caution, saying that my inclination was to refuse. They felt that the publicity opportunity was too good to miss, which I totally understand. Michael made his presentation at the 2003 anniversary weekend in Waltham Abbey. He stayed for the Gala Ball, and was filmed socialising with the group and chatting with individual members.

The footage that eventually made it into the final programme showed the TPC and some of its members in a less than flattering light. Oh well, that's showbiz, but at least they got the name right.

I actually quite liked Michael. He had a passion and enthusiasm for his cause that I recognised. It was like watching me, only smaller.

Alex Heaton and his mother Gidea also featured heavily in one of the programmes. Gidea had been the Club's contact for tall teenagers, children, and their parents. I don't think she was allowed to refer to the TPC during her interviews. If she did, it ended up gracing a cutting room floor. Coincidentally, she had given birth to Alex on 1st August 1991, the exact date on which I launched the Club. I really should have sent him a birthday card every year.

And so I launched into organising our own anniversary celebrations for the last time. It was made easy for me as Swallow Hotels had recently acquired a new site in Liverpool, and had asked whether we would help them to publicise that the hotel was equipped with 6ft 9in beds throughout. Naturally I agreed, and as part of the deal we negotiated some exceptional rates for our event in the city.

A Beatles Convention takes place in Liverpool on the August Bank Holiday, so hotel accommodation is hard to come by under any circumstances, let alone at the rates that we were given. With so much going on it was not difficult to put together a full and varied programme of events.

During the weekend, Carol once again proved her dedication to the Club. BBC News 24 had requested a live interview at 08.00 on the Saturday morning. Neither Carol nor I are morning people, so I left her to sleep as I crawled out of bed and made my way to the function room in which the news crew was ready and waiting. It was only twenty to eight, so I grabbed a cup of coffee from the waiter who had been sent to look after the crew.

While waiting for the signal from Broadcasting House I chatted with the interviewer. When he discovered that Carol is just 5ft 3in he asked whether she was in the hotel, and would she be willing to be interviewed as well.

Full of trepidation I called our room. The semi-coherent and less than polite response left little doubt that I would be on my own for this one. I informed the interviewer, who assured me that he understood and that it would not be a problem.

At three minutes to eight Carol stomped into the room, her face like thunder, and growled "Coffee, black, as soon as we're done," at the waiter who was nervously backing away.

She took her position at my side, while the interviewer thanked her and apologised profusely for having disturbed her sleep. Our interview was intended as a fairly lightweight and entertaining item, and he was much less confident about the prospects for that. Grumpy interviewees do not make for good television.

The signal came from Broadcasting House, and he told us to get ready. Carol's expression did not bode well. He began the countdown: "Five, four, three…"

That's when Carol's face lit up with a beautiful smile, she became charm personified. He visibly relaxed, and completed the countdown silently and on cue; the interview began.

Everything went exactly as he had hoped for. We did our bit, getting over the serious points, while maintaining good natured banter with the interviewer and with each other. After five minutes he drew the interview to a close and handed back to the studio.

As soon as he announced "Ok, we're clear, thanks everyone," Carol's face resumed its pre-interview state. She turned away and called out to the waiter: "Right! Gimme coffee now, and no-one gets hurt!"

The waiter stood ready, holding a cup of coffee at arm's length, and retreated to a safe distance as soon as she had taken it.

The interviewer smiled at me: "That is some lady you've got there. She's great, isn't she?"

Who was I to argue?

I made some more local radio and press appearances, and so missed virtually all of the Beatles Convention events. It was probably just as well. Carol told me that I would have spent a fortune in the guitar exhibition, especially as there were several nice Rickenbackers on offer.

The end was in sight, and I decided to make my last visit to a TCI event, the Chicago weekend, organised by the Paramount Tall Club of Chicago. I had been twice before, and both visits were enjoyable and very productive. I was always urged to promote our events as though we were all part of the same community which is, after all, supposed to be what Tall Clubs are about. TPC and TCI members had become frequent visitors at each other's events, thanks in no small part to the relationships developed at these weekends. Sadly, this time even that event was tainted for me by petty trivia.

At the final dinner and dance they present a number of awards and prizes for various accomplishments. The prizes are of no great value, perhaps a bottle of bubbly and a token souvenir or two. One of these is the travel prize, awarded to the Club whose members have in total travelled the furthest to be there. Say 20 members have travelled from a club that is 500 miles distant, that club scores 10,000 miles; you get the idea.

With air travel cheaper than ever, more Europeans have been attending, and carrying off the travel prize. At around 3,500 miles per member attending, it doesn't take too many to rack up the miles, and for most of the preceding years the prize had gone across the Atlantic, usually to Germany or Britain. Not so that year.

Jim Nelson, making the announcements and presenting the awards on behalf of the Paramount tall Club, surprised quite a few people when he said: "We have decided that this year we are going to keep the travel award as a domestic competition."

Someone did ask very loudly how a supposedly international organisation can have a domestic competition, but was ignored.

As I said, it was trivial, but yet another example of an organisation saying one thing and doing another. The only way to make sure that a TCI member Club won the prize was to change the rules. Never mind that the European visitors went to more trouble and spent more money to be there. It may have changed again, I don't know, but that is what happened then.

Top Right: August 1953 - all kids love an ice cream

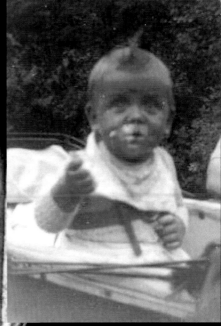

Bottom Right: September 1954 - A little Blondie with a little Brownie

Above: 1956 – With my father and sister outside the St Heliers Arms in Carshalton, which my parents managed at the time. This is one of the few pictures I have of my father.

Below: About 1958 - My first School Photo at Benhilton School in Sutton, Surrey. I'm the one on the right.

Top: My Grandad

1961 - Outside the staff dining room at Libury Hall with my first brand new bike. A bit low on street cred, but mother knows best. I think it had 28" wheels.

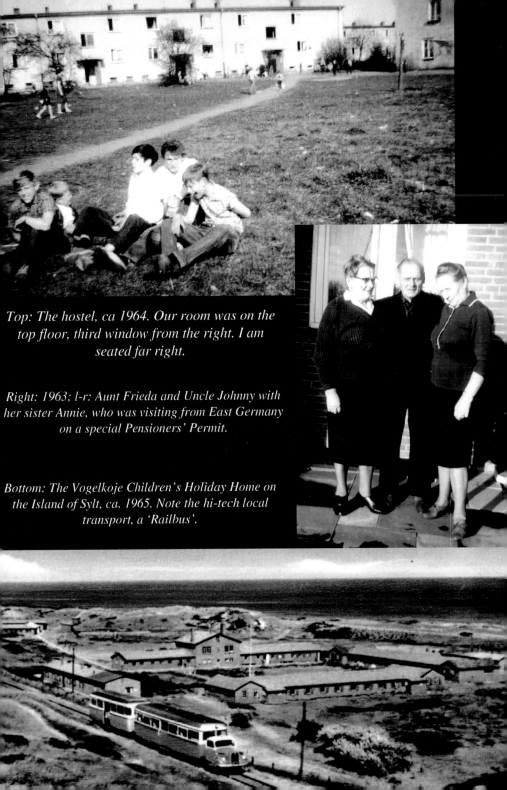

Top: The hostel, ca 1964. Our room was on the top floor, third window from the right. I am seated far right.

Right: 1963; l-r: Aunt Frieda and Uncle Johnny with her sister Annie, who was visiting from East Germany on a special Pensioners' Permit.

Bottom: The Vogelkoje Children's Holiday Home on the Island of Sylt, ca. 1965. Note the hi-tech local transport, a 'Railbus'.

Top: 1964, Class M7. I am far right (position, not politics). Sigrid, who gave me 'that' telling off two years later, is largely obscured by Frau Sass...

Left:... but Sigrid in 2006 doesn't remember the incident

Bottom Right: 1976 - Mum and George get married. With them, my then girlfriend's children, l-r: Karon, Keith, Joanne.

Below: Me with Werner, my recently discovered brother

Top Right: 18th August, 1987 - Carol and I get married in the Red House, Port of Spain, Trinidad. One of us wore white.

Bottom: I get my own piece of Berlin Wall, December 31st 1989.

Top: In the recording studio

Left: ...on stage

Right: Presenting
a programme at
Hereford Hospital
Radio

Bottom: Performing 'Molly Malone' with the
Hatband at my 40th Birthday (l-r 'Bobby John'
Williams, me, Mick Mullins, George Copper

Mr Phil Heinricy,
Founder of 'the Tall Persons Club of Britain',
HEREFORD (somewhere- please help Post Office)

Top: I didn't make it up – Posted in Doncaster at 4.45pm, it was delivered the following morning!

Above: Day 1; Glasgow – l-r: Scottish rugby international Gordon Brown (1947-2001), me, Chris Greener; front: Seana, the researcher.

Right: "Oh yeah? Well my dad's bigger than your dad!" – Chris Greener and Rob Bruintjes, then Holland's tallest man, during our first anniversary weekend.

Top: All dressed up with somewhere to go.

Below: ...and we went by horse and carriage.

Left: We used this bridge in countless photoshoots

Above: At Munich Airport, 1993 – In Height Order: Chris Greener, Dave Conroy, Charles Frost, me, Mike Harrison, Dave Firman, Terri 'Olive' Gleeson, Patsy O'Rourke, Lin Davies (now Gardiner), Mary Noakes, Val Sims (now Johnson), Pippa Boulton, Elaine Barnes, Heather Buttle, Margaret Moore, Carol.

Bottom Right: Charles Frost and Godfrey Fane ride the slide in the Berchtesgaden Salt Mines, Europatreffen 1993.

Below: Carol with Sandi Allen (1955-2008), at the launch of the 1994 Guinness Book of Records

Top: Carol, the Queen of Etiquette, suffers a momentary lapse of concentration - but it was such a yummy pudding

Below: A bus full of Tallies - knees everywhere!

Bottom: Monday morning; another great weekend. With us, the two Wojcik boys, who attended many events, and wanted to be taller than their 6ft 6in dad. I could name everyone, but I won't.

Top: When Tallies go Karting, carnage ensues

Above: Harry Galloway (1946-1996) - he of the Harry Galloway Member of the Year Award

Right: Feeding Imogen the 6 month old giraffe at Longleat, August 1996

Left: The famous
walkway at the
entrance to
Colditz Castle…

Right: The new European President
makes his speech. Now you know where
Tony Blair got that hand gesture.

30. EUROPA - T...
Dresden 1997

Left: One of dozens of pictures of Carol
cuddling Uwe Seyler – is there
something I should know??

Top: Europatreffen 1998:. Some members of the team settle their differences amicably. Back l-r: Bill Skinner, Andrew Smith, Matthew Palmer, Paul Escott, Peter Matthews; Middle l-r: Pippa Boulton, Mary Noakes; Front: me.

Above: During our shopping trip to New York, 1997; l-r Karen Sneade, Jackie Elliman, Jo Bates with a funky chicken.

Right: The Band of HM Royal Marines, Britannia Royal Naval College, Dartmouth; Europatreffen 1998, London

Top Left: Rosario Rigutini, our Italian member, with Carol. He travelled from Rome for many an event.

Below: Mary Noakes works hard to improve International Relations with Christian Schimdt

Bottom: Eighteen Giants; l-r Matt Langmaid, Paul Hitch, Mark Gray, Pete Diamant, Wiert-Jan Huttema, me, Harry Galloway, Julie Miller, ??. Front: Mine Hosts and a small waiter.

NINE GIANTS

Top Left: With Sue, our landlady, at a party. I've not told her yet we can't make next month's rent.

Right: Short partners welcome! 5ft Jean Galloway lost among the Tallies.

Left: First one to mention 'The Three Stooges' gets a slap! - l-r: Me, Uwe Seyler and Toby Brown

Top: Life after the TPC; my company car, well, one of them, anyway.

Left: I just can't help myself - doing a piece on limo driving with Wesley from TV's Central News South.

Above: How could you not love that face? Oscar, Bertie the dog's favourite chew toy.
Photo by Charles Frost and used without telling him (yet).

Bottom: Carol's 50th Birthday present to herself, 2008. A match made in heaven.
Photo by Jim Briggs

The TCI website states that it operates in the USA and Canada and that makes it "...truly an international organisation". Yeah, right. There is also some stuff about all Tall Club members being welcome, whether locally or from abroad. I think they must mean Canada, or maybe Hawaii?

Even so, among the rank and file of TCI I met many wonderful people over the years. It is they who always showed me the generous hospitality and friendship on which Americans justifiably pride themselves.

Our membership had finally realised that I was serious about stepping down, and several good people came forward to form a steering committee. They were to decide on the future format of the TPC, and on who exactly would assume the positions of responsibility.

The final planning meeting for the handover took place in an hotel on the Hagley Road, in Birmingham, which may be considered as the birthplace, or at least the place of conception, of the TPC Mk II.

On the day of the scheduled final meeting I told everyone at the outset that I intended for us to leave the room that evening at 6.00pm, with all of the major decisions made. One or two people scoffed at the idea, saying that it would take at least another meeting or two to get to that stage.

The day progressed, as does any of its ilk, with lots of talk and lots of coffee and biscuits. With twenty-five minutes to go before we had to vacate the room no decisions had been made.

I said: "Right, folks, we need to decide on a legal structure for the Club. The general feeling so far seems to be in favour of a Company Limited by Guarantee. Does anyone disagree?"

No-one had any strong feelings against the idea, so I asked for a show of hands; carried.

We had already discussed who might be on the first board of directors, so we held a secret ballot; decision made.

I worked my way in similar fashion through all of the points I had announced at the start of the meeting.

At two minutes to six I announced that we had achieved what we had set out to, thanked everyone, and officially closed the meeting.

We gathered in the bar for a final drink before going our separate ways. Pippa Boulton asked: "How on earth did you manage that? I thought we were going to end up scheduling another meeting."

Andrew Smith agreed: "When you started off by saying what you wanted to get done today I thought you had no chance."

As I drove home I felt a little strange. I felt like a parent who had told his offspring to move out, but felt uneasy when they announced that they were actually going to.

But the TPC was my baby. I had reared it, and nurtured it through the early years, and brought it to a point at which it could make its own way in life. Sure, it wasn't going to be easy, and there were bound to be troubles along the way, but I would still be there in the background to help out if needed. It could still come to me for advice, even if it would ignore some of what I said and do what it wanted. It was going to make mistakes, and hopefully would learn from each one. It was time to let go.

One piece of advice it ignored was to leave the headquarters in Hereford. Our PO Box (PO Box 200; 200cm = 6ft 6½in - geddit?) was well established, and listed in all sorts of media. Sue and her staff were already handling most of the routine admin, so it made sense. No-one believed that I would be able to resist interfering, so it was decided to move head office well out of my reach. They couldn't have known then what an expensive mistake it would turn out to be, albeit due to factors that could not have been foreseen. Had they known me better, they would not have worried. When I let go of something, I really do let go. Sink or swim; unless you scream for help, I'm staying out of it.

Someone said to me much later that it was as though I had dropped off the face of the earth as far as the Club was concerned. I never made contact with the board. If they wanted me, they had my number. That I would make such a clean break was inconceivable to most people, and they were taken by surprise when I did.

In the end I beat my target date for the handover by a generous margin. On the day I handed over all of the records, paperwork, boxes of files and pieces of equipment I didn't feel sad. I don't remember exactly how I felt. I just knew that the time was right, and that I was doing the right thing.

I had already begun to organise the following year's anniversary celebrations. Suzannah Weeks was taking over that duty, so I arranged a meeting at the venue where I introduced her to the relevant people.

At that year's anniversary event the Club presented Carol and me with a beautiful armorial sundial, an Edinburgh Crystal clock and a cheque for the balance of all the money that had been collected for the presentation. Almost £800 came in from TPC members, as well as from some other European and North American clubs. We were stunned. I knew that the Club meant a great deal to a lot of people, I just hadn't realised how much. Carol and I were especially touched by the member who sidled up to us during the evening and said: "Here, take yourselves out for a meal on me," and pressed a substantial cheque into my hand.

The sundial now has pride of place in our garden, while the clock stands front and centre on our mantelpiece.

The next three years or so were a rocky time in more ways than one. Carol and I were not exactly excluded from the Club, but we were certainly left to feel no longer part of it. There were the odd telephone calls from board members requesting information or advice, most of which was totally ignored, which was fine with me, but that was more or less that.

Members who had been part of the Club since the early days commented that the whole atmosphere had, in some inexplicable way, changed. I had always known that it would, and was apprehensive about how that change would manifest itself. I knew it wouldn't be the same, nor could it ever be. New leadership brings a new direction. My baby was not my clone. It was developing its own identity, and making its own way in life.

As the years have passed and my baby has grown up, Carol and I now once again feel very much part of it. The atmosphere is different, yes, but in so many ways it's still the same. I love the way one long time member put it: "We aren't a club, we're a family."

We have many close friends who started out as Club members. The odd membership may have lapsed but the friendships continue. New ones develop as we continue to attend the anniversary weekends. The Club is, and always will be, a big part of us just as we are a big part of the Club.

I still smile when I remember the exact date of the handover. It was in no way deliberate, it just happened to work out that way.

April Fools Day, 2000.

The Aftermath

The weeks that followed the handover in April 2000 were a strangely serene time for me. I had been feeling the pressure of late, and to be suddenly free of the relentless schedule of publication deadlines, annual events, membership administration, advertising sales deadlines, paying the bills, plus the additional obligations of media appearances, contact with other Clubs around the world, being generally available to our members, and all the other little things that had been part of my daily life for the past nine years actually left me with a huge sense of relief.

I had my life back. That makes it sound as though I didn't enjoy running the Club, but nothing could be further from the truth. I enjoyed every minute of it. But I was only too well aware that I had been running out of steam for a while, and that I was no longer pushing the Club forward. I knew that the effect on the Club would inevitably have been a negative one, and that it was time to make way for fresh blood and new ideas.

As if to put a final exclamation mark to my efforts, just three weeks after the handover the BBC transmitted *Happy Birthday Shakespeare*, a two part drama featuring Neil Morrissey and Dervla Kirwan. One of the scenes required Neil to be at the back of a crowd of people watching a procession, but unable to see because of the people in front of him. Neil is, I believe, 6ft 2in so that was not easy to achieve. I was contacted by the BBC to ask whether we could provide some extras for filming, which we were happy to do. The final cut showed several members obscuring Neil's view, and all of them wore Tall Persons Club T-shirts. The Tall Persons Cub had been immortalised in a work of fiction – what more could I ask?

Actually, it can't be mere coincidence that in the past decade or so more retailers have added 'tall sizes' to their range, or increased the maximum leg length or shoe size they routinely stock. Sizes in general seem to have improved in favour of the tall person. Just the other day, Carol bought me a cardigan which fits beautifully, with long enough sleeves and body, and just £8 from Primark! During my last few months in office I was speaking with a trousers and jeans manufacturer, who remarked on how the demand for his tall sizes had increased beyond expectations. Yes, the Club and the publicity it generated really has made a difference.

My mother died in mid-April, at the age of eighty. It was not unexpected, as she had been suffering from cerebral atrophy for some time. The symptoms are not unlike those of Alzheimer's disease, and she had been a resident of a local nursing home for the past four years. Her condition first became severe in the week running up to our annual event in 1996, which made that weekend particularly difficult to deal with.

The private hire business had been growing quietly, and we had acquired a stretched limousine, the first in the county. I had plenty to do, and could concentrate on earning a living again. Carol and I had been living in our house for sixteen years, and we decided it was time to move, lest we still found ourselves there in our dotage. The process was well underway by the time we attended the Club's annual event in August.

The new board knew full well that I would always be available with help and advice if needed. Only a couple of times was I asked, which was a good sign. On both occasions my advice was ignored, which wasn't so good, as it turned out. The details are unimportant. The new board was not me, and was doing some things differently from the way I would have done them. That's not a criticism, but a simple fact. They were doing what they felt to be right, and I would never hold that against them.

In 2001 the annual event took place in Sheffield; we weren't able to attend. I had taken over the limousine business as a sole trader in addition to buying my own Hackney Carriage, so funds were on the tight side. Even so I made a flying visit on the Sunday evening to meet up with old friends after the dinner and dance. Most other Clubs had a tradition of inviting their founders to the annual dinner and dance; the new board had chosen not to, as was their right.

The venue was Manchester in 2002, and this time Carol and I were there. Our presence was not even acknowledged, which I will admit hurt. I wasn't expecting anything grand, but I had hoped for simple recognition of the fact that we were there and, particularly for the newer members, our role within the Club.

During the evening a member who had joined the Club in the first six months sat down beside me, crossed her arms, looked at me seriously and said: "It's not the same."

She was right; somehow the atmosphere had indeed changed. The close sense of togetherness we had all known and loved was somehow not as strong. It was bound to happen. For the first nine years the Club had been personality led. Now it was being run, in effect, by a committee. Even I was surprised at just how much that had diluted the sense of unity that we all used to feel. It's difficult to explain clearly; I guess you just had to be there.

Over the years the composition of the board changed as directors resigned and were replaced, or reached the end of their maximum term and had to stand down. I began to be consulted more often, and even made the odd media appearance on behalf of the Club. I was happy to feel useful and valued. The feeling of isolation from the very organisation we had created was replaced by one of belonging again. I almost felt like the proverbial prodigal son who was accepted back into the fold. The board even presented Carol and me with a complimentary place at the 2007 annual dinner, which we appreciated enormously.

We maintained private contact with a number of people who had become first and foremost friends rather than Club members. It was through them that we first heard about the rumours that began to circulate after we moved. Apparently, the fact that we moved to a larger house just months after giving up the Club raised a few eyebrows. You can guess the nature of those rumours. The only variation was in the amount of money I was supposed to have siphoned off from the Club. The record was £250,000, claimed by an ex-member who told someone who at the time also happened to be on the board.

"I put her right," he told me. "I told her to work it out. With subscriptions as low as they were then, if you had taken every single penny of the Club's income over the nine years it wouldn't have been as much as that. Mind you," he laughed, "it would have been a neat trick, to have published over 40 magazines, three directories, covered the Club's operating expenses, arranged the annual bash and to come away with a quarter of a million quid in your pocket."

As you might expect, not one person asked us outright about the truth or otherwise of the rumours. Had they done so, we could have shown them that we had bought a house for £25K more than the one we sold, and taken out an additional £45K on the mortgage. I guess that means that it cost us about £20K to start and to run the Club.

I have often been asked what made me start the TPC, and that is not actually that easy a question to answer. In all honesty, I have to say that it was more or less an accident. I just happened to be in the right place at the right time, and it all came together. I could have viewed it as a business opportunity, to be operated purely for profit, but that would have meant I could not have made it as affordable as possible for the largest number of people. All I ever wanted to do was to make sure that it could provide the services that were so obviously wanted and needed at a price that allowed it to cover its running expenses. I never anticipated how quickly it would grow, nor the demands that it would make on my time.

Was it all worth it? You bet your sweet backside it was. I was privileged to spend my time doing what I enjoyed, to not dread getting up in the morning to face yet another day at the office, to relish each and every new challenge that each passing day seemed to bring. I know that what I did, together with Carol, has changed lives. None of us can ask for more than that from a life. But no-one has gained more from the Club than I have. It helped me to grow as an individual, to become more and to achieve more than I ever thought possible.

Even so, I am not the person some people seem to think I am. To be placed on a pedestal fills me with dread, for the higher the pedestal the greater the fall. I am no guru or sage - I am just me, with as many, if not more, human failings as anyone else. I shall be happy if, come the day, my life can be summed up in just four words: "He Made a Difference". As epitaphs go, that's good enough for me.

Above all, I was lucky to be supported all the way by Carol. I don't think most women would be prepared to make the sacrifices that she made in order to help the Club become as successful as it was, and I trust will continue to be.

I suppose it's the ultimate irony: the Tall Persons Club GB & Ireland owes its existence in no small measure to a woman of 5ft 3in (and a bit).

Tall Man Talking

Part Two

The Practical

The People

The Medical

Growing People - Shrinking World

We all know that successive generations have been taller than their predecessors, and statistics confirm it. But why rely on statistics? If you need proof of how recent generations have been increasing in height, then all you need to do is to wait outside any school and watch the fifth and sixth formers emerge. By the time you are arrested and taken away for questioning you should have noticed that most of them are taller than your grandparents. Come to that, take a look at your own circle of friends and family. Most adult children will be taller than their same sex parent, i.e. sons taller than their fathers, and daughters taller than their mothers.

A visit to a museum exhibit of clothes from the Victorian era should provide the final proof, assuming that you still need to be convinced.

At this point I need to make a brief diversion into the murky world of statistics. Stick with it, because it is all relevant, and I promise it will be over soon. If you want to skip forward two or three pages, that's fine by me too.

By the very nature of the subject, any discussion of average heights will involve a raft of statistics; and there's the rub. We have all heard the quote about "Lies, damned lies, and statistics", I shall, however, resist the temptation to crack the age old joke that 73% of statistics are made up on the spot.

Bugger; too late!

Statistics must be treated with extreme caution. They are all too easy to manipulate and to apply in a way that suits the purposes of the individual or body quoting them. Statistical correlations can be found even where none exist. My favourite example of this is one I stumbled across during my psychology studies. It showed a direct correlation between the salary of Methodist ministers in Massachusetts and the price of rum in Hawaii. I leave you to judge the significance of that one for yourselves.

While running the Club, I had to deal with huge amounts of information involving statistics. After a while I started to take as much interest in the way the information had been collected and collated as I did in the figures themselves.

When some official or academic body sets out to calculate the average height of a population, it does not visit everyone in the country to measure them; it would be impractical. Instead, they satisfy themselves with what they consider to be a representative sample. In the case of population surveys, this will normally amount to around 500-600 individuals. Where and how they find these individuals is anybody's guess.

Why is that important? Well, depending on the socio-economic make up of the total sample, the result can be skewed one way or the other. Surveys into the Health of the Nation are carried out at regular intervals by the Health and Social Care Information Centre, part of the Government Statistical Service. When I first encountered them in the 1990's they were conducted by The Office of Census and Population Surveys (OCPS), and included average heights by age, sex, socio-economic background and geographical region. The differences are significant in some cases, with individuals in the more prosperous South East being taller than their counterparts in parts of Northern England, and managers and executives generally taller than manual workers.

I believe that samples were taken from each age group and each sex. Whether a separate sample was taken for each region, as I suspect, or a single sample was broken down by region, thus reducing statistical significance, wasn't clear. Like it or not, racial background also makes a significant difference and I could not establish whether each sample was taken to mirror the ethnic mix in a region.

One can't even depend on race in isolation to produce accurate and meaningful results. The prime example of this is to be found in Korea. The country was divided at the end of the Second World War. North Korea was ruled by a communist dictator, and became isolated from the rest of the world, while the South enjoyed economic prosperity. In the 1990's a series of famines wreaked havoc on the population of the North. Millions died, millions more suffered from disease and malnutrition. The regime refused all help from outsiders. The population of the South did not endure the same hardships.

Accurate and reliable information about the North and its population is almost impossible to come by. Most data have been collected from refugees and defectors, therefore representative samples are impossible to guarantee. However the differences that have become manifest from the data that have been collected are significant, and cannot be ignored. The 70+ age group is the last to reliably show final height comparable between the two populations, as it is the last to have reached final adult height under similar economic conditions. I have seen sources quote current differences between North and South for adult males and females aged 20-30 of well in excess of 10cm and 8cm respectively. Other sources quote nearer double those figures but, in view of what I have already said about statistics, I am not going to make any definite claims. Whichever figure you choose, environment, nutrition and healthcare do make a huge difference to final adult height.

One height survey from the United States revealed in the small print that the sample had been taken exclusively from clerical and administrative personnel in the US armed forces. It was not clear whether it included those in supervisory and management positions. How does this kind of selective sampling affect the end result? I am loath to speculate on all of the possibilities.

During its short and horrendously expensive life, the Millennium Dome exhibit included a machine which took anthropometric measurements of all who stepped inside it, all done with lasers and electronics. The data were then sold to commercial companies for use in design of a wide range of products, including clothing and furniture. All very laudable, were it not for one minor detail: no-one over 6ft 6in could get in! Whether that was with shoes on or off, the statistics resulting from the exercise were skewed towards the lower end of the height range.

It's true that only a fraction of 1% of the population exceeds that height, but as everyone at the lower end of the height range could enter the machine, the results will inevitably be biased in that direction. Thanks to the location of the Dome, its visitors would not have been a representative sample of the British population either, located as it was in the South East and frequented by a high percentage of tourists. I'm sorry, PC Brigade, but if you run a few thousand Japanese tourists though the machine as part of the study you might as well kiss goodbye to any hint of statistical relevance as far as the population of Britain is concerned.

Ultimately, anthropometric statistics assembled by whatever means are unlikely to vary by huge amounts, but they will vary. I trust that this goes some way to explain why some of the figures I use may be at odds with other published surveys.

The late Dr Stephen Pheasant was acknowledged for many years as this country's leading expert on anthropometrics and ergonomics. He published many books, papers and other learned works on the subject. During a conversation I had with him in the mid-nineties, he revealed that the data he was using in much of his work were collected during the 1960's and 1970's. I questioned the validity and the application of some of his more recent work as a result, and he became more than a little irritated with this ignorant layman who was daring to question his expertise. There followed much muttering on his part about standard deviations and the like.

With input from both sides, we eventually agreed on all the major factors that contribute to increasing average height, and that although differences between the population then and now were unlikely to be huge, they existed nonetheless. Some of those differences could become significant when applied in product design.

Our conversation ended with him extending an invitation to come and meet him at one of the regular gatherings of ergonomics experts with which he was involved. Regrettably that meeting did not take place, as Dr Pheasant died not long after our conversation. No, there is no direct correlation between the two events, so don't start looking for one.

The main point I made which led to the invitation, and a more sympathetic ear from the good Doctor, was straightforward. I suggested that when collecting and collating data for use in most product design, only data from individuals between the ages of 20 and 40 should be included. My reasoning was this: adults in the 18-20 age often achieve the final half an inch or so of their final adult height in those years, and would therefore reduce the overall figure, albeit only slightly. People in their forties and fifties are already known to be generally shorter then those in their twenties, and are already over half way through their allotted span.

From the time that the data are gathered and collated to the time that they are published and then used and applied by designers, several years may elapse. The design and development process for some products may be measured in years rather than months. That product may not only be on the market for several years, but have a practical life span of several years more. This currently means that by the time some items have been in use for five or ten years or so, half the people for whom they were designed are dead.

If that sounds rather drastic, consider that in England the difference in average height between a 25 year old male and a 75 year old male is currently around 8cm, or 3.25 inches. A visit to www.ic.nhs.uk, where you will find a comprehensive set of statistics under the heading "Health Survey for England", will provide confirmation.

Dr Pheasant conceded that point, but questioned the practicalities and economics of collecting and publishing data in such a specific way. He reiterated his assertion that the differences were likely to be quite small and to therefore have only minimal long term effects.

I think the clincher was when I quoted from one of his own books, *Ergonomics – Standards and Guidelines for Designers* (ISBN – 580-15391-6), published by the British Standards Institution, in which he made the following statement about the height of kitchen worktops: "The 900mm standard height for kitchen worktops was originally set as an interim measure. It has subsequently acquired an air of permanence. Ergonomically this is undesirable." His recommendation that worktops in a kitchen should be of different heights to accommodate not only users of different heights, but also different tasks, merely strengthened my case. A higher surface is better when cutting up ingredients, but rolling out pastry is better done on a surface at least ten centimetres lower.

Dr Pheasant and I began to find more common ground.

What all of this illustrates, I hope, is that most statistics should come with some sort of Government Truth Warning: "Warning! Statistics! Use with Scepticism!"

On another occasion I was talking with the then Head of Design at Rover Cars. More flexible design in cars is one of the regular issues raised by the Tall Persons Club, and this conversation illustrates beautifully how our higher education system, instead of encouraging open and flexible thinking, more often forces people into predetermined thought processes.

He felt that slightly longer seat runners, which would allow for a greater range of height among potential drivers, were not a realistic option, as the driver's seat would intrude too far into the rear passenger space. I pointed out that, according to accepted wisdom, the vast majority of car journeys were made by single occupants. A little discomfort caused by moving the driver's seat forward when the rear seats were occupied would surely be a minor issue. Although he felt that safety requirements would influence the feasibility of simply lengthening seat runners on current models, that it should not be an insurmountable obstacle if tackled at the design stage.

We then talked about the top of the range models and higher specifications of base models. The higher the specification, the more likely the car is to have thicker padding on the doors, seats and roof lining, to have a centre console, and all manner of other extras which intrude into the cabin's interior, and thus reduce the amount of space available to the driver. The drivers of such cars are statistically likely to be taller then average, I told him. Didn't it therefore make sense to allow for that at the design stage?

"Are you sure about that," he asked?

"You work in a large office complex, with lots of other managers along the same corridor as yours, don't you," I asked?

He confirmed that he did.

I continued: "Aren't these exactly the kind of people you are aiming these top of the range models and specs at?"

"Absolutely," he said.

"And how many of the managers who work on the same floor as you are under 6ft tall," I asked.

There followed a deathly silence of several seconds, before he said: "Oh my God, I never thought."

It was another of those promising starts to a relationship which ultimately came to nothing, thanks to the demise of Rover Cars.

Once again, I deny everything! It was nothing to do with me; honest.

I wish this kind of conversation were an isolated incident. I experienced many more which confirmed my suspicion that most people have two very different ways of thinking. One is their normal everyday common sense way, the other is the official corporate line which has nothing to do with common sense, the real world, or the customers' needs.

A good example of this is a kitchen unit manufacturer who shall remain nameless, because I think they are still trading and can doubtless afford much better lawyers than I can. Their one good point was that their units could be supplied with a set of adjustable feet which allowed the worktops to be installed at a height between the usual 900mm and 1000mm. I think the parent company was Dutch or German, which went some way to explaining this innovation.

The British division manufactured its own products in addition to the range from the parent company. Their marketing materials made little of the innovative adjustable feet, but I thought they should be listed in the Club's Supplier Directory all the same. I called one of the senior managers, and invited him to advertise with us, and to make more of this feature. He declined, as was his right.

As we chatted, it became clear that the company didn't feel the adjustability of their units to be particularly important. I foolishly asked whether they had ever considered producing a range of kitchen units at 800mm that could then be combined with drawer units of 100mm, 150mm and 200mm. This would give the customer the option of different worktops heights for different users and tasks, while at the same time increasing the flexibility and usability of the units. There was also the chance of add-on sales for people who only want to remodel a small part of their kitchen. I am ever the salesman, looking for new ways to sell familiar products, and was quite pleased with my idea.

"What? You mean have different worktop heights in the same kitchen," he asked.

"Yes", I said.

"Oh no, we couldn't do that," he said.

"Why not," I asked.

"Because it would look stupid," he replied.

Aesthetics over ergonomics; how could I possibly argue? I could have, I know, but it was towards the end of a long hard day, so I let it go.

I knew that I wasn't going to sell this man any advertising, but wanted to maintain a friendly relationship with him. There was always a chance that I could persuade him in the future. That's when his private as opposed to corporate train of thought emerged on to the tracks. He asked me more about the Club and what we were about, at which stage he became positively animated. In great detail he told me about his friend's teenaged children who were already taller than their parents, how the kids at school are so much taller today, and that we are clearly becoming taller as a nation.

Had I been able to reach down the telephone and throttle him, I would just about be coming up for parole now.

I didn't fare much better with office furniture or bed manufacturers either.

Desks first: the height of an office desk doesn't appear to have changed much since the 1930's. It might be just my imagination, but I am sure that surfaces on some old Edwardian roll top desks were actually higher than some standard office desks today.

In 1991 I visited the Netherlands to meet the then leaders of the Dutch Club. Rob Bruintjes and Wiert Jan Huttema were at the time the most active campaigners in Europe lobbying commercial and political organisations, with some success, for change to accommodate the needs of their members. They had arranged a meeting with an office furniture manufacturer, Ronal Project, where I was to see the kind of product readily available on mainland Europe.

To say I was impressed is an understatement. I took a seat at one of the desks in the showroom, and found it to be higher than anything I was used to in Britain. It was still a little too low, so I lowered my chair. The man from Ronal immediately stopped me. He reached under the desk top and folded out a small handle, which he cranked, and the desk rose as though by magic, to the right height for me. Not content with that, he then returned my chair to the appropriate height and adjusted the armrests, so that I was sitting comfortably, shoulders neither hunched nor slouched, and my elbows supported in just the right position.

Impressed as I was, it was just as well I was sitting down when I asked the price, because I was taken by surprise yet again. The price was comparable to a standard non adjustable desk in the UK!

"If you want to save money," said the man from Ronal, "we have desks with a simpler adjustment mechanism."

He led me to a desk which stood on two telescopic pedestal type feet. Adjustment was accomplished by means of a simple locking nut; they even supplied the spanner and a clip under the desk in which to store it!

Upon my return to the UK I immediately set about finding British suppliers of comparable office furniture. Yes, of course there were a couple of potential suppliers, but the prices! You would think that making desks adjustable required them to be gold plated as well.

Discussions with various manufacturers and retailers met with a combination of two arguments. The first was the kitchen worktop argument: we can't have desks of different heights in the same office because it would look stupid. The second was the Catch 22 argument I have encountered time and time again.

It goes something like this: manufacturers don't make adjustable desks because office furniture suppliers don't stock them; they don't stock them because office furniture buyers don't ask for them; the buyers don't ask for them because the office layout designers don't specify them; the designers don't specify them because manufacturers don't make them, which is why the stockists don't stock them for the designer to be able to specify them so that the buyers can ask for them from the stockist., who would order them from the manufacturer…

I trust that's clear to everyone?

Lest you think that this whole adjustable desk idea is new and innovative, let me tell you about Michael Harper, a Club member who was sent to work in Finland by his company. Upon arrival at his new workplace he was shown to his office. His boss apologised profusely for the old desk he would have to make do with until the new one arrived. It dated from the 1960's and was showing the wear and tear one might expect, and yet it was adjustable to suit someone of almost 7ft if necessary! The Scandinavians have been doing it right for 50 years or more, while the Brits can't even get it right today.

So why is an adjustable desk so important? Surely it is just a matter of comfort?

Ah, wish that it were. I now have to introduce two words that strike loathing and hatred into the hearts of managers, executives and business people everywhere. No, Value Added Tax is three words! I am talking about Health and Safety. I suppose technically that's three words as well, but I wasn't counting the "and".

The Health & Safety Executive (HSE) offers only basic advice on setting up an office chair correctly. It doesn't appear much concerned with desks. After all, so many workplaces contain things that can kill, crush, burn, poison, maim or disfigure you in such a wide variety of exciting and interesting ways that desks seem somehow rather dull by comparison.

I had conversations with H&S officers in several companies, but most were members of staff who filled the H&S role in addition to their normal duties. One made it quite clear that, no matter how much he might agree with me, if he started to pressure the company to spend money on things they didn't want to spend money on, office furniture for example, then his main job would be in jeopardy.

One full time health and safety man was most concerned that higher desks would disadvantage shorter employees, and leave the company open to accusations of discrimination. Here was a man who understood the most complex of safety procedures, rules and regulations, but couldn't grasp the concept or purpose of adjustable desks. As far as he was concerned, all tall people had to do was to lower their chairs.

Talking of lowering chairs: in the late 1980's or early nineties the people responsible for standards within the European Union lowered the standard for the height of office chairs by 10cm! A chair built to the new standard was given by researchers to a group of office workers to try out. It was found to be too low by everyone over 5ft 2in!

For a tall person, there is a problem with just lowering the chair. If the chair is set up correctly in accordance with HSE recommendations, lowering it increases the load on the lumbar region leading to backache. If he or she has to stretch out their legs in order to get their knees under the desk the load increases further. Neck and shoulders also have to endure higher loads, as posture is altered to accommodate the unnatural position it is necessary to adopt in order to work at the available height. It is not only unusually tall people who suffer. Most people over 5ft 10 would benefit from using a desk that is higher than the current standard.

Club member Lin Gardiner, Davies as she was then, called me one day to tell me about her new job in a large blue chip company. She is 6ft 2in and a dead ringer for Kirsty Ally.

"I'm finding it pretty stressful," she told me. "I end up with a headache most days."

"Raise your desk, I told her. "Get some old telephone directories or something like that, and stick them under the feet of your desk. It's more likely to be poor posture stressing your neck and shoulders than anything else."

Her boss didn't much like the idea of telephone directories, and told her to ask the maintenance workshop to make her some suitable wooden blocks. The newly raised desk attracted attention from colleagues throughout the offices. Many tried it and found it to be more comfortable for them too, even though most of them were shorter than she is. The only complaint Lin heard was from the poor maintenance man who spent several days making and fitting yet more wooden blocks to numerous desks.

When she called me again, it was to let me know that since raising her desk she had not suffered a single headache, was feeling much better generally, and she was getting more work done than before.

I gave the same advice to many members, including one whose boss refused permission for her to raise her desk, because "...it wouldn't look right." She went ahead and did it anyway. He didn't even notice for over three weeks. Point proved; desk still raised.

Millions of working days are lost each year to undiagnosed backache, at a cost to the economy running into billions of pounds. One would expect employers to take comfort and safety in the office more seriously. Instead most figure that a desk is a desk is a desk, except when it is for the MD, when it becomes an executive mahogany work station, and price is less important.

Few employers appreciate the difference between price and cost, especially as the economic benefits of a more efficient office environment within, say, a heavy industrial plant are not always easy to recognise and to quantify.

Persuading suppliers that it is worth not only stocking, but actively promoting, adjustable desks is not easy.

"It's a very price sensitive market," said more than one. "Price is everything. Customers will never spend any more than they absolutely have to."

This from a man who drove a Jaguar when a Ford would have done the job equally well. Hypocrite!

The manufacturers weren't much better. The mere suggestion of improving their product to make it suitable for a much wider range of users met with protestations about the huge potential costs involved. One did admit that economies of scale would reduce the unit cost of adjustability to well within affordable levels, but felt that the higher price would make him less competitive, despite the additional benefits to the customer. This would damage his business in the long term, he told me, and wasn't worth the risk.

When I pointed out that the Scandinavians and Continentals have been making adjustable desks for decades, the best response he could come up with was: "Ah, yes. But they're different."

Whatever happened to offering a superior product, doing more for your customer, being an innovator and leader?

Sorry, this is Great Britain we are talking about, an island both geographically and mentally. That's why we have such a successful car and motorcycle manufacturing industry, isn't it?

The situation is no better when it comes to beds. The 6ft 3in bed has been with us since the mid Victorian age although by the 1990's the 6ft 6in so called King Size bed was accounting for an increasing share of the market. The 4ft 6in width common in earlier decades was also giving way to those of 5ft wide. Super King size, 6ft by 6ft 6in, was a rarity other than in the top grade rooms of some major hotels, but it is gradually becoming more common.

The National Bed Federation, an association of bed manufacturers in the UK, used to publish its own leaflets offering advice on buying the right bed. In the first leaflet I received the advice stated that a bed should be six inches longer than the user's standing height. The survey of the Health of the Nation published in the early nineties already showed that best part of 20% of adult males were reaching 6ft in height, and well over half exceeded 5ft 9in. This meant that the standard 6ft 3in bed was too short for over half of all adult males and the so called King Size bed was failing to satisfy the needs of almost 20%. Taking into account that the height of adult males was on the increase, this did not bode well for the future.

Naturally, I made a strong point of this in the many media appearances I made at that time. I also pointed out that as managers and executives were likely to be at the upper end of the height range, and were also the principal customers of major hotel chains, it was the hotel operators who should be flexing their buying muscles and putting pressure on bed manufacturers to improve their products.

The only hotel chain to take notice was Swallow Hotels, who in 1999 equipped their new hotel in Liverpool with 6ft 9in beds. Swallow Hotels was a large, family owned, hotel chain which sold most of its sites to the Marriott chain not long after. I had become a big fan of Swallow Hotels, having organised major events at their locations in Newcastle, in Bristol twice, Grantham, Glasgow and Liverpool. Unfortunately, the new owners did not maintain the innovative, customer centred thinking of their predecessors. Just my opinion, and if it makes Marriott feel any better then I can report that a couple of Hilton hotels I used were even worse.

A couple of years later I was sent another leaflet about beds, which I recall as also being published by the National Bed Federation. The publicity that the Club had generated about the shortcomings of beds seems to have had an effect. The advice now was for a bed to be *three inches* longer than the user's standing height. They had simply changed their guidelines to ensure that the customer fitted the product rather than encourage their members to make their products suit the customer.

I should stress at this point, in order to avoid being sued, that I am relying on my memory in respect of the leaflets. I relinquished all of the materials I collected in my time running the Club when I handed over to the new board in 2000, and they are therefore no longer in my possession. If I am wrong I apologise to the Federation, but I have the distinct feeling that a delve about in their archives would turn up copies of the leaflets in question.

These days, the Federation's website refers users to the Sleep Council website. Their advice is that a bed should be four to six inches longer than the user's standing height, so I suppose we are moving in the right direction again.

The Sleep Council further suggests that anyone over 6ft (1.83m) should consider a 7ft bed, and states that many manufacturers now offer these as an option, while others will make special sizes to order. Yet the National Bed Federation's website search facility doesn't allow for searches for any bed over 6ft 6in in length, and nowhere could I find reference to special sizes. Why am I not surprised?

Some of the major manufacturers do mention, tucked away in some dark recess of their literature, that they will make special sizes to order. Because this involves interrupting the usual manufacturing process, slowing down or even stopping expensive machinery, the costs can be, quite frankly, exorbitant.

Smaller companies are usually more accommodating, especially those which make mainly wooden frame beds. Many waterbeds are 7ft long as standard, and worth considering. Waterbed design has come a long way since the early days of them being little more than enormous water filled balloons, and are now engineered and produced to exacting standards.

In an ideal world, two people should be able to lie on a double bed with their hands clasped behind the head without their elbows touching. Length should be not less than six inches more than the standing height of the taller user. For most tall people this could mean that a 7ft x 6ft bed is the minimum size they should consider.

I hear the cries already: "That won't leave much room to walk about in the bedroom."

So what? You spend a lot more time in the bed than you do walking about in the bedroom, and I know which is more important. A good night's sleep matters. It benefits your general health and well being, and reduces the chances of you getting on first names terms with your local chiropractor.

In Britain, the average Victorian woman and man were about 5ft 0in and 5ft 5in respectively. Even that was a slight increase over previous generations. An interesting piece of information I was sent concerned the recruiting records of the Durham Light Infantry for 1793. It made reference to the heights of the new recruits, citing most at around 5ft 4in to 5ft 5in, but gave a special mention to a very tall man of 5ft 8in and, if my memory serves to recall the precise wording, a "…veritable giant of 5ft 9in…" As was so often the case, I had Harry Galloway, my favourite librarian, to thank for that one.

There have been a few reports in the general press of finds of human remains dating back thousands of years which suggest that the particular individual may have been around six feet tall. However, one individual does not a population make. It is not yet possible to deduce accurately from such remains whether a height related medical syndrome may have been at work all that time ago. Only speculation and deduction can throw light on the occasional individual. I recall a suit of armour in the Tower of London which appears to have been made for in individual who may have been suffering from acromegaly (more on that condition in a later chapter).

Today the averages for men and women have risen to about 5ft 5in and 5ft 10in. Even that does not put British people in the upper strata of height. The average Dutch male is already well in excess of 6ft tall, with some sources quoting 6ft 1in as the figure. The Scandinavians are not far behind. In the Far East a huge acceleration in average height has been noted, particularly in Japan, probably due to the change in diet over the last generation or two. Western fast food now forms a much larger part of a Japanese teenager's diet, and whilst this has resulted in a less healthy populous, it has led to an increase in average height in that age group of around 4in within a generation or two!

In Europe, the increase in average height in the past century has been ascribed to a better diet, nutrition, and better healthcare. Yet in Japan we are seeing a population which is becoming taller, but less healthy, with so called Western diseases such as heart disease and the like on the increase.

Note the contradiction: with so-called better nutrition we have ended up with a population that is taller, but less healthy.

I dislike the concept of 'better diet and nutrition' as a contributory cause of increasing height. It would be more accurate to think of a 'more plentiful and healthier diet' as having started it, but the higher calorie intake most people now enjoy has little to do with a healthier diet. There is nothing healthy about the burgers and fries, and other assorted junk and processed foods that are now the staple diet of the average Westerner, and increasingly the Japanese. It is this perversion of good food which is leading to a taller but less healthy population.

Better healthcare has, without doubt, played a major part in the process. Take a look at any film footage of 1930's working class Britain or America and you will see the proverbial 'snot nosed' children running about in the streets. Healthcare was rudimentary at best for the working classes. For most it was beyond their means. A look at perinatal mortality rates for the period are most revealing, especially when separated according to socio-economic demographics.

When a child is ill, growing goes on hold, while the body deals with the illness. Once the child has recovered, growth returns to normal, but the deficit is never made up.

Measles, mumps, whooping cough, rubella and more, were a routine part of any childhood until little over a generation ago. These childhood illnesses were all good for a couple of weeks off school, and were shared generously within every community. Allowing for the incubation period, the active period, and recovery time, each of these would slow the body's growth rate for a couple of months. Add in a few colds and other minor ailments, and it is easy to see that growth rates were reduced for a total of at least twelve months, if not longer, during childhood. The result was of course an adult who was not as tall as he or she might otherwise have been.

So many factors play a part in the post war increase in average height. New houses are better constructed, while old houses have been improved to become less draughty and damp. Central heating, running water, improved sewerage disposal and more, are now the norm and have all contributed to a cleaner and healthier environment. How many of us today use an outside toilet with no flush, or draw our water from a pump in the yard?

Further confirmation of the effects of improved healthcare can be found in the slight acceleration in the increase in average heights which ties in to the introduction of childhood vaccination programmes in various countries. Naturally, that acceleration was soon negated, as the children of that generation became adults.

And yet, with all of these obvious trends, the size of some of the most obvious and basic objects in everyday life remain resolutely unchanged for decades, even centuries in some cases.

I once had a flat in an old Victorian building. The house had not been especially grand, even in its heyday. It was just one of those semi-detached town houses with a basement where the kitchen was. Bigger than a worker's terraced house, it was still much smaller than the 'Grand House on the Hill'. And yet all of the internal doors were 7ft high.

A Victorian terraced house we owned had all of its original doors, all of them 6ft 6in high. Built in 1897, the first male occupants would have had an average of over 12 inches clearance.

The house we live in today was built in 1991, when the average male already exceeded 5ft 9in in height. Its doors are the same height as those in that Victorian terrace.

Why should it matter; doesn't that leave most people almost 9 inches to spare?

Well actually, no it doesn't. Everyone ducks when something intrudes into their line of sight, and when it is something as rigid as a doorframe, they definitely will. Allowing for the thickness of any carpet and underlay that may be fitted, the height of heels on a pair of shoes, and that a spring in the step will further reduce the available clearance, and it is easy to see why most people over 6ft 2in duck when going through doors.

It may not strike you as much of a hardship to duck through a door and, to be perfectly honest, it isn't. But when you have to duck through doors fifty or a hundred times a day, it becomes a very different matter. The head is a heavy old lump, and having to constantly tilt it to duck through doors puts a strain on the neck and shoulder muscles, as well as on the cervical spine.

If the Victorians could have 12-14 inches of clearance, why can't we? Using today's average height figures, 7ft doors would fit the bill perfectly.

You already know there's another one of those 'battles fought' tales coming, don't you? I'll waste no more time then.

The Club approached the Royal Institute of British Architects on the matter, and met with a contradictory response. On the one hand, specifying 7ft doors in certain types of office building was seen as the right thing to do, but in a domestic situation 6ft 6in was deemed adequate. Have I missed something here, or do we all become taller when we leave for work?

It was the same old story: Builders won't fit them because architects don't specify them; architects don't specify them because the manufacturers don't make them; the manufacturers don't make them because the builders' merchants don't stock them; the merchants don't stock them because the builders don't ask for them; the builders don't ask for them because the architects don't specify them...

Doesn't that have a ring of familiarity about it, and did you notice the deliberate mistake?

The manufacturers do make 7ft doors, because they are used in some types of commercial buildings. However, architects don't specify them for domestic applications, because they are made to higher safety standards to comply with fire regulations and the like, and are therefore more expensive than the basic domestic version. There's that eye on top quality again: don't use the good stuff, it's too expensive.

I spoke with the MD of a building company which specialised in smaller housing developments, sites of no more than 200 houses, often less than 100. I asked him about the cost of fitting larger doors at the building stage. It was no problem, he said, as long as he knew in time to make sure that the right frames and doors were on site.

What about the cost, I wanted to know. In his opinion, the additional cost would be so negligible as to be not worth bothering about.

"Anyway, we'd save a few bricks and brick-laying time if we use bigger doors," he laughed.

"If you came on site when we were still doing the foundations, and told me that you would buy a particular house as long as it had 7ft doors, I would fit them at no extra charge," he told me.

He went on to say that, if fitted as standard in all new houses, the build price would be virtually unaffected, because the manufacturing price would come down on that volume of doors.

So why didn't he do it anyway?

It would seem that architects get very upset with builders who do not adhere to the plans they are given. They are also a little precious about having a Royal Institute to belong to, because that elevates them above the status of mere tradesmen.

The Club did approach a couple of the larger, nationally known developers, but with no real success. We couldn't get to talk with anyone who might have been able to wield influence. The best (only) response was from someone in a design office who told us that they had to give the customer what he wanted, and that what he wanted was what he knew, and was familiar with.

That response made me wonder how we ever got en-suite bathrooms and fitted kitchens.

By now some people will be wondering why I haven't mentioned airline seating, or any other form of public transport seating, for that matter. Well, I have been resisting it because it has been, and continues to be, one of the most frustrating battles the Club has ever fought.

We have established, beyond reasonable doubt, that the average height of the population continues to increase. I wonder why, therefore, the busses currently in use by London Transport or whatever it currently chooses to call itself, have less room per passenger than the older models of the sixties and seventies? This pattern is repeated across the country and across the transport industry.

In the South East, a fortune was spent redesigning commuter trains. Out went the rows of facing seats to be replaced by modern aircraft style seating. At least when the seats faced one another the passengers could interweave their legs and get reasonably comfortable. Now, even getting into most seats requires a degree of contortionism normally associated with novelty variety and circus acts. I have travelled on many a train on which I couldn't even get into the seat comfortably, and had to sit with my body twisted so that I could leave my feet in the aisle. By the time I arrived at my destination I was ready to consider hip replacements. I have on occasion been barely able to walk.

I suffered that same fate on a charter flight from Florida during a business trip. Not one seat on the aircraft was suitable for anyone over about 6ft 3in. The flight attendant was most apologetic, and assured me that I could have as many free drinks as I wanted on the journey. What a waste; I don't drink much at the best of times, and never when travelling by air. I spent the nine and a half hour flight with my feet in the aisle, and the edge of the seat in front digging into my leg just above the knee. The bruise took a couple of weeks to fade, the discomfort even longer.

This is going to sound really snobbish, but it's true: the demographic of those taking cheap package holidays on charter flights to Florida is such that they tend to be at the lower end of the average height range. Those who favour more exotic, and more expensive, locations on scheduled flights are more likely to be from a higher socio economic background, and therefore taller and slimmer. If you don't believe me, watch a holiday programme in which holidaymakers are interviewed: the people in Bali, Sri Lanka or the Maldives are very often taller and slimmer than those at Disneyland. That's why the seat pitch on charter flights is less than on most scheduled flights.

If you think that is an outrageous assertion, I refer you to *Freakonomics* (ISBN 0-141-01901-8). Aided by Stephen J. Dubner, the noted economist Steven D. Levitt wrote this wonderful little book in which he demonstrates numerous examples of cause and effect between two seemingly unconnected phenomena. Some of them make my ideas seem positively mundane.

The Club attempted several times to compile a database of the bests seats on each airline, but fell foul of that most basic of marketing ploys, the 'Bait and Switch'. An airline advertises its wonderful economy class legroom, and when it has attracted the extra passenger volume it was looking for, out come several rows of seats, and with them the extra legroom they were advertising; back to square one.

Such was, and still is, the price sensitivity of air travel, that few airlines are willing to lead the way by making comfort and safety the priority. The ludicrous lengths some people will go to in order to save a few pounds on a flight was brought home to me by the man who bragged that he had got his flight £20 cheaper by travelling from a different airport. It had cost him an extra £40 to get to and from the airport, which was 100 miles further away, but he had saved £20 and was extremely pleased with himself.

Most aircraft have a few seats, usually those on emergency exit rows, which have extra legroom. The Civil Aviation Authority (CAA) insists that it is the responsibility of the airline to ensure that they are occupied only by passengers who speak English, are capable of opening the emergency door, and are willing to assist with the evacuation of the aircraft in the event of an emergency landing.

I have often been on flights on which these rules have been ignored. The worst example was when I saw a man of about 5ft 4in, in his seventies, with two walking sticks and a straight right leg which had obviously had the knee joint fused sitting in the emergency exit row. I raised the issue with a member of the cabin crew only to be told: "Oh well, he's there now, so never mind."

I wish it were an isolated example, however it's anything but.

Only once have I been on a flight on which the rules were strictly adhered to; well, almost.

I had managed to get a seat in the emergency exit row, and had settled down nicely when a member of the cabin crew approached me and a fellow passenger.

"You know that you are in an emergency exit row, don't you," she asked.

I assured her that I did.

"Have you read the special instructions? Do you know what to do," she continued.

"Yes," I said. "Pull that handle, throw the door through the hole, and shout "Follow me"".

"Close enough," she smiled, and left us to it.

I related some of these incidents to the man from the CAA, but he simply said that it was the responsibility of the airline to ensure compliance with the regulations. So why does the CAA have and publish regulations if it does nothing to enforce them? He went on to tell me that tall passengers who want more legroom should fly business class. The CAA would not involve itself with the needs of the tall passenger, as it was only a question of comfort and not one of safety.

The same attitude was taken by politicians in both Westminster and Strasbourg. Those same politicians have passed laws to ensure that no-one is discriminated against on the grounds of disability, age, colour, race, sex, and lawyers only know what else. Yet tall people are fair game, or so it would seem. Clearly, we tall people are 'non-people' in their eyes. They fail to see that it amounts to overt financial discrimination against tall people, and consider it totally acceptable. Just a thought: if we really are 'non-people' do we still have to pay tax?

I have lost count of the number of times I have been told by an airline that in order to secure the exit row seat I should turn up at check-in early, as these seats could not be allocated until check-in. I have been first in the queue, only to find that the seats had already been allocated days beforehand. The rule seems to apply in theory only. In practice it is a very different matter.

It was not long after the Club launched itself on an unsuspecting world that the issue of deep vein thrombosis (DVT) first appeared in the popular press. Sitting in a confined space for a prolonged period without moving, such as on a long haul flight, can cause the blood to form clots, which may later move to and lodge in the heart or lungs. The latter is known as a pulmonary embolism. Post mortems carried out on individuals who had died during or shortly after a long haul flight revealed that almost a third of them had died as a result of such blood clots.

The risk of developing a DVT became prominent in all media. The Club was frequently involved in the publicity, and raised the issue whenever an opportunity presented itself. The airlines naturally denied any connection between long haul flights and DVT, because they are allergic to being sued. Eventually the evidence became so overwhelming that most airlines now offer advice on avoiding DVT in the in-flight magazine.

It would not be fair for the Club to claim the credit for this, but it was certainly influential. I lost count of the number of radio, television and press interviews Club members gave on the subject.

Since those days further research has implicated the poorer air quality on flights since the blanket smoking ban, rather than the confined sitting space. When smoking was allowed planes used to pull in fresh air from outside, as opposed to recycling a high proportion of what was already inside, which is what happens now. The airlines save around 6% of their fuel bill in this way, so the economic incentive for them to do so is strong.

It makes me wonder who exactly paid for that research. Whilst I do not doubt that it may be relevant to some degree, the original hypothesis cannot be dismissed. The link between DVT and long haul flights was first observed at a time when smoking was still permitted on most flights. The US only banned smoking on all domestic flights in 1988 and international flights in 1990. Many international airlines didn't ban smoking until some years later, well after the link had been established.

But nothing is ever as clear as it may at first appear. After all, smokers are considered to be at higher risk of developing a DVT. Wouldn't a smoking ban therefore reduce the risk? Is that possible reduction in risk offset by the poorer air quality argument?

Can research actually prove whatever you want it to prove? Is anyone totally right or completely wrong?

It is also claimed that the reduced air quality is responsible for increased incidents of 'air rage' and the spread of all manner of diseases and ailments, such as flu, sore throats, chest infections and more besides. But that is another story altogether.

The fact cannot be ignored that tall people have less room in an economy seat on an aircraft. Movement is even more restricted, and thus the risks increase. That's why it is an issue of safety, and seats with the most legroom should be allocated to the tallest passengers as of right. Why should we pay more to fly business class, just so that we can reduce the risk to the level that someone of average height would be at in a standard economy seat?

It is discrimination, plain and simple.

An additional complication arises in that a woman is more likely to have longer legs than a man of the same height. For example, a 36in inside leg is as common for a 6ft 2in woman as it is for a 6ft 6in man. Therefore, if any rules or regulations are brought into force to cover the allocation of seats with legroom, this difference would have to be taken into account.

My favourite "tall passenger" story concerns the 6ft 1in man who whilst checking in at a BA desk was most insistent that he was tall, and therefore had to have an exit row seat. The check in clerk agreed to summon the check in supervisor, who just happened to be Mary Noakes, 6ft 1in plus heels. She walked up to the man, and stood before him as the check in clerk relayed his request. Mary peered down at him, and said simply: "No!" He accepted the seat he was given without another word.

A final thought on safety for airline passengers. It is actually safer for passengers to face the rear of plane, a configuration which is, I'm told, the norm on RAF passenger flights.

I once flew on a Ryanair plane which did have a couple of rows of seats which faced one another, which had the added benefit of increasing legroom significantly for the passengers in those seats. In the early days of air travel this layout was common. Airlines are loathe to use this configuration on commercial flights today because apparently passengers dislike the feeling of being tilted forward during take-off. Those passengers are clearly unaware of the safety benefits.

I saw an interview with Sir Bobby Charlton, in which he recounted the horrors of the 1958 air crash in Munich which killed eight members of the Manchester United team. He told how those who were killed were all in forward facing seats. All of those who survived were in seats which faced the rear of the plane.

In an age when children must wear goggles to play conkers, and actors must be given soft mats to fall on when they have been 'shot', a no cost solution to increasing survival rates in aircraft crashes is ignored for no good reason. I for one would be more than happy to be tilted forward for two minutes or so during take-off, secure in the knowledge that if the worst case scenario were to occur my chances of survival would increase maybe tenfold.

It has been suggested that tall people above a certain height might be classed as disabled, and thus claim protection under the relevant laws. I do not agree with this proposal. The Oxford English Dictionary defines "disable" as "to make unfit". By that definition we are not disabled; it is our environment that disables us.

Some tall people are disabled, and should have the appropriate protection in law, but it is important that height of itself should not be viewed as a disability. It is part and parcel of the rich variety of sizes and shapes that make up the human race.

The truth is that it's time to stop making people fit the environment, and to make the environment fit the people; and I don't just mean tall people, I mean all people.

While editing this chapter I came to a conclusion: I sound like a right whinger! I don't mean to; it's just the way it's turned out. Anyway, if I don't whinge then someone else will have to eventually.

This country can't go on pretending forever that we can make do with standards as they are today, and have been since the early Stone Age. Even the royals are getting taller. Henry VIII is said to have been over 6ft tall, and a current heir to the throne has surpassed that by quite some way too. Do we have to wait for our first 7ft King before we get...

Oh, never mind, you can see where that one's going already.

Perceptions and Distortions

While researching sources for this section on the internet, I had the strangest experience: I found a site on the search page which gave a two line summary that sounded like just what I was looking for. I clicked and was taken to an article that I wrote about twelve years ago. Spooky!

Because this is not intended to be an academic work, this chapter is not knee deep in references to the work of others. Most of what follows is information I came across while running the TPC and in general reading. I do not always recall, or have been unable to locate, the source of the original information, much of which predates the internet and World Wide Web. Most of it is fairly well known to the specialists anyway, so if you want to follow up any of the examples, ask a psychologist. All of it is, of course, interwoven with a liberal sprinkling of my personal views and experiences.

I wonder whether I am really the right person to be talking about perceptions of height. After all, even my perceptions have shifted over the years. I too have at times wished that I were not as tall as I was. It was a process of learning and self-acceptance that taught me to enjoy what I now consider to be one of my greatest assets. The most fundamental difference between those of us who see their height as a positive feature and those who do not is their perception of themselves: are they a tall person, or a person who happens to be tall?

Research into the self-perception of tall people is limited. I found just one document which dealt with that specific subject. It was part of the course work of a German university student who is himself tall. He found that, on the whole, tall people have a very positive self-image. However, his sample size was very small. The tallest was 6ft 10in with most subjects less than 6ft 6in and they were either fellow students at his university or fellow members of the local tall club. Whilst this does not invalidate his findings, it does present the likelihood of sample bias. Were the students confident because of their height, in spite of their height, because they had achieved well academically, or because they came from a sound socio-economic background; were the tall club members at peace with their height having learned self-acceptance from other members or were they happy with their height before joining the club?

In my experience, a negative self-image is more likely to be observed in those tall people who fall into the top 1% of height distribution. It is they who are most noticeable and who will inevitably attract the most attention. Socio-economic background also influences self-perception, with those coming from the lower end of the scale more likely to have negative feelings.

The perceptions of others often determine how tall people perceive themselves. If the person did not enjoy familial and peer support during their formative years they are more likely to view their height negatively. This in turn leads to negative body language and submissive behaviour patterns, which invite unwelcome reactions from others, reinforcing the negative perception of self. It's a vicious circle which not everyone finds easy to break.

I was fortunate in having good support throughout most of my life. I now view the brief period during which I felt dissatisfaction with my height as nothing more than a normal teenage reaction to what I perceived as a prominent and undesirable feature. Had I been of average height I may fixated on my upturned nose, slightly prominent ears, my lean build, or something else. Most teenagers are dissatisfied with some aspect of themselves, and I doubt that I would have been any different.

My height has now become such a small part of who and what I am, it no longer figures in how I perceive myself. I have lived with it for so long that it is nothing out of the ordinary.

"What's it like to be so tall," is one of the questions most commonly asked in the many interviews I have given, and my answer is always the same: "I have absolutely no idea!"

Stunned silence from the interviewer. Think about it though: I am tall, that's a simple fact of life. I have no idea what it is like to deal with the world as a person of average height, because the last time I was average height was at the age of about 11 or so, and then only for a year or two. At that time I did not have to worry about buying clothes, cars, or booking airline seats. All of the things which inconvenience tall people weren't an issue for me then, so I have nothing with which to compare my current experience.

To me, the world functions at around chest height, and has done so since I was about 15. Nothing strikes me as even vaguely unusual about that, because it is all I have ever known. I am only aware of how unusually tall I am when someone reminds me of it, a shop assistant, for example, or one of the regular jokers.

Occasionally I will catch the reflection of a crowd of people in a shop window, and notice that one person in the crowd sticks out head and shoulders above the rest. My reaction is always: "Good grief, look at the size of… oh heck, it's me!"

It is only then, and sometimes when I see a photograph of myself with other people, that I am overtly aware of my own stature.

In my mind I am not a tall person – I am just a person who happens to be tall. You will get sick of hearing that, I know, but it's a truth that applies to us all and one that may also be applied to other physical features.

When it comes to judging the advantages versus the disadvantages of being tall, it all depends on how one applies that judgement.

Financially it is, without question, a disadvantage to be tall. We have already established that tall people either have to or are expected to pay more than a person of average height for certain products or services. When it comes to clothing and the like I understand that the market is smaller, therefore the demand is less, and unit production costs greater than they are for the mass market. Unfortunately, some suppliers like to maximise the profit to be made from that simple fact. I have no problem with paying a little extra, but when I am faced with prices that are double, even triple those of a comparable average size item, my limits are well and truly exceeded. There is such a thing as a fair price, and then there is blatant exploitation of a niche market.

The main disadvantages are, to me, lack of comfort in most environments and the implication by too many product and service providers that it is in some way my fault.

The greatest benefits of being tall are, to me, intangible. I love being tall, and the attention it attracts. Granted, it can be a bit tiresome at times, but on the whole I enjoy the attention. I never have to start a conversation because someone will always come and talk to me. I am remembered almost wherever I go, and because I make a point of not slouching or trying to hide my height in any way I appear confident and am treated accordingly. I have found a great deal of humour in my height, and the occasional crack on the head from a lower than expected door frame is just part of the deal.

For the most part, I control the perceptions of the people I know and of others I come into contact with. Of course, there are those people who see me but do not interact with me, and whose perceptions may be very different. They may see me as threatening because of my height, or perhaps different in some other indefinable way simply because I do not conform to their idea of what is 'normal'. However, once we interact in any way I am back in control, and their perceptions usually change.

Granted, the change is not always a positive one. I have strong character traits, some of which can make people feel uncomfortable. Anyone who thinks that this tall guy is the proverbial quiet gentle giant who is easily kept in his place has a nasty shock awaiting them. Don't misunderstand me; most of the time I am that gentle giant, but when it's time to fight my corner I am no pushover.

Naturally this means that some people don't like me. So what? I don't expect to be universally liked. None of us is perfect. I expect only to be afforded the same respect as anyone else, regardless of their height.

I know full well that not every tall person is as comfortable with their height as I am. Tall women especially may find themselves subject to additional pressures, more often than not at the hands of insecure shorter men. It is true that the most fragile thing in the known universe is the male ego. When faced with a woman who is significantly taller than he his, the average male will subconsciously revert to the time in his life when the most influential and powerful woman was also much taller than he was; he called her 'mother'. It's just like watching a grumpy teenager, as he complains bitterly about the 'overbearing Amazon'.

Many people still labour under the misapprehension that being a tall woman is the most wonderful thing in the world. After all, aren't all those supermodels over 6ft tall themselves?

As I regularly pointed out in interviews when this point was made: it's one thing being a 6ft supermodel earning a six or seven figure income, quite another being a 6ft 2in secretary in Berwick-upon-Tweed.

I have lost count of the numbers of times I have heard how male bosses will ask a taller female employee to sit down when they have something important or personal to discuss. Many men find it difficult to look up at a woman while giving her a telling off.

Conversely, I have met many tall women who assume that they are sometimes perceived as masculine purely because of their height. The scenario frequently involves a cashier or someone sitting at a low desk, and whose sightline does not extend above the waist of the person they are serving. Once again, it is general perceptions which can lead to such misunderstandings.

For example, if you saw someone of 6ft 1in wearing a motorcycle helmet, dressed head to toe in motorcycle leathers, and riding a large powerful motorcycle, wouldn't your first expectation be for it to be a man? After all, girls don't ride big beefy motorbikes, do they? Well, actually, they do. However, because men are more commonly associated with such machines than women are, it is an understandable mistake to make.

Returning to the cashier at the supermarket check-out: from that low perspective, and while scanning the contents of the 237th trolley that morning, peripheral vision is not going to extend much beyond the waist level of whomever is standing opposite. If all that is thus visible is a pair of jeans, a T-shirt and the bottom part of a jacket, only the waist band will provide a basic estimate of the height of the customer. As only a small percentage of women are over 6ft, the likelihood is that if someone appears to be that height or above, they are more likely to be a man.

Let's revisit the same scenario and this time, although the height is the same, the customer is wearing a beautifully styled dress and a casual wrap around cardigan. What are the chances that she will be mistaken for a man now?

Many tall women see these occasional misperceptions as a negative aspect of their height, whilst in fact the misperception is based on a much wider, but still limited, range of information, which statistically favours the individual being a man.

Perceptions are always comparative; there are no absolutes in perceptions. How do you know someone is unusually tall? Only because you can compare them with lots of other, not so tall, people, both visually and referentially. Perceptions also depend on environment. A 5ft 10in man may be only of average height in Britain, yet were he a member of the Pygmy tribe, he would be positively gargantuan.

Just to confuse the issue, preconceptions may also influence our perceptions.

Two groups of people were invited to attend identical presentations by the same speaker in the same lecture theatre, and afterwards rate the presentation and describe the speaker. The first group was told that the speaker was a well educated successful businessman, the second that he was a manual worker with an average education; the speaker dressed appropriately for each role.

The first group rated the presentation more highly in terms of its content and delivery than the second. Interestingly, they also estimated the speaker to be about two inches taller!

Similar experiments have been conducted many times, and always with similar results. It says a great deal about how we perceive people on the basis of limited information.

What has consistently surprised me is the small margin which separates those of us who are 'admirably tall' and those who are considered 'unusually tall'. A man of 6ft 3in is generally viewed as the former, though one of 6ft 8in is likely to be seen as the latter.

Let's put that 5 inch margin into perspective. Extend your middle finger at an angle to the rest of your hand, and consider the distance from fingertip to knuckle. Mine is about 5 inches. The difference between admirably and unusually tall is the length of a middle finger.

On a daily basis we deal with people with a range of height at least double that, and yet we think nothing of it. However, as soon as that 5 inch margin occurs at one or other extreme of our standard frame of reference, we are taken aback. What a huge difference a few inches can make (and you can wipe that smirk off your face right now; I'm trying to be serious here)..

With all of that said, we must be wary of accepting the results of all psychological research without question. It is true that as long as rigorous procedures are followed and the hypothesis to be tested is properly isolated, the results should prove reliable. Unfortunately, because researchers are themselves only human, the results of their research can easily be tainted by the same human foibles their research so diligently seeks to illuminate. The 'causation fallacy' is not always as easy to eliminate as we may like to imagine. Likewise, the necessity to generalise the final summary of what is fundamentally excellent and meaningful work may cause the real conclusions of the work to be lost in a fog of generalities. On the other hand, the attempt to express everything as accurately as possible makes most research documents difficult to read and even more difficult to comprehend.

We may like to think that language allows us to communicate clearly, but often the opposite is true. It may be what we leave out, rather than what we say, that holds the key to what we wish to convey.

Actually, psychology and pantomime have a great deal in common.

Researcher number one does his experiments, and then publishes his results, saying words to the effect of: "This is how it is."

Along comes researcher number two with his results, and shouts: "Oh no it isn't." Enter researcher number three with his results, and a cheery: "Oh yes it is."

A lot of supposed psychological facts are really just majority decisions. Fifty researchers say one thing, six say the opposite, and democracy rules. Actually, the same is true of most science. If it weren't we would never question or test accepted wisdom, and our knowledge would never increase.

A great deal of research is repeated time and again. One topic that saw the TPC regularly invited to comment in the media was one that I believe was originally commissioned by a major commercial company, and has been repeated many times since. It beats me how researchers manage to bag research grants to test hypotheses which have already been proven beyond reasonable doubt, but I suppose all that research money has to go somewhere.

"Tall People Earn More" announce the headlines, citing the work of whichever University is the latest to tackle this old chestnut. The results show that on average a tall man will earn more than his equally qualified shorter counterpart. The rate is usually expressed as a percentage per inch of height although reference to absolute sums is also made. The latter must be viewed in the context of the economic circumstances prevailing at the relevant time and place.

Brace yourselves, because I am about to quote a proper source, just like real researchers do. The study by Persico, Postlethwaite and Silverman (University of Pennsylvania, 2003) goes into great detail, and proves that it is not just height per se that appears to affect eventual earning potential, but height in teenage. In doing so, they have added to what I have previously seen published on the subject. They concluded that it is those who are tall in their mid-teens who tend to come out at the upper end of the earnings scale. Those who were late in achieving their final adult height and were of average or below average height in teenage are more likely to be nearer the average as adults. Their research does include reference to race and gender, but concentrates its conclusions on white males. They also make every effort to determine the influence of many other factors in conjunction with height.

The researchers suggest that it is height and self-esteem in teenage that influences the observed trend. Tall teenagers who follow athletic pursuits are the most likely to come out at the top of the scale. Achievement on the sports field translates into the long term self esteem that enables the individual to outperform his less athletic peers once school and university are but a distant memory. Teenagers whose extra curricular activities are of a more intellectual nature, say the chess club or a debating society, come out slightly behind, but still significantly ahead of the average.

The original research document runs to over 70 pages and includes detail about chosen professions, family backgrounds and much more. Out of necessity I have, of course, drastically simplified its findings here. If you want to read the whole thing, there is currently (September 2007) a download available at *http://www.econ.upenn.edu/Centers/pier/Archive/03-036.pdf.* Be warned: if you don't have a degree in mathematics or statistical analysis you will find parts of it as comprehensible as an insider joke about quantum mechanics.

In conclusion, this particular study ponders whether the treatment of children with HGH (Human Growth Hormone) to increase their adult height, and thereby potentially their adult earnings, would be a financially sound investment. The argument is also countered with the observation that should such treatment become widespread the effect of the height premium would ultimately be negated.

Perhaps it was just idle speculation on their part, but I find that kind of thinking worrying.

Now for the part that I have been banging on about in every interview in which the 'Tall Men Earn More' point has been raised – and there have been many.

Yes, it is true that tall men earn more, but what every bit of research that I have seen on the subject leaves out is this: at around 6ft 6in it starts to go into reverse. Were it not so, then most 7 footers would be coining it in, but they aren't. A more accurate summation might be: Taller than average men earn more, while unusually tall men do not.

Why is this minor detail left out? The reason is quite simple and logical really. In any research which involves demonstrating conclusions by means of statistics it is customary to exclude all data at the extreme ends of the range. This prevents a small number of extreme data skewing the overall result in one direction or another; sensible statisticians' practise. Messrs Persico, Postlethwaite and Silverman *et al* use this device to make sure their conclusions are applicable to as large a part of the population as is feasible. Unfortunately, those of us who are members of Tall Clubs would virtually all fall into that top percentage of height distribution which is excluded from the calculations.

Anyway, now we have ascertained that being 10ft 6in at 16 years of age will not necessarily lead you to rival Bill Gates' earnings in adulthood perhaps we should look at the reasons why. Whether or not a suitable methodology can be established I don't know. Necessarily small sample sizes will always leave results open to question, but should be good for a few more research grants which, after all, does save the researchers going out and finding proper jobs.

By the way, if I need to refer to Messrs Persico, Postlethwaite and Silverman again I shall refer to them simply as Messrs P,P & S, because I can't be bothered to write their names out in full every time. If I do not refer to them again then it will have made writing this paragraph a total waste of time.

IQ and the Tall Person

A great deal of research appears to confirm that tall children tend to have a higher IQ than their shorter peers.

The whole concept of measuring IQ by means of IQ tests is a touchy subject. Much of the early work on the subject has been discredited. Even today many organisations refuse to allow their use, as the results are too easily misinterpreted, misunderstood, or misused. An example off all three is the tests that were administered to immigrants entering the USA through Ellis Island in the early 20th century. Eastern Europeans, among others, performed well below the expected average, and were consequently labelled "feeble minded". Immigration officers were even granted legal powers to return such "feeble minded" individuals to their place of origin.

The problem was that at least part of the test was dependent on a reasonable command of the English language. Naturally, people for whom English was a completely foreign language did not fare well. Because the test also included questions relevant to US culture, immigrants who were not already familiar with the culture again performed well below expectations. This led to the theory that certain races were of lower intelligence than Caucasians, unthinkable today, but perfectly acceptable in the early part of the 20th century.

It has also been established beyond reasonable doubt that IQ is not a fixed quantity. A child may perform at one level, but at a higher or possibly lower level at later stages in life. Experiences, environment and motivation all play a part.

I wish I could remember the source of one particular piece of research I came across during my first year studying psychology. It was twenty years ago, and as far as I recall, the main facts were these: Two groups of young people, one black the other white, were given IQ tests. In the first test the white children performed slightly ahead of the average, while the black children came out slightly below average. The two groups were then combined and taught and encouraged to socialise as a single group. A second IQ test, administered some time later (I think it was about a year, although it may have been more) showed the scores of both the white and the black children to be virtually identical, and to have risen above the score achieved by either group in the first test.

A nurturing environment, one which not only encourages but recognises ongoing achievement, is one within which it is easier and more rewarding to learn, and to acquire new skills. Performance in IQ tests will tend to improve in a positive learning and social environment

The influence of sub-culture with particular reference to language was explored in another experiment. A standard IQ test was given to two groups of teenagers, one white, the other black. The white group scored significantly higher than the black group. The test was repeated, but this time with the test paper written in language more familiar to the black group, the colloquial language of what the experimenters referred to, I believe, as "black street-culture". The results of the second test were virtually reversed, with the black group scoring higher than the white group.

Another complication is that general IQ tests do not necessarily differentiate between particular talents, abilities and personal preferences.

A quick word about pleasure: how and why we experience pleasure is down to brain chemistry. This is a complex subject, which I shall not even attempt to précis here. The point is that, as we all know, learning can be pleasurable. Our brain chemistry may therefore predispose us to favour one pursuit over another. A neurosurgeon and a mechanic are likely to have very different lifestyles, but may well have a similar IQ.

This introduces the idea and definition of motivation into the equation. Society generally expects people to strive for "success", but almost invariably defines that success in terms of either financial rewards or recognition by ones peers. What about the individual's own definition? Without knowing and understanding what motivates an individual it is impossible to say whether they have been successful or not.

Many people in the upper echelons of the IQ range can be found doing relatively undemanding and financially not very rewarding jobs. Does this mean they have not been successful? What if that person has an interest that they do not wish to pursue professionally? They may be doing an undemanding job simply to pay the bills while leaving themselves enough free time to devote to that interest. They see no need to gain recognition from an academic institution in order to do what they enjoy doing most, and may well be as skilled and as knowledgeable as someone who holds a degree in the same subject.

I once heard success defined as "Being able to do what you want, when you want, and being able to afford it". By that definition many a so called under-achiever is actually very successful indeed.

Perhaps these people have recognised that the whole concept of "success" is merely a modification of pack hierarchy observed among other animals which live in social groups. They have made a conscious decision to not play that game, and have instead chosen to step outside the constraints of society's expectations. Our society does not deal well with anything or anyone who strays too far from a predetermined norm. Most of us need to feel at ease within our social group. Non-conformists have to be labelled in some negative way so that they become non-threatening to all that we know and hold dear.

On a personal note, any time I see an article focusing on so called underachievement by people with a high IQ, I feel it is more likely to be the writer, rather than his subjects, who has a problem.

Let us not confuse intelligence with common sense. Supposedly intelligent people frequently overcomplicate simple tasks, or are even totally defeated by them. This is beautifully illustrated by a story I came across while researching for this chapter.

Mensa is a society for people who have tested in the top 2% of the population for intelligence. A group of members was having lunch when one of them noticed that the salt was in the pepper shaker and the pepper was in the salt cellar. How to transfer each condiment into its appropriate container was just the kind of intellectual challenge they enjoyed. They discussed the problem in detail and devised a clever solution involving a saucer, a serviette and a straw (I can't work out what the straw was for either). They were pleased with themselves and wanted to show off to someone how clever they were. When the waitress arrived with their bill one of them said: "Look, the salt is in the pepper shaker and the pepper is in the salt cellar, but we have got...."

He didn't get a chance to finish, because the waitress said, "Oh, I'm sorry about that," unscrewed the tops from both containers and switched them.

The importance of past experience is often overlooked. Consider the university don whose car got stuck in a patch of mud. As he tried to drive out, the wheels just kept spinning, and were soon a tyre's width down in the mire. He called a recovery vehicle, which soon arrived. The driver climbed into the car, and by delicate coordination of accelerator and clutch gently rocked it back and forth until it gained enough momentum that he was able to drive the car straight out of the patch of mud. It took less than a minute. The recovery driver's experience rather than his intelligence saved the day – or did it? Perhaps it should be called 'selective intelligence'?

If you are still with me, I would like to conclude this short exploration of IQ and IQ tests with a final piece of brain mangling.

Silverman and Silverman's assertion that "Doing experiments with people is like doing chemistry with dirty test tubes" should be a mantra for serious practitioners of psychology everywhere. The desire of a test subject to please the researcher and to therefore not necessarily respond or react in the way they might have done were they not being observed has skewed many a set of results. We also need to remember that experimenters are people too and it is therefore not always possible to eliminate 'researcher bias'. Even some of the greatest names in the field have succumbed to the urge to be more than a little selective in both methodology and data selection in order to prove an hypothesis. This is especially relevant in the interpretation of results. Many a piece of research has fallen foul of what is referred to as the 'causation fallacy', identifying a cause and effect link where in fact none exists. It is also often expressed as "correlation does not imply causation".

In its simplest terms, the causation fallacy might run something like this: Ice cream consumption rises in summer; more people drown in summer; therefore people who eat ice cream are more likely to drown. Clearly this conclusion is erroneous. The common factor is summer, and you shouldn't need me to explain any further than that.

Apply this to the observation that tall people generally have a higher than average IQ. The question is now: if a higher socio economic background produces both taller people and people with a higher than average IQ, do tall people tend to have a higher IQ because they are tall or because they are more likely to come from a higher socio economic background? The original observation has been repeatedly confirmed by numerous researchers, but the effects of background and a positive nurturing environment cannot be ignored.

Higher socio economic origins generally indicate better nutrition and healthcare, both of which contribute to greater final height. Better health means less time wasted being ill, and therefore more time for learning and gaining new experiences. A positive learning environment with access to a wide range of books and other learning tools may be more readily found higher up the social ladder. How important is one versus the other? We just can't be sure. Ultimately, so many factors play a part and interact in such a wide variety of subtle and complex ways, that it is almost impossible to completely isolate each from the others.

The preceding pages may be summarised thus: Beware of IQ tests, and approach all psychological research with an open mind and a healthy degree of scepticism.

I know I could have said that in the first place, and I may well have already done so, but if I had you would probably have asked "Why?"

I can't escape this section without telling a couple of personal stories, which serve to illustrate further intelligence versus both common sense and experience.

My first mobile phone, back in the eighties, was a trans-mobile. It was huge by today's standards. The handset fitted into a cradle on a base station which also held a battery the size of this book. Try as I might, I could not get the handset into the cradle, unless I pushed it in very firmly with the flat of my hand. After three weeks of watching me grunt and swear every time I tried to hang up the phone, Carol took a look at the problem. Within seconds she had spotted the small slot in the handset and the little lug on the base station. With the slot fitted over the lug, she gently nudged the handset into the cradle with her index finger. Duh!

I went to pick up Carol from work one evening. The medical centre where she works is part of a large engineering works. When I arrived, her colleague was struggling to remove the screw top from a flask. Both the flask and top were made of stainless steel. A burly maintenance man had also tried and failed, and promised to return with a strap wrench which he was sure would do the job. I boiled a kettle and, while holding the flask on its side wrapped in a thick cloth soaked in cold water, carefully poured boiling water over the top. Then with a dry cloth, I grabbed the top and unscrewed it easily. All those physics lessons at school weren't wasted after all. Metals expand and contract when heated and cooled. By keeping the flask cool and heating the top I caused the lid to expand just enough for me to be able to unscrew it.

The first story demonstrates a complete lack of common sense on my part, while the second shows that learning and experience may solve a problem that brute force can't.

Tall Children, Teenagers and Adults

Thankfully most tall people are so for genetic reasons. Some, however, will have been affected by one of the medical conditions which are outlined in a later chapter. I shall not discuss the details of those here, nor their specific effects on the tall child.

I suppose it's as well to start with some general observations. First and foremost has to be that the more that is made of a child's height, whether positive or negative, the greater and more long lasting the impact will be. Many adults influence a tall child's life and the individual attitudes of each of those adults, including the parents, will impact on the child. Whether that impact is positive or negative depends on more factors than I can list here without inducing total brain meltdown.

The old saying 'Give me the boy until he is seven and I will give you the man' is uncomfortably true. If a child is made to feel that its height is in some way an undesirable quality and an inconvenience that is the attitude it will learn and maintain for life. I have known far too many examples of parental conditioning of this kind.

I have already said something similar many times in these pages, and I shall say it a few times more, no doubt. It bears repetition because it is the most fundamental truth in the development of any child, not just a tall child.

A woman told me how her parents always made a big thing of her height from an early age, and not in a positive way. To make matters worse, it continued as a sort of family joke until well into adulthood. It was not until she plucked up the courage to say 'enough is enough' that her family finally realised the damage they had been doing and how hurtful they had been over the years. The woman's experiences within the TPC taught her that she was not the only one to feel that way, and that it was not her fault. She learned that it was possible to overcome that early conditioning, that it was alright to be tall and to be proud of it. Once she had learned the new attitude it became easy for her to face her erstwhile tormentors, and to tell them the truth. The new positive attitude she adopted carried over into other areas of her life too.

Another TPC member seemed rather stand-offish, her manner almost brusque, when I first met her in hospitality during a television discussion show. Approachable she most certainly wasn't. It was a defence she had adopted in response to the unwelcome attention she had become accustomed to attracting, courtesy of her height. She hadn't been a member long, and had yet to become involved with her local group. Over the following two or three years I watched as she changed, revealing her true personality, a wonderfully kind and good humoured nature. The only time I ever saw real aggression in her was in a go-kart race, when she wasn't going to let me pass, no matter how I tried. She eventually married another TPC member, and they now have a daughter.

Further confirmation of the wonderful lady she is came out of the blue. It was a year or two after I had stepped down from leading the TPC. I was doing some business with a couple, and the subject of my height was raised. I answered their questions, and then the wife said: "We stayed at a lovely B&B in Weston-super-Mare last year. The couple who ran it were really tall too. They were so nice, wonderful people. They made us feel so welcome."

I mentioned their names, and that of their daughter; you can guess the rest.

The road to self acceptance is not always an easy, nor a clear one; it can be long and arduous. It is, however, a journey well worth making. The lessons learned along the way are of benefit in all areas of life.

Tall Children

This is not going to be an intellectual discussion on child rearing, so I won't pretend to be the latest version of Dr Spock (he's the one without the pointy ears). If you need hints, tips and guidance on that subject, just watch a few episodes of *Supernanny*.

Up to the age of five it is more likely to be the parent who will have a problem dealing with a child's height. If the parents are not unusually tall themselves, there will be the natural concern about whether everything is in order, whether the child is in some way ill. In some cases, of course, they may be, but in the vast majority of cases it is not so. So why do difficulties occur?

During infancy, a cheery district nurse declaring "You've got a right little monster here," or "She's awfully big, we'll have to keep an eye on that," does little to ease the mind of a shiny new parent. If that does happen, it's worth keeping track of the child's growth, by plotting it on a growth chart. It will quickly become apparent whether the child is so far from the expected pattern of growth that further investigation is merited.

Next comes that age that all parents enjoy and savour, but only ever as a memory: the 'Terrible Twos'. That is the age at which a child begins to develop a sense of its own identity and its ability to manipulate its environment.

In itself, the Terrible Twos is just one of those phases that all children and their parents have to go through, but when your two year old is already the size of many a five year old, their temper tantrums can attract unwelcome reactions from people who are unaware of the child's actual age.

At that stage, age misperception probably impacts more on the parents than it does the child. They can be made to feel that it is they who are at fault, that something is horribly wrong with their child, or it is in some way developing abnormally; nothing could be further from the truth.

Survive that period and the child then faces nursery school, and the values and attitudes of secondary carers.

A mother told me how her three year old son was left to play on his own at nursery. The carers had separated him from the other children of the same age. They were afraid that he would hurt them, as he was so much bigger than they were. He was sent to play with the older children, but they wanted nothing to do with him because he was still a baby in their eyes. So the boy spent his days sitting alone, amusing himself.

"He looked so lonely and lost when I saw him," his mother said. "It broke my heart to see him like that."

Parents have to be aware that situations like this can and do occur. To educate those secondary carers, many of whom may hold a professional qualification, is not easy. No professional likes to be told by a lay-person that they are mistaken in their practices and beliefs; it both questions and undermines their authority. Tact, patience and understanding are required. In the long term it is not only the child who will benefit, but all the future tall children, as well as other children who do not conform to some perceived norm.

Conversely, adults who interact with the child in line with its apparent, rather than its actual age, can help to speed the child's development. They unwittingly provide the more stimulating and challenging environment known to be conducive to improving IQ. This is generally positive, but it can bring with it unforeseen difficulties.

Although intellectual development is accelerated, emotional development does not necessarily keep pace. Should the two diverge significantly, the child may begin to experience difficulties in social interaction with its intellectual peers, who may be two to three years older than they are.

The idea of tall children being on average more intelligent than their peers is well established. Apart from the influence of nutrition and health care, it is likely that the expectations of others set standards to which the child feels it should aspire. By achieving and living up to those standards its development is enhanced, with an obvious knock on effect on the child's IQ.

Parallels may be observed in both only children, who get more individual attention from their parents, and in children born to older first time parents. In the latter case, the parents are more mature and at peace with themselves. They may have already achieved many of the goals they had set for themselves, and are therefore more inclined and more able to spend quality time with their child. It is not uncommon to find that only or first born children born to older parents learn to read well ahead of their peers. Eldest children usually have a higher IQ than their younger siblings. For a while at least they were, of course, only children, which may go some way to explaining this phenomenon.

In school a whole new set of perceptions come into play. It is common for teachers to expect more from a tall child, based on nothing more that its physical size. He may be expected to show greater maturity, and to accept more responsibility than his peers. "You're a big boy, you should know better," is an observation usually based on nothing more than height.

On the other hand, many tall people report that as children they were often the first to be accused of misbehaviour. "I stood out a head above the rest of the class, so I usually got the blame for everything," said one.

Bullying occurs in all schools, whether they admit to it or not. Any child who is notably different is a target. Wearing glasses, having ginger hair, being a 'swot' or unusually tall is all it takes to attract the bully's attention. Any child with a passive and non-confrontational nature is an obvious target.

How or whether the school deals with bullying effectively is a separate discussion.

A brief word of warning about literature available on bullying: some of it makes reference to the aggressor usually being the taller child. To a degree there is some truth in this, but if the child is exceptionally tall it is far more likely to be the victim.

Tall Teenagers

Difficulties can occur as the tall child approaches teenage, especially if it has favoured socialising with others who are a year or two older. Physical development is likely to leave the tall teenager performing at a lower level in physical activities, such as informal games of football and the like. With the onset on puberty, priorities within the group also change dramatically. Whilst previously members of the opposite sex held no particular appeal, suddenly they become extremely interesting indeed. The tall child, although still on a par with its intellectual peers, suddenly finds itself completely divorced from their new principal interest. It is, after all, still a year or more away from undergoing the hormonal changes that trigger that sudden shift in focus.

Suddenly the tall child finds itself on the fringes or even completely excluded from the group that was previously one of its social centres. Rejoining those who are at the same level of physiological and emotional development is not always a satisfactory option, as the intellectual gap may be difficult to bridge.

I know that in my case I felt extremely isolated for a couple of years, until time and biology sorted out the dilemma.

Bullying may also become more of an issue in teenage. Roles within any group tend to polarise and become more distinct as the hormonal changes of puberty impact upon established group dynamics. Alpha males and females emerge within the group and both are likely to enforce and defend their new positions, either physically or psychologically.

No matter how much we like to kid ourselves that, as humans, we are in some way separate from and superior to the rest of the animal kingdom, we are subject to the same impulses as any group of primates. Fundamentally, we are still animals, mammals, primates. Whilst we have the intellectual capacity to modify some of our behaviour patterns, we do not have the ability to override or to eliminate them completely. At times of great stress, such as during the hormonal upheaval of puberty, more basic instinctual behaviour patterns do emerge.

Tall teenagers fall into a number of distinct groups. Those who are athletically built, and star of the sports team, are just the kind of future high earner that Messrs P.P. & S. identified in their research (writing that paragraph wasn't a waste of time after all; great!). The admiration of their peers builds self-esteem and confidence, which serves them well both at school and later in life.

Tall children who are not athletically gifted may find an outlet in other activities. This will still afford them status within a particular group and, whilst it may not attract universal admiration, does build confidence and an awareness of the ability to achieve.

Exceptionally tall teenagers are often gangly and uncoordinated. Their physical development is out of kilter, as the body grows but the muscles fail to keep pace. Should some form of recognition elude them, height will become their primary identifier. The nicknames that all too often accompany that feature are rarely flattering.

Thankfully, attitudes appear to be changing among PE teachers. The old Sear'nt Major breed is slowing making its way to that great parade ground in the sky, to be replaced by a more enlightened and aware generation. I have heard countless tales of PE teachers who were far worse than any playground bully. Any child's failure to perform was highlighted and ridiculed. That included not only exceptionally tall children, but also the fat kid or the scrawny little weakling who couldn't climb the ropes, or execute even a simple vault over the pommel horse. Once a teacher openly ridicules a child it becomes fair game for the bullies too. After all, if the teacher does it then it must be ok.

The humiliation such children feel quickly carries over into other areas of school work. Failure to achieve according to the expectations of other teachers can bring more unwelcome attention. Exceptionally tall children suffer more than most, as their height leads to unrealistic assumptions about their potential. Failure to live up to those expectations destroys self-confidence. Ironically, the child may well be performing better than others of the same age, but because of unrealistic demands and expectations still feels like a failure. This process may begin in childhood, or not until teenage. Whichever it is, the effects are likely to be long lasting.

Self-imposed isolation is a common response, leading to inhibited social development. Discomfort in social situations, especially unfamiliar ones, is an understandable consequence. Once learned in teenage, such behaviour becomes difficult to modify in adulthood. We now have the reason why the 'Tall Men Earn More' idea falls apart above the 6ft 6in mark.

Within the TPC I met many members who initially felt uneasy in social situations, but were unable to explain why. In most cases they put it down to self-consciousness about their height. The more they talked about themselves and their past experiences the more apparent it became that it went much deeper than that. Without having gained some form of recognition, height became their principal identifier. Even though they were intelligent people, their lack of self-confidence gave them a lesser sense of self worth.

Here is yet another example of the cause and effect question: as teenagers did they lack the self-confidence to strive for some form of recognition, or did the lack of recognition result in lack of self-confidence?

Of course, nothing is ever that simple, and the issue can become complicated by failure to accurately identify the problem. A tall teenager may express overt dissatisfaction with his stature, and claim it to be the reason for everything that he feels to be wrong with his life. Being such an obvious feature, a parent may truly believe that it has to be what lies at the root of the obvious difficulties the teenager is experiencing, and what is putting such a strain on their relationship. They will direct their efforts to solving the 'problem' for their offspring, blissfully unaware that in doing so they are actually reinforcing the negative perceptions which began as nothing more than a convenient excuse.

I shall never forget the call from a concerned mother who told me all about the problems she was having with her 6ft 4in 15 year old son.

"It's his height," she told me. "He hates being so tall and it's affecting his whole life."

I listened as she told me about his sullen and uncommunicative behaviour, his moodiness, and about the grumpy young man he had become since beginning the latest growth spurt. He hated being so much taller than all of his friends, he hated being different. She told me of the regular arguments they had, the trouble he was in at school, and how he would hide away in his room for hours on end, emerging only to wordlessly raid the fridge, accompanied by the odd primeval grunt.

Now, I realise that many of you are probably way ahead, but hang on in there.

I listened as this worried mother unburdened herself to the first person she had found who was willing to listen without being judgemental, someone who was himself tall and almost certainly understood what her son was feeling. I could hear the tension falling away as she let go of everything that had been troubling her. It made her feel better, and she thanked me for my patience and understanding.

"May I ask you a question," I said?

"Of course," she replied.

"What were you like as a teenager?"

"Oh my god," she said. "I was horrible. I am still apologising to my mother to this day for ever having been a teenager."

She began to tell me about her own teenage, her own appalling behaviour, the arguments with her mother, but then slowly petered out to total silence.

"Oh," she said after a few seconds. "I've just realised. It's got nothing to do with his height, has it? He's a teenager. He's behaving like any boy his age. I was so worried, I just didn't think. I thought it had to be his height. It seemed so obvious."

And there you have it: an individual's height is so obvious, so unmissable, it is all too easy to lay the blame for everything at its feet.

I have come to believe that height is often nothing more than a highly visible hook on which to hang all of the excuses for a less than perfect life. Psychologists refer to this as 'learned helplessness'. The real reason may not always be as clear, as easy to accept or to confront. The poor self-image and low self-esteem some tall people have often has little, if anything, to do with height. It is more often the people around the tall person who lie at the root of the true cause. Their attitudes and behaviour are far more influential than the individual's height alone.

Height may be a symptom but rarely is it the real, nor the whole, problem.

Tall Adults

Tall adults are, for the most part, nothing more than tall teenagers, but older. Actually, the same probably applies to all adults. The attitudes we have developed by teenage tend to stay with us for the rest of our lives. Of course, as adults we all look back at how different we were as teenagers, and cringe at some of the things we got up to. But in truth, the underlying attitudes were already in place, although often subjugated to peer pressure, or to a need to look cool and to find acceptance.

For the tall adult, height can become a defence behind which to hide unwelcome truths, a camouflage for experiences and memories they would rather not face. Unusually tall girls in particular may find that age misperception can lead them into situations which they are neither physically nor emotionally equipped to deal with. Such experiences may be so traumatic that the after effects persist well into adult life, and may never be properly identified and dealt with.

I once received a call from a consultant psychiatrist, asking for help. A 6ft 3in woman had spent several months in his unit, and had made little progress. She put all her problems down to her height, and wanted nothing more than to have height reduction surgery. She had convinced herself that life was unliveable as an exceptionally tall woman; if only she were 5ft 11in, all her problems would disappear.

The doctor was compelled to respect patient confidentiality, so we talked about height in general, and examined some hypothetical possibilities. We concluded that the issue of height had to be removed from the equation. He had already suggested that she make contact with the TPC, and possibly attend a social event, but she was not willing to do either. However, she was not averse to meeting another tall woman, probably in the hope that she could thereby confirm everything she claimed to feel about her height.

I arranged for one of our members to visit. A 6ft 6in woman who held a responsible job within her organisation, had an active social life, and had lived and studied in the USA, she also made sure that she did not wear flat shoes for her visit.

A few weeks later the doctor called again, but this time to thank us for our help. At long last he was making progress with his patient, and was optimistic for her future well-being. It had taken just a couple of visits before she stopped focusing on her height. With that defence removed she had been left nowhere to hide, and finally began to confront the real problem.

When childhood and teenage conditioning carries over into adulthood it will affect every aspect of life. Yet it can be modified, or broken if you prefer. Either the person finds a niche within which they can achieve the success that previously eluded them, or someone else recognises their potential, helps them to believe in their own abilities, and offers encouragement to break free from the shackles of past conditioning.

A good example is the 6ft 10in 21 year old man who had risen to the dizzy height of stores manager in a small manufacturing company. He had started as a stores assistant and taken over the top position upon the retirement of his immediate boss. The job included responsibility for all stock purchase and control, and was certainly a notch above the kind of jobs done by most of his friends.

He was a regular caller at TPC HQ, often calling for no more than a natter. I realised very quickly that here was a man who had no idea of his potential. As far as he was concerned, he had achieved as much as he was likely to, and could see nowhere else to go. I suggested he consider a change of career.

He was a smart dresser who oozed confidence and bravado. Back then, it was largely an act, but a role he played to near perfection. His personality was such that he found it easy to talk with people, and to sidestep their usual obsession with his height. I was certain that he could have a successful career in sales and management, and recommended that he look out for entry level sales jobs with a large company.

He wasn't sure, but I pointed out that he already dealt with a lot of salesmen in his position as buyer for his company. "Is there anything special about them to make you think you couldn't do their job," I asked him?

His answer made it perfectly clear that there wasn't. It took a while, but he called me one day to announce that he had an interview. His current employers were behind him all the way, and wished him well. They were surprised only that it had taken him so long to make the move. I wasn't in the least surprised when he got the job.

In the months that followed I think I must have heard from him almost as much as his manager did. Yes, I'm exaggerating, but not by much. Within a couple of years he moved on to another company, and a more challenging environment. When we last met he was a regional manager for a major white goods manufacturer, leading a team of several salesman, and responsible for an area covering the North of England and the whole of Scotland. Since then he has worked in Russia and Ireland for other companies and is now UK national sales manager for his latest employer.

He paid me the greatest compliment at the 2003 anniversary when he said to a new member: "I would not be where I am today if it weren't for Phil."

Sometimes all it takes is for someone you trust to show a little faith in you. I'm sure he would have eventually made that initial break without my encouragement. All I did was to help him to make the decision sooner rather than later.

Another was a 6ft 7in man in his forties. A quiet and passive man, he had been in the same job as a lowly stock control clerk for many years. At the regular staff evaluations he was told that promotion was not an option for him, as he did not exhibit the leadership skills of a supervisor or manager. That was his employer's loss. Had they seen him in the role he adopted within the TPC I am sure they would have felt very differently. He was prominent in his local group, arranging gatherings and organising outings, welcoming new members and generally representing the Club in any way he could. When I scheduled the Club's national event in his area he provided invaluable support, locating venues and arming me with whatever information he could to ensure that the Club got the best deals around.

His employers had become so accustomed to seeing him in the role he had occupied for so long, they were incapable of acknowledging the changes in him as they happened. At the next staff evaluation his confidence was such that he actively questioned the lack of promotion. Again his manager trotted out the same old tired arguments, saying that he was doing a good job where he was, and that a supervisory position would not suit him.

Whether he finally plucked up the courage to embark on a different career with a new employer I do not know. The last I heard he was staying put, as he had built up too many years of excellent pension rights to forsake them lightly. He was nearing fifty by then, future security was important to him, and I can understand his caution. Even so, in other areas of his life he became more assertive and adventurous. In dealing with his landlord he stood up for his rights when previously he would have been more inclined to submit to the demands being made. He found new energy for his hobbies. Previously they had been solitary pursuits, but he sought out other people and groups with similar interests, and became actively involved with them.

If he had been encouraged more in teenage, his life may have turned out very differently.

Exceptionally tall people are few and far between. That's why the TPC is the perfect environment in which to lose that sense of isolation, of being the only one who knows what it is like to deal with the day to day hassles of being very tall. Many members feel no need to attend a social event, and are just happy to know that they aren't the only tall person around; it's all the confirmation they need.

For some tall people a single positive encounter with another tall person is enough to change their perception of themselves. I sometimes wonder about a young man I met when I was in my mid-twenties. Conrad was 6ft 7in, and serving with the RAF, stationed at RAF Credenhill, near Hereford. The camp has since become the headquarters of the SAS, one of the army's elite combat forces.

I was in a local pub with some friends. Most were sitting around a small table near the door, while I sat at the bar chatting with the staff. The door opened, Conrad walked in, and immediately attracted my friends' attention. They called out to me: "Hey, Phil, you've got competition."

I watched as Conrad, aware of being the focus of attention, hunched his shoulders as he walked up to the bar. He hadn't been standing particularly straight in the first place, and was trying hard to disguise his height even more. As he stood next to me, waiting to be served, I looked up at him and said: "You ought to stand up straight, mate. You're doing your back no good at all."

He gave me a disdainful look. "It's alright for you," he said, "You don't know what it's like."

"Oh, I think I do," I said, and stood up next to him.

For a moment he looked shocked then he too stood to his full height, and smiled. We chatted for about half an hour, and he relaxed more and more as time went by. My friends and I moved on to another of our regular haunts, and I never saw him again. I wonder whether he eventually saw the TPC featured on television and, if he did, remembered our meeting all those years ago. Whether it made a long term difference to him I shall never know, but I hope it helped.

The right words at the right time in teenage can make for a very different adult.

Actually, the right words at any time can trigger positive changes. Unfortunately, we never know what words will trigger the change, and sometimes we will not even know of the change for which we have been the catalyst. Think back to my experience with Sigrid: her words changed my entire attitude to the opposite sex, yet she has absolutely no recollection of the incident.

Hold on to that thought as we launch headlong into the next (very short) chapter, which originally appeared as an article in '6ft+', the magazine of the Tall Persons Club.

It's Only Words...

...or is it?

I know that you believe you understand what you think I said, but I'm not sure whether you realise that what you heard is not what I meant!

Read it again, because it does actually make sense.

Often it is all too easy to hear what is being said but to miss what is actually meant. As tall people, we are subjected to more than our fair share of overt comments. Because of this we are sometimes inclined to react inappropriately, be it towards the person making the comment or, even worse, toward ourselves. For example, the 'weather' joke, or some variation on that theme, is not necessarily a cheap crack at our expense, but is rather the end result of a complex set of physiological and psychological reactions to an unfamiliar situation by the 'joker'.

There is no point in pretending that our mere physical presence does not have an effect on those around us, especially if they are not accustomed to us. We are different, we do stand out, and that is of enormous benefit, if we choose it to be.

I can hear the cries of "West Coast psychobabble" accompanied by eyes glazing over already, but bear with me, and I shall attempt to explain.

First of all I want you to recall an occasion when you were watching a thriller or similar film. Remember when something drastic and unexpected happened that made you jump. What did you do? First, you almost jumped out of your skin, then took a sharp intake of breath. Your heart rate leapt, but then your rational brain took over, and reminded you that it was just a film, and that therefore no threat existed. You relaxed back into your seat, took a breath and gave a chuckle or nervous laugh before admitting that you weren't expecting that. You may have even made a joke about it. Sound familiar?

What happens to some people when they unexpectedly encounter a tall person is not dissimilar. No, we are not something out of a horror movie, but we can unintentionally jolt someone's comfort zone. Looking at the process involved, it might go something like this, and please note that when the descriptions use the male gender, they apply equally to women.

Situation: A tall person walks into a room. An average height person reacts.

Reaction 1: Wow! I suddenly feel very small. This person has an imposing physical presence, and could be a threat. I have to be ready to defend myself in case of attack. That's silly. This isn't the jungle, it's a meeting. I know. I'll make a joke to show I'm not scared. Then I'll smile and show some teeth, just like submissive chimpanzees do, to show that they aren't a threat. That'll do it. Here goes: "What's the weather like...."

Reaction 2: Hey! That person is really tall. They have attracted all the attention in the room. I can't have that. I am the alpha male around here. This calls for action. I'll just have to make that person feel really small, to show everyone how clever and important I am. I'll say something clever. That will do it. "Hey! What's the weather like..."

Reaction 3: Wow! Look at that person. They are tall, carry themselves well, look confident, and really attractive. I have to get to know that person. How do I start a conversation? I know nothing of their tastes in music, food or film. Politics and religion is far too risky to start. I know! I'll say something about the one thing we are both aware of: their height. That should get things going. Then I can get to know them better. Who knows where that might lead?

That covers some of the likely reactions, so what of the response a tall person might make?

Response A: Oh god, no! Someone's made a joke about my height. Everyone's looking. I feel awful. I want to go home, to crawl into a deep hole, and to never go out ever again.

Response B: Someone's made a joke. Oh well, it's to be expected. It's a normal reaction, and it's better to be noticed than to be ignored. I'll come back with a good line, or just smile benignly. Either way, I can show them that I've heard them all before. Stay composed. Show you have dignity and self-confidence. Now let's move the conversation to something less tedious.

Response C: I wish they'd think of a more original approach line, but I suppose they have to start somewhere. Not bad though. Good looking, well dressed. Could be interesting. Accept comment with good grace, change the subject. Get talking. I wonder how they like their eggs for breakfast?

Body language will tell you a lot about the nature of the initial reaction, and you can gauge your response accordingly. Your own body language will usually determine how people will react to you in the first place.

You are probably sick of hearing this by now, but it bears a repeat airing. If you adopt a submissive or defensive posture to the world about you, it will treat you in line with the image you project. The basic rules for a tall person are simple, as they are for everyone. Of course it takes time to practice and to perfect the techniques that make the big difference, but perseverance will pay dividends.

Clothes maketh the (wo)man, they say. If you have ever watched Trinny and Susannah on the rampage you will already know the truth of that. A simple change of image and style can make a huge difference to one's confidence and presence.

Posture tells the world how you feel about you. Erect, confident posture says 'I like me', and it's difficult for someone to like anyone who doesn't like themselves. If you act confidently, you will be seen and treated as confident.

Slouching, huddled posture, with eyes fixed firmly on one's toes says 'I am not worthy – please treat me like dirt'. Guess what? Convey that message, and people will happily oblige.

Now go back to the first sentence of this article, and something else may occur to you. The words are true in many areas of our respective lives. But what could be easier in a discussion than to stop and to recap, to agree or disagree point by point, and to make sure that what we are saying is actually being understood; and if not, then why not?

Words are the means by which we communicate clearly with one another, at least that is the theory. We take our language so for granted that we often fail to spot the hidden meanings and messages our words may or may not convey. Even when the meaning seems to be clear, the interpretation that we choose to place upon those words can make a huge difference to the way that people see us and, more importantly, to the way that we see ourselves.

Above all, the message is:

No-one can make you feel bad about yourself without YOUR permission.

This article was inspired by the words of a Club member who told me that something I had said to her had changed her entire attitude to the people around her, and thus their attitude towards her had also changed dramatically. Now, I say a lot of stuff, and so had to ask her to elaborate.

She told me that she'd been having a good moan to me about the oiks who couldn't think of anything better to say to her than to make a comment about her height. I pointed out that, men being men, we are not overly imaginative when it comes to trying to start a conversation with an attractive woman. The only thing we can think of is to state the blindingly obvious. By cutting them dead with a sarcastic comment, as she had been, most immediately slunk off, defeated and demoralised. Apparently, I suggested that she go a little easier on them, and at least give them a chance to prove that they weren't worthy of her time before she cut them dead. That way, she wouldn't waste time with total oiks, but would perhaps get to know some really nice guys. She tried it, and it worked.

There's another point to this story. I have no recollection of the conversation we had, yet what I said obviously had a positive effect on her and on her life.

We often have no idea of the effect and influence we can have on someone's life with just a few words. Whether that effect is positive or negative depends on the words we choose.

Remember, there is a world of difference between "My darling, when I look into your eyes the hands of time just seem to stand still," and "Honey, you've got a face that could stop a clock!"

"It's Only Words", sang the Bee Gees. I beg to differ.

What Happened Next...

After this article appeared, I attended the Club's anniversary celebrations. A woman said to me – and I paraphrase: "I read your article, and thought it was a load of old twaddle (or words to that effect). My friend read it too, and she thought there might be something in it. When we went out that weekend, a guy came up to talk to me, and started with the usual comment about my height. I was about to cut him dead when I remembered your article, and I thought I would at least give it a try. You know what? He turned out to be a really nice guy, really sweet. He kept apologising, and bought me drinks all night. I hate to admit it, but you were right."

I rest my case.

Incidentally, I would like to thank the lady for telling me that story. It's always good to know that something you said or did helped someone else.

Thoughts on 'Counselling' and 'Therapy'

During my time running the TPC, I spent many hours in an informal counselling role. I say 'informal' because I have no formal training as either a counsellor or therapist, and yet many of the people I spoke with under those circumstances told me afterwards that they made more progress with me in an hour or two than they had done in months, or even years, of formal sessions.

I looked into training as a counsellor, but decided against it after realising that I would have to fundamentally change my approach to everything I did in that role. Several organisations offer formal qualifications in Counselling, but all of the courses I looked into favoured a passive approach. Each viewed the counsellor as a facilitator, a sounding board, someone who would, without actively guiding them, allow the client to find their own resolution. No wonder some people end up seeing counsellors for years on end. I know of one clinical psychologist, who describes most counselling as "…nothing more than you can get from a night in with a good friend and a couple of bottles of wine." Actually, he said some other things as well, but none that can be repeated in polite company.

In my experience, the need for counselling arises most often because someone has backed themselves into a corner to the point that they can longer see a way out. They can no longer see whatever was, or still is, troubling them. Granted, sometimes it is not that they are no longer able to see, but they have instead decided consciously or unconsciously to not see. The human mind has a wonderful capacity to either bury or to totally ignore anything it does not wish to deal with.

Counselling is supposed to encourage the person to open up and to talk about what is troubling them, which is why 'passive counselling' is ineffective. How can you 'passively encourage'? It's a contradiction in terms. If the person doesn't feel comfortable or able to talk with the counsellor, than the whole thing is a complete waste of time. Notice I said and meant 'talk with' and not 'talk to'.

Imagine, if you will, a person blindfolded in a field, looking for the gate in order to escape. When the person stumbles about, bumping into things, and falling over, the traditional, passive counsellor will sit down with him for a lengthy discussion about how it feels to crash into things and fall over; hardly a productive approach.

A counsellor who simply says "Walk forward twenty steps, turn right, walk thirty steps and there is the gate," may help his client find his way out of the field, but teaches him nothing in the process.

The counsellor who takes a more developmental approach won't give directions to the gate, but will instead offer hints and tips on how it may be found. For example: "Try listening for traffic; the gate is most likely to be on the side of the field leading to the road. Keep talking. The reflected sound will change as you approach a hedge or similar object. When you bump into something, reach out and feel it, find out what it is, as it might give you a clue as to how close you are."

Good counselling is about helping the client not only to deal with his current dilemma, but teaching him techniques to help him deal with future situations.

An old friend was going through a particularly difficult period in his life, both professionally and personally, full of emotional turmoil and indecision. He decided to get away from it all by spending a weekend at our home, during which naturally we talked a great deal. The biggest problem, or as fashion now dictates we call it "issue", was his perception that he had no control over any aspect of the situation in which he found himself. The respect, awe even, he felt for some of the people involved had rendered him a powerless passenger in his own life rather than being its driving force. Aware of how those around him had always perceived him as co-operative and compliant, he felt unable to take any positive action. He was concerned that, by no longer behaving in that predictable way his friends and colleagues had become accustomed to, they would no longer relate to him as they had previously done.

What he failed to recognise was that when we continue to do that which we have always done we will continue to get the same as we have always had. Change never happens of its own accord; someone makes it happen. The only question now is whether we wait for someone else to initiate that change, and accept that it may not be the change we are hoping for, or we initiate that change for ourselves. By doing the latter, we are in control of the changes. Of course, those around us may feel uncomfortable or disorientated by our actions, which they may see as uncharacteristic, but that is no bad thing. In fact, it increases our control over the situation, as others try to adjust to the different person we seem to have become. The differences might well be small and very subtle, but people will become aware of them, and will be taken off guard though they won't always understand why..

During our late night chats I introduced him to a few simple concepts; the first I have just outlined. Here it is again, because it is important:

If you always do what you always did, you'll always get what you always got

The second is simple enough, but few people find it easy to accept.

The past may have influenced who we are, but it does not affect what we choose to become in the future.

The only person who knows all about your past is you. Most of the people you come into regular contact with have no idea what you went through as a child or at some other time in your life. They will see and react to you the way you are now. If you carry and display the baggage of the past, of course it will continue to affect your present and your future. Modifying ingrained behaviour isn't easy; it will not happen overnight. However, the negative and destructive patterns of the past can be changed over time, and with persistence. As with any skill, practice makes perfect.

I am not saying that we should forget all about our past; quite the contrary. We must learn from it, and use what we learn to guide us constructively into a positive future. An old Russian saying sums it up: If you keep one eye on the past you are blind in one eye, but if you forget the past you are blind in both eyes.

And finally......

Learn to be objective rather than subjective.

213

Turbulent times in life are like being lost in a maze. You can neither see where you are, nor where you want to be. Yet it is easy to see the right path if you are standing outside and above the maze, looking down on it, and taking in the overall view. Likewise, the artist who works on some fine minute detail of a painting will step back from time to time, to view the whole picture, and to make sure that the detail fits in with whole.

When wondering what to do about some troublesome aspect of life, it can be helpful to imagine that it is someone else's life instead, and one is giving advice to a friend. Become the observer rather than the subject, and the view suddenly becomes a whole lot clearer.

With this approach, you learn to experience a situation, rather than to endure it or suffer because of it. There is a great deal of truth in the old saying that what doesn't kill you makes you stronger. Each situation faced and dealt with teaches something for the future and whatever it might bring.

My friend returned home and in due course came through his troubles. During a 'phone call several months later he told me of some other difficulties he was then dealing with, which I would have expected to cause him some distress. Instead, he seemed very relaxed about it all, and I commented on his very different attitude.

"I learned that from you," he told me. "Before, I used to worry about everything in my life. I always wanted things to run smoothly, and to work out right. I know now that isn't the way life works, and I treat each new set of problems or difficulties as a learning process. I no longer worry about these situations; instead, I choose to experience them."

Sometimes people ask me whether these techniques really work, and I have to be honest and tell them: "No they don't – not all the time."

Above all, counselling of any kind only works when the person wants them to work. Another of those old maxims, which holds true in every area of life, is that you cannot help someone who does not want to be helped.

Counselling has its place, but no-one will ever convince me that the passive approach is as effective as a pro-active one. In fact, you would be better off talking to your dog. At least then you would also get some affectionate cuddles to reassure you that someone really does care about you.

For a final thought on the subject, I hand you over to my friend George, the vet, who kindly checked this manuscript for errors, and provided valuable guidance along the way. In his words (although I suspect he probably borrowed them from someone else):

Ask three questions about any particular situation:
1. Is there a problem?
2. Does it matter?
3. If it matters – what do I DO about it?
4. Once you have decided what to do about it, get on with it!

That last one was mine again, because I just can't resist having the last word.

Idle Musings on Psychotherapy

With my tongue firmly wedged I my cheek, I would like to make the following observations.

I have heard it said that anyone who has not undergone a full course of psychotherapy is screwed up to a greater or lesser extent.

In order to become a fully qualified psychotherapist one has to undergo a full course of psychotherapy with someone who has already qualified. This begs the question: with whom did the first psychotherapist qualify?

As there was no-one with whom he could have undergone a full course of psychotherapy, he must have been screwed up. Therefore, anyone who qualified with him will most likely have been screwed up by him, and the same would be true for all who followed. Are therefore all psychotherapists screwed up?

Anyway, when you think about it, why would you entrust your mental well-being to someone who styles themselves "Psycho-the-Rapist"?

Removes tongue from cheek and continues.

Medical Matters

The information presented in this section is intended as general information only and should be viewed neither as personal medical advice nor as a substitute for the advice of a suitably qualified physician. Some of the opinions expressed are mine, and should be treated as exactly what they are: not fact, but merely opinions. I retain the right to exercise my democratic right to be wrong!

A list of organisations which can provide information and support is given in the Appendix.

If you are a hypochondriac do not read this chapter!

Medical students frequently develop symptoms of the ailment they are studying, and I don't want you rushing off to the doctor claiming to be suffering from all manner of interesting disorders.

Fact is that the majority of tall people are so for no sinister reason. Familial tall stature, and all of the environmental factors that contribute to tall stature, are largely responsible.

In recent years, with the rapid progress of molecular genetics, more of the causes of syndromes that are known to be associated with accelerated growth and tall stature have been identified. However, some of these conditions are such that height is just one small factor in a wide ranging and complex set of symptoms. The affected individuals and their parents may face difficulties beyond those caused by tall stature alone.

In others, height is the most obvious feature, and the syndrome may have little, in any, effect on the person's life. In fact, a great many people go through life without ever knowing that they have some condition or other, as it has no significant impact on that person's life or well being.

I shall give only the salient features of some of the better known and more commonly encountered conditions. At the end of each I shall include any relevant experiences I have had, and observations I have made, which I hope will add a little more flesh to the bones of the information.

I shall avoid using too much medical jargon and terminology. At times I may even seem to be over simplifying explanations, but I want as many people as possible to be able to easily grasp the basics. If you are a medical professional who dislikes the simplified explanations that's just too bad.

Think of them as the back of an envelope sketch, rather than the fully detailed technical plans.

Genetic research has come on in leaps and bounds since I was involved full-time with the subject of height, and I see nothing to be gained by giving you chapter and verse on the technical stuff.

You think you can handle that stuff? Alright then, try this for size: the molecular genetics as they apply to Sotos syndrome: Gene Symbol NSD1; Chromosomal locust 5q35; protein name Histone-lysine N-methyltransferase, H3 lysine-36 and H4 lysine-20 specific.

I did warn you.

Returning to basic English, I shall cover only the more common conditions which may cause an individual to become significantly taller than expected. That begs the question: what is significantly taller than expected? Before we get into the detailed stuff, I shall attempt to clarify that point.

What is Unusually Tall?

I met a man of 6ft 5in who wasn't unusually tall; I met a man of 5ft 11in who was.

Does that sound like gibberish? At least I have got your attention.

If a 6ft 4in father and a 6ft mother have a 6ft 5in son, no-one should be in the least surprised. However, if a 5ft 5in father and 5ft mother have a 5ft 11in son, there is good cause to ask questions.

It is only possible to establish whether a child, or an adult for that matter, is unexpectedly tall by having some idea of how tall they were expected to be in the first place. One way to do that is to make reference to the parental height or, more accurately, the mid-parental height.

Mid-parental height is simply the average of the height of both parents. For example, a 6ft father and 5ft 6in mother give a mid-parental height of 5ft 9in. As a rough guide, and depending on which expert's figures you believe, generally a son will grow to a couple of inches above that height, a daughter an inch or two below. The margin for error is quite wide. Plus or minus 4 inches for a boy and 2 inches for a girl is considered acceptable.

The main drawback of this method is that it implies no ongoing monitoring of the child's height. Without a reference point along the way, it is difficult to know whether growth is progressing normally or not.

It makes sense always to plot a child's growth on a growth chart.

Growth charts are available from most doctors' surgeries. These show the average rates of growth from childhood to adulthood. Once the mid-parental height has been plotted, it will be clear where in the overall scheme of things they fall. Say the mid-parental height is on the 75th percentile, one would expect a child's height to not divert significantly from that figure throughout its period of growing. If, for example, the child's height were instead to register at around the 95th percentile it could be a sign that further investigation into a possible cause may be merited. The same applies if it were around the 50th percentile. A significant divergence in either direction deserves attention.

Another means of estimating a child's final height is to measure a girl at the age of two years and three months or a boy at two years and eight months, and then to double that figure. The final height is likely to be within a couple of inches either way of that figure. The reason for the difference in age between the two sexes is that girls tend to reach their final height slightly sooner than boys.

The medical profession likes to use bone age to determine a probable final height. An x-ray of the bones of the hand will give an indication of how far from final fusing the ends of the long bones are. Fusing takes places at the end of the pubertal growth spurt, and once completed the person should not grow any more. Two difficulties arise with bone age x-rays. First, the physician needs to be very familiar with the procedure. Second, in cases in which one of the syndromes outlined below is at work bone age x-rays have on occasion proved less than reliable.

Finally, it is important to remember that height is as much relative as it is an absolute. Investigation is merited when a child is significantly taller than might reasonably be expected based on mid-parental height. If both parents are unusually short, then offspring of average height, although not tall when compared with other children of the same age, should be viewed as taller than might be expected.

Syndromes

A few words about syndromes in general:

A syndrome is a collection of symptoms which, when observed together, allow a physician to identify a particular condition.

An individual may display one or more of the symptoms associated with a particular condition without actually being affected by that condition.

Not all those affected by a syndrome will display all of the symptoms known to be associated with that syndrome.

Not all those affected will display the same range of symptoms as others who are also affected.

Not all those who display symptoms will display those symptoms to the same degree as others who are also affected.

The same clinical symptoms may occur in more than one syndrome. This does not mean that the individual is suffering from any or all of the syndromes.

Right then, now that we've established that being tall doesn't automatically mean that someone is ill, we can move on to the more practical stuff.

There is nothing to be gained by withholding information about a syndrome from those who have been affected. They should be made aware of how the syndrome is likely to affect their lives, what the implications are, and how they may need to adjust their lifestyle accordingly. Treating them with kid gloves will only cause them to worry about what is really wrong, and can add stress where it can be easily avoided. Even young children can understand more than adults generally give them credit for. Explain everything in simple language with simple analogies, and ultimately both the parents and the child will benefit.

It is impossible to say with any great degree of accuracy how frequently genetic inconsistencies occur. Some of the more obvious ones, such as Downs syndrome, are practically impossible to miss. Many others produce effects so minor that they can easily go completely unnoticed. Even the estimates of incidence which are given for many syndromes cannot be taken as gospel, because we simply don't know how often the syndrome is missed. Not until every child is genetically tested at birth will the figures have true meaning.

Some syndromes are said to occur only 1 in 1,000,000 live births, while for others the incidence may be as high as 1 in 500, possibly even more. Add up all the different syndromes, and one might be forgiven for thinking that so called genetic mutations are actually verging on being the norm rather than the exception. Take man's obsession with identifying and naming anything that doesn't conform to some generally perceived norm, and the picture becomes ever more muddied.

Take, for example, ADHD syndrome. No doubt some children do have a chemical imbalance which affects their behaviour, but I cite as an example a friend's youngest son, who was diagnosed with the condition. He was disruptive at school, constantly in trouble, and always getting into some sort of mischief. Yet when he was alone with adults and given an interesting task, he would work diligently and creatively for hours on end. He was bright, intelligent, always willing to learn, interested in wildlife documentaries and history programmes, and responded well to acknowledgement of a job well done. This kind of experience makes me wonder about children with ADHD: do they really have some kind of disorder, or are the adults around them simply too thick, or too threatened, to recognise highly intelligent children who are bored out of their skulls?

The more we develop the capacity to identify almost anything that doesn't conform to a predetermined norm, the smaller the range of so called 'normal' becomes. Perhaps it's only a matter of time before those we now consider to be normal will be identified as abnormal, because there is nothing wrong with them.

Returning to the matter of height related syndromes, many researchers make reference to overgrowth during the early years, but then state that adult height will be within the normal range. I suspect that these researchers have treated height as an absolute rather than relative. Height may ultimately be statistically within the normal range, but is still likely to be greater than expected based on parental height.

The appearance of similar or even identical clinical symptoms in different syndromes is referred to as 'clinical overlap', and makes the whole business of accurate diagnosis difficult. A physician may diagnose a condition in accordance with whichever one he is already most familiar with.

It seems that so many syndromes have such a large degree of clinical overlap that, in practice, the principal difference between them comes down to molecular genetics.

Management and treatment of a condition is more dependent on the nature and severity of the symptoms than it is on the name; perhaps a case of 'A rose by any other name...'

Marfan syndrome

Marfan syndrome is a disorder of the connective tissue, first described by Dr Bernard Marfan in 1896. It is genetic in origin. The condition is autosomal dominant, which means that an affected parent has a 50% chance of passing on the gene to their offspring, although 25% of cases occur as a result of spontaneous mutation. It affects several body systems, including the eyes, and both the cardio vascular and skeletal systems.

The gene mutation responsible for Marfan syndrome has been identified. It affects the production of fibrillin, which is an important constituent of muscles and tendons. In the UK, genetic testing is rarely carried out. In the USA families with a history of Marfan syndrome are more likely to be offered genetic testing. Some symptoms associated with Marfan syndrome are also observed in other conditions which therefore may appear to be similar to, but are in fact quite different from, Marfan syndrome. Diagnosis by a specialist physician who is familiar with the condition is imperative.

Great advances in the management of Marfan syndrome have been made. With proper monitoring and treatment, life expectancy is now considered to be in line with that of the general population. There is currently no known cure.

Salient Features

Musculo-skeletal

Tall lean stature, with longer bottom body segment; growth rate is accelerated during the first five years of life after which it returns to normal; puberty has been observed to occur at the early end of the age range, in which case the individual may not become as tall as may have previously been predicted. Arachnodactyly (long thin fingers with prominent joints); joint hypermobility (the thumb may be pulled back to touch the wrist with relative ease; a thumb held inside a closed fist is likely to protrude from the fist by as much as the entire first joint); wingspan usually exceeds height by several centimetres, but can be the same or less. Unusually narrow and malformed chest (either pigeon chest or funnel chest); scoliosis and/or kyphosis (curvature of the spine); stretch marks are not uncommon.

Oral

High arched palate; crowded teeth.

Ocular

Dislocation of the lens of the eye (subluxation); detachment of the retina; myopia (shortsightedness).

Cardiovascular

Dilation of the ascending and sometimes also the descending aorta, possibly leading to eventual dissection; aortic aneurism. Mitral valve prolapse, possibly with regurgitation (backwards flow of blood).

Pulmonary

Pneumothorax (collapse of the lung) is not uncommon.

Genetics

Although usually inherited from an affected family member (in 75% of cases), Marfan syndrome can occur spontaneously (in 25% of cases). Severity can vary substantially between affected members of the same family.

Treatment and Management

Due to the complexity of Marfan syndrome it is important that it should be monitored by a physician who is totally familiar with the condition. A regular echocardiogram (NOT electrocardiogram, although this may also be required in certain situations) is recommended. This too should ideally be administered by the same person each time to ensure consistency. Surgical intervention to repair the aorta and the mitral valves may be required at some point. Ocular problems may also require surgery to replace the lens and to reattach the retina. Glasses and/or lenses can help to correct some visual defects. Medication, including beta-blockers, can help with management of Marfan syndrome. Physiotherapy can help to strengthen muscles, and may also be required, possibly in conjunction with bracing, to support the spine. Lifestyle adjustments are essential; contact sports, long distance running, heavy manual tasks and the like should be avoided. A good general level of fitness is to be recommended.

Note: A great deal of clinical crossover exists between Marfan syndrome and Beals syndrome, also known as Congenital Contractural

Arachnodactyly. The latter is separate and distinct from Marfan syndrome, as it is caused by a different gene mutation. Although the two are clinically similar, the cardio vascular implications appear to be less severe in the case of Beals syndrome. Without full genetic investigation it is difficult to establish a clear distinction.

Personal observations:

Although I have not seen this stated in any of the literature on the subject, I have noticed that in particular some, but by no means all, young women between the ages of approximately 16-25 with Marfan syndrome may suffer a degree of depression (*Please note: I am not aware of any case in which a diagnosis of either clinical or chronic depression was confirmed. There is no increased risk of any form of mental illness or disorder with Marfan syndrome*). This appears to lessen with the passing years, maybe due to acceptance on the part of the individual concerned. Good family support makes a huge difference. Counselling may be of help. Contact with support groups can also have a positive effect.

General Practitioners may not be familiar with Marfan syndrome, although I believe that the condition is now included in doctors' training. Older GPs in particular may therefore have not encountered the condition. One cannot expect all GPs to be familiar with every last syndrome or condition, so one must be prepared to ask questions and to insist on referral to a suitable specialist if symptoms warrant it.

I cite as an example the case of a woman in her forties whom I met at a business lunch. As she reached across the table for the salt, I noticed her lean and spindly fingers – classic arachnodactyly. I noted her overall build and asked: "You're short sighted, aren't you?"

She looked surprised. "I'm wearing contact lenses," she said, "How did you know?"

"You get out of breath going up two flights of stairs too, don't you?"

She confirmed that she did.

"I bet you can pull your thumb back to your wrist," I said.

"Like this, you mean," she said, as she did exactly that.

I suggested that she ask her GP for referral to a specialist, who might be able to throw some light on the subject.

She called me a few weeks later to tell me that her GP had admitted that she had suspected something wasn't right but, as she knew nothing of Marfan syndrome, had not known to whom she should refer her. A visit to a cardiac specialist had confirmed my suspicions, and she was due to have mitral valve replacement and aortic repair surgery within weeks rather than months.

It was only after successful surgery that her specialist told her that our meeting had been more fortuitous than either of us realised at the time.

I should add that not all people with Marfan syndrome will experience shortness of breath after moderate physical exertion. However, severe mitral valve prolapse and regurgitation does affect the flow and thereby oxygenation of the blood, thus shortness of breath can result.

If you suspect something is wrong, it is better to ask questions than to say nothing. In the words of my own GP: "I would rather see you twenty times about nothing than not see you the one time that something really is wrong."

Sotos syndrome

Also known as Cerebral Gigantism, Sotos syndrome was first described in 1964. It is characterised by increased head circumference and overgrowth during the early years of life. Paradoxically, despite the overgrowth, muscle development is delayed resulting in poor motor skills, and delays in speech development. Poor cognitive and social skill may lead to a diagnosis of autism. A degree of autism may occur, symptoms of Asperger's syndrome are not uncommon, but either should be dealt with as part of the larger developmental picture.

The developmental gap appears to close as the child progresses into adulthood. Growth velocity slows to normal after the initial growth phase, around the age of six. Adults with Sotos syndrome are likely to be within the normal range of intellect, although height is likely to be greater than expected based on mid-parental height.

Many genetic conditions are easily identified at or shortly after birth. This is rarely the case with Sotos syndrome. An accurate diagnosis may only be made after months or even years of awareness that something is not quite right, vague assurances that all is well, albeit delayed, and uncertainty about whether the child will ever develop 'normally'.

Salient Features

Physical Development

Accelerated growth during the first five years of life, after which growth velocity returns to normal; increased head circumference. Hydrocephalus may be suspected but is rarely confirmed.

Oral

High arched palate and crowded teeth; teething may begin early. Tendency to drool; dislike of sucking – breastfeeding may be difficult. Children seem to dislike chewing and will swallow rather than suck things like a boiled sweet. Poor muscle tone and delayed muscle development may be the principal reason for these observations. It is also likely to be at least partially responsible for delayed speech development.

Appearance

Large head; narrow and tall skull; thin hair and high hairline; prominent forehead. Flat bridged nose; eyes wide set and slanting downward at the outside edges.

Skeletal

Bones mature faster than is usual, bone age in advance of actual age; hands and feet may appear large when compared to the rest of the body; flat feet or feet that collapse inwardly are not uncommon; scoliosis may develop. Greenstick fractures, in which the bones splinter rather than break, have been noted.

General Development

Due to the delay in muscle development motor skills take time to develop and refine; coordination may remain poor into adulthood – this will often be viewed as simple 'clumsiness'. Drooling for prolonged periods and mouth breathing may be observed. Children often show reduced sensitivity to pain and discomfort; bruises and even fractures (usually greenstick fractures) may be sustained without complaint. Extremes of temperature are often casually endured (the child's hands and feet may be blue with cold, but they show no sign of discomfort). Comprehension of language is often well ahead of speech development, which may lead to frustration, as a child knows what it wants to communicate but is not able to. This can initiate temper tantrums and outbursts, which can be disturbing as the child is physically larger than others of the same age. Intellect may be impaired, and specialist teaching may be required – the range varies widely between those with Sotos syndrome with many showing average intelligence. Emotional development is often delayed. Inappropriate responses to emotional and social cues can lead to difficulties. Many children with Sotos syndrome grow to lead normal and independent lives as adults.

Treatment and Management

Physical and occupational therapy to promote muscle development is essential. Speech therapy will aid effective communication. Alternative strategies to aid effective communication and mobility will help to build confidence and self-esteem. Appropriate play in a structured environment can help a child to develop essential skills without distraction. Completing at first simple and then more complex tasks will build a child's self confidence, and aid developmental progress.

Personal observations:

I met a young woman of 22 who was eloquent and good humoured about living with Sotos syndrome. She explained how, as a youngster, even taking her dog for a walk was fraught with potential danger. A sharp tug on the lead by the dog was all it took to fracture her wrist. The majority of fractures she sustained as a child were so called greenstick fractures. Because of her insensitivity to pain she rarely noticed anything was wrong, but her parents soon realised than any significant amount of bruising made an x-ray examination advisable. Social Services raised a collective eyebrow at the number of injuries she sustained, but their fears were allayed by her doctor, who explained the reason. Her parents had been most encouraging, helping her to exercise and to be as active as possible. She had attended a mainstream school, completed a college course, and gained recognised qualifications.

"I'm still a bit clumsy," she told me, "but it's only bad when I am really tired."

When we met, she had just moved into her own flat, had a good job with a large company, and had her eye on a certain young man. I have no doubt that his fate was sealed.

At the other extreme, I met a family whose son had many other difficulties in addition to Sotos syndrome. He would never lead an independent life.

How easy the syndrome is to miss became clear to me courtesy of a letter I received while I was still running the TPC. I had published an article about Sotos syndrome in the Club's magazine about three months prior.

I paraphrase his words, but in essence the man told me this: "We had always known something was wrong, but couldn't work out what. The doctor said he was just a slow developer, but we knew there was more to it. When I saw the article everything became clear. I showed it to our doctor, and he referred us to a specialist, who confirmed a diagnosis of Sotos. We know there is no cure, but now that we know what's wrong we can deal with it. It's still not easy, but at last our son is making good progress, because now we know what to do to help him. I don't know how independent he will become, but at least now he has a chance."

Parents can make a huge difference, simply by being aware, and applying common sense. I attended a meeting of parents of children with Sotos, at which a father told me about his young son: "Once we knew that delayed muscle development was part of it, I figured that it was probably why our son was so slow to learn to talk properly. He knew what he wanted, but couldn't tell us, and that made him frustrated and angry. I started playing silly games with him, trying to touch the tip of my nose and then my chin with my tongue, and got him to copy me. He loved it, and we laughed a lot. It helped to strengthen the muscles around his mouth, and his talking came on in leaps and bounds."

Having a child with Sotos syndrome is not the end of the world. With understanding, patience and the right support, good progress can be made. The results of perseverance can be immensely satisfying and rewarding for both child and parents.

Klinefelter syndrome

First described in 1942 by Dr Harry Klinefelter, the syndrome that bears his name is characterised primarily by an additional X chromosome, confirmed by research in the 1950s. Instead of the usual chromosome formation of 46XY, a male with Klinefelter syndrome will present with 47XXY. Of all the height related syndromes, it is probably the one most likely to remain undiagnosed until adulthood; if indeed it is diagnosed at all. This is both good and bad news. Good, because it is clear that effects of the syndrome are such that they have little impact on the life of many affected individuals. Bad, because infertility or greatly reduced fertility is one of its effects, and may only be detected well into adulthood.

It is a syndrome which affects males only, although some females do have an additional X chromosome, in which case they are sometimes referred to as Triple X females. Symptoms are similar to Klinefelter sundrome, but fertility in females appears to be unaffected.

Males with the chromosome formation 47XXY in only some and not all of their cells are said to display Mosaic Klinefelter. In very rare cases a male may have more than one additional X chromosome, and display the formation 48XXXY or, even more rarely, 49XXXXY.

The syndrome seems to occur in about 1 in 1000 live male births. However, it is also thought that many cases escape diagnosis, so the incidence may be as high as 1 in 500-700.

Salient Features

Physical Development

Accelerated growth during the first five years of life, after which growth velocity returns to normal; longer bottom body segment. Build is usually lean although some children develop "puppy fat" and a pear shaped body. Small testicles and occasional failure of the testes to descend have been noted. Children will tend to begin puberty within the normal age range, but progress may be slow, with secondary male characteristics slow to develop. Voice may "bend" rather than break; hair and beard growth is often sparse. Some boys may develop breast tissue during puberty. This rarely becomes a problem, but in those incidences in which it does, plastic surgery may be indicated. It is vital that the surgery is carried out by a proficient surgeon, as residual scarring can have greater detrimental effects than the breast tissue itself.

General Development

Accelerated growth may result in the body outpacing the muscles, and so the child may be uncoordinated and ungainly. Intellectual development is within the normal range for most, but can vary widely. One group tested produced a range of IQ from slightly below average up to 131. Children may be quite passive and non-assertive, leading them to be viewed as dreamers at school. They may therefore miss out on a degree of intellectual stimulation which, in turn, may impact on IQ scores.

Fertility and Sexual Development

By its very nature, Klinefelter syndrome may lead to a slight degree of feminisation. Males will have either no or very few viable sperm. In a very small number of cases males with Klinefelter syndrome have fathered children (confirmed by blood testing) but this is the exception rather than the rule. IVF is an option for some, while for others adoption is the principal route to a family of their own. Libido tends to be normal, and although the testes and testicular volume may be slightly smaller than average, the principal male genitalia is most likely to be of normal size. Testosterone is produced in the testicles. Reduced testicular size and volume may impact on the production of the hormone, slowing down completion of puberty.

Management and Treatment

There is little that can be done for the child, other than to encourage physical fitness and development by means of exercise and sporting activities, and intellectual development by means of a stimulating and supportive learning environment. Some boys with the syndrome show reduced levels of testosterone production. As a result, puberty is slow to progress, and a testosterone supplement may be required to help with completion of sexual maturity. In addition, this will also aid the ends of the long bones to fuse correctly, and is therefore likely to reduce final height. Parents must be made aware that administering testosterone supplements can lead to increased aggression, which can be cause for concern in an already moody and possibly belligerent teenager.

Other Implications

Even academic sources do not agree unreservedly on other conditions which may or may not be more likely to occur in males with Klinefelter syndrome. Several sources quote a list of conditions of which those concerned should be aware. Others say that no associated health implications have been identified. It is probably best to say that general health issues should be noted and treated as and when they occur.

Personal observations:

I have known many cases in which Klinefelter syndrome was only diagnosed after a man presented with fertility problems. Some had, during their childhood, been checked for a height related syndrome. In most cases Marfan syndrome was initially suspected, but soon dismissed. Further investigations were rarely carried out, as only Marfan syndrome was considered major cause for concern.

It is true that Klinefelter syndrome is not life threatening. However, some couples find the sudden revelation that the man is infertile so traumatic that it causes a major strain on their relationship, that strain leading to eventual breakdown of the relationship.

That is not to say that Klinefelter is completely without its difficulties. A mother told me of her son, who had started his growth spurt at the normal time, but was still growing steadily at the age of 21. His growth velocity was never particularly great, but it was consistent and for much longer than is the norm. Her doctor had assured her that nothing was wrong, even accusing her of being a neurotic mother. Once again '6ft+', the magazine of the TPC came to the fore. She took a copy of the magazine containing an article about Marfan syndrome to her doctor, sat down in front of him and resolutely refused to budge until he had read it. He grudgingly admitted that she might have a point, and referred her son to a growth specialist. Within weeks he had been diagnosed with Klinefelter syndrome. Exceptionally low levels of testosterone had prevented him from completing puberty normally. Consequently his long bones were extremely slow to fuse, and he had continued to grow for much longer than is usual. He had also remained the

233

same sullen and moody young man that he had been as a fifteen year old, in fact a typical teenager, even though he was 21.

The mother was in tears as she told me: "They put him on testosterone supplements six weeks ago, and he has changed. He is once again the way I remember him. Thank you for giving me my son back."

Had the young man's height been plotted on a growth chart throughout his childhood, his unusual growth rate would likely have been noticed much sooner. The difficulties he eventually faced could have been avoided. Of course, he still has to deal with the implications of his infertility. I believe that he was fairly philosophical about it, saying that he would deal with the issue at such time as it became relevant.

A Bold Hypothesis

Pseudo Klinefelter?

I first mentioned the following observations in *6ft+* in the mid-nineties.

Among TPC members I encountered several males who displayed classic Klinefelter syndrome symptoms. In addition to the usual physical and developmental features, almost half also had astigmatism. All had tested negative for both Klinefelter and Mosaic Klinefelter. None was totally infertile, but all had sperm counts and motility so low that they were considered, to all intents and purposes, infertile.

I am the first to admit that as a sample size the number involved is far from statistically relevant, however, many syndromes were first identified from a very small number of individuals who shared a set of symptoms.

Of course, it is still possible that Mosaic Klinefelter might be at work. When carrying out the test only enough cells are checked to make the result statistically relevant. In some cases only 30 cells are checked, which means that a negative result is only 95% reliable; that 5% chance cannot be ignored, and may well render my hypothesis redundant.

In simple terms, 46XX produces a female, 46XY a male, therefore 47XXY changes balance away from the nice and tidy 1:1 to a ratio of 2:1 in favour of the X. In Mosaic Klinefelter not all body cells are affected. Even so, within the total of all body cells the ratio would still be much closer to 2:1 than 1:1.

Are you with me so far? I hope so, because here comes the hypothesis bit: If there were some kind of fault somewhere on that final Y chromosome that changed the effective balance between the X and Y chromosomes in favour of the X, might that not cause male development to mimic that observed in Klinefelter syndrome without displaying an extra X chromosome in any cell?

I discussed this idea with a couple of doctors, one of whom was an endocrinologist, the other a growth specialist. One felt it to be unlikely, but feasible and worthy of investigation, if only to eliminate it from enquiries. The other dismissed my idea pretty much out of hand, saying he could see no way in which it was possible. I asked him why this was the case. His reply: "If it were the case, then someone would have found it by now."

I followed up with a couple of questions about the nature of other conditions known to be caused by genetic mutations, and asked about possible parallels. No matter how I tried, I could not get a satisfactory explanation as to why and how my hypothesis was flawed.

I repeat: it is perfectly possible that my hypothesis is completely wrong, and that we are dealing with some form of low level Mosaic Klinefelter. However until my question is answered by results from tests and investigations, no-one can be sure.

But what if I am right? Klinefelter-Heinricy syndrome anyone?? They would probably wind up calling it something really boring but descriptive, like Flawed Y syndrome.

XYY syndrome

XYY syndrome is characterised by an additional Y chromosome, giving the configuration 47XYY. It was first identified in 1961, and is thought to occur in about 1 per 1000 live births. Because the syndrome does not impact significantly on the physical well-being of the individual, it is probable that many males with the condition remain undiagnosed, and the incidence may therefore be much higher. It has, in the past, been the subject of some highly questionable research leading to the appellation "the criminal syndrome". It was thought that the additional Y chromosome would lead to higher levels of aggression. This was "backed up" by the discovery that the number of men with XYY syndrome in criminal institutions was well above the population average. It has been difficult to shake this misconception, despite considerable research which has proven this particular hypothesis to be untrue.

Salient features

Development

Males will usually be taller than expected, often with a build similar to that of a man with Klinefelter syndrome. No obvious distinguishing physical features have been noted. Boys may be physically more active than others of the same age, and this energy needs to be channelled productively. Emotional development may be delayed. Slight learning difficulties have been observed in a number of cases. With good familial and teaching support, these are readily overcome.

Fertility

Males appear to have no fertility problems. There is no evidence to suggest that the condition is hereditary.

Acromegaly & Gigantism

Acromegaly and Gigantism, the latter sometimes also referred to as Giantism, are basically the same condition, distinguished only by the timing of their onset.

The following is an article I originally wrote for publication in *6ft+*, the magazine of the TPC, and provides a basic explanation of the condition.

Gigantism: growth hormone is secreted by the anterior lobe of the pituitary gland. It controls the rate of growth of the individual, as well as determining the timing of sexual maturity. Sometimes, usually due to a micro-tumour, the gland continues to secrete growth hormone for much longer, and in greater quantities, than it should. The affected person will continue to grow upwards, as well as outwards, until secretion is stopped, by medical or surgical intervention. If unchecked, the person will take on the characteristic appearance of one suffering from acromegaly.

Acromegaly: when normal growth is complete the ends of the long bones fuse, and the person has reached their final height. If the pituitary starts to produce excess growth hormone, the person will experience some upwards growth but, due to the fusion of the long bones, many bones, such as the lower jaw, will grow outwards. This leads to a characteristic appearance of the lower jaw and lips, thickening of the fingers and feet, and enlargement of cartilage structures, such as the nose and adams apple, the latter resulting in a deeper than normal voice.

The condition is not hereditary, i.e. is not passed on from parent to child via the genetic material, however, some people believe that a set of conditions, or family tendencies, can be passed on, which may make the child more likely than normal to develop the condition. In one case, a man reported that several members of his family have had several pituitary related problems: - diabetes and cryptorchidism (undescended testes), for instance.

A person with the condition will take on a certain appearance, with large hands and feet, larger facial features, jaw, and cheekbones, and of course excessive height, if affected at or before puberty.

The stature and weight attained due to gigantism can cause a reduction in mobility, and make movement awkward and slow. It can be important to maintain some form of exercise programme, to counteract this.

Salient Features

General
Coarsening of facial features. The nose and lower jaw may broaden, the lips thicken. Enlarged hands and feet, thickening of the joints, particularly of the finger may be observed; carpal tunnel syndrome. The larynx may enlarge causing the voice to become deeper and more sonorous. Excessive sweating and oily skin; general tiredness.

Cranial
Headaches are not uncommon.

Ocular
Vision disturbance. In some cases the tumour may become large enough to exert pressure on the optical nerve, affecting vision.

Causes and Diagnosis
Tumours of the pituitary may occur spontaneously, or as the result of head trauma. Diagnosis is frequently delayed because of the rarity of the condition. Any sudden increase in height in adulthood must be taken seriously, as it is the most obvious indication that something is amiss. Unusual growth rate pre-puberty should always be investigated. Early diagnosis will greatly improve any prognosis.

Treatment and Management
Pharmaceutical regimes can achieve satisfactory results in some cases, while in others surgical intervention may be required. Advances in technology have allowed surgical techniques to become far less invasive than they were even twenty years ago. Even so, specialist physicians will not always be in accord when it comes to deciding upon the most appropriate course of action. Some will favour a tried and tested procedure, while others

may prefer a newer alternative. A wide range of factors, including the degree to which the condition has advanced and the general health of the individual, will influence the decision.

Height Restriction and Reduction

Height restriction means limiting growth of an individual to stop them attaining the height they might have otherwise done. Height reduction means reducing the height an individual had already attained.

Once again I have raided my personal archives of articles written for *6ft+*, the magazine of the Tall Persons Club GB & Ireland. This one concerns height restriction only. I shall then deal with height reduction separately. The article has been edited, as the original was written in the mid 1990s, and some minor changes have occurred since then. You will gather from the tone of the article that this is, for me, an emotive subject. I make no apologies for that, but hope that the factual information answers all of the questions you, the reader, may have about the subject.

What I find particularly satisfying (in a smug 'I told you so' sort of way) is that the concerns I raised about these procedures back then, and which were largely waved aside by medical professionals, are now acknowledged as requiring serious consideration before embarking on such treatments.

Height Restriction

There are three principal methods of restricting the final height a child might achieve, and all of them depend on the treatment being started before puberty. Two of these methods are pharmaceutical, one is mechanical. There are recorded cases in which drug treatments were begun too late, resulting in the child becoming even taller than it would have done had it been left untreated.

Artificial Advancement of Puberty

By administering quantities of the appropriate sex hormone to trigger puberty, the pubertal growth spurt is also triggered ahead of time. Final height is therefore also achieved sooner, and should be around two to three inches less than would have been expected without treatment. Parents often panic when shortly after starting the treatment the child heads north at an alarming rate, contrary to their expectations. This is perfectly normal, as it is the pubertal growth spurt, brought on early, exactly as intended. Because the growth spurt also ends earlier than would have been the case without treatment the child's terminal height is reduced.

The advantage of this method is that it has been in use with generally satisfactory results for some time, and its effects are reasonably well understood. The disadvantages are not so well documented, nor do many doctors tell the parents exactly what the long term implications might be. Because these treatments were only begun within the past couple of generations, we are only now seeing those who were treated reaching middle age. We will not have the full picture until a good number of those people have completed their allotted span on this earth.

First, and most importantly, high levels of sex hormone in women has been linked with a higher incidence of cervical and other gynaecological cancers. Second, it has been reported that in approximately 10% of cases in which high levels of sex hormone have been identified the women have become infertile. These points must be discussed with the doctor, and cannot be ignored when making the decision to begin growth restriction treatment.

One must also consider that the child is effectively being pushed into puberty at a time when it is unlikely to be psychologically ready to deal with it. A ten year old girl suddenly blossoming into full womanhood may not be what you want for your daughter, while a fourteen year old boy resplendent with beard growth and deep voice finds it much easier to get served in pubs. Along with the sudden physical development comes all the joy and happiness associated with having a teenager in the house, the mood swings, temper displays, and the generally obnoxious behaviour most of us have either been through ourselves, or remember from our dark and distant past. Imagine facing an angry and aggressive fourteen year old who has the body and musculature of a young man, but not the maturity to recognise what is happening and why.

Inhibition of Growth Hormone Production

A number of drugs are now available (though not all of them in the UK) which inhibit the production of growth hormone in the pituitary gland. Naturally, with lower levels of the hormone being produced, the final height of the individual is also held in check.

Different drugs are likely to have different side-effects and, as most of the drugs will be relatively new, some of the possible long term effects may not become fully known and understood for many years

Leg 'Stapling'

A pin or staple is inserted into the long bones of the leg, in order to encourage the ends to fuse. The amount of height restriction would appear to be slightly less than with an appropriately timed drug intervention, but the time at which the treatment may be commenced is a little less critical.

Few people have reported major side effects with this method, although one has to take into account that the bones are being deliberately damaged, albeit minor damage, which may produce effects in the event of severe injury, or later in life as the body ages.

Should We? Shouldn't We?

This is the most difficult question of all. There is no doubt that in some cases treatment is wholly appropriate, especially when the child is expected to reach an extreme height as a result of a medical condition. The human body is not designed to be infinitely tall. Muscles, joints, and circulation have limits as to what they can reasonably deal with, and growth restriction might be necessary rather than just desirable. The following paragraphs are intended to deal with routine cases of cosmetic and psychological height restriction, and will not necessarily apply to those who have a medical condition.

Most growth clinics have reported a drop in the number of cases presenting for restriction in the last decade, as people are becoming more aware of how the population generally has increased significantly in height this century. The motivation to restrict a child's height for no more than cosmetic or psychological reasons is not as strong as it once was.

If you are considering growth restriction for your child, you need to ask yourself why. Is it because you are fairly tall and had difficulty adjusting to that fact? Did you not have the support of other family members to help you to deal with being a little out of the ordinary? Are you now transferring your anxieties on to your child? It is important that you are honest with yourself in answering these questions, because even if you have your child treated it won't, for the most part, change their lives to any vast extent. Let me say that again: you aren't going to make much difference by having your child's growth restricted.

Can that be true? Think about it: if a boy is heading for 6ft 10in, and the treatment stops him at around 6ft 6in or so, he will still be tall by most standards, he will still have trouble getting clothes and footwear to fit, the jokes will still be made, legroom will still be at a premium wherever he goes, beds will be too short, and desks too low. The same applies to a girl who might have been 6ft 2in, and has been stopped at 5ft 11in. So would the treatment be totally pointless? Not necessarily; life will be a little easier, but probably not noticeably so.

What happens to the next generation? If your child has had its growth restricted by a few inches, it will make no difference to its genes, which will still be carrying, and will pass on, the gene for the unrestricted height. Do you want your grandchildren to be treated, and their children, too? Think also about the attitude you are teaching your child: they are receiving medicine to stop them being 'too tall', therefore to be tall is to be sick, because only sick people take medicine. Simplistic? Yes, but that's how children think, and that which they learn in childhood they will often carry with them to their graves. "Give me the boy until he is seven, and I will give you the man," applies here as much as anywhere.

Talking of the next generation, we are all aware of how people are still becoming taller, so although you might have been tall twenty years ago, by the time your children reach adulthood they may well no longer be considered as unusually tall. Far better, then, to support them with the knowledge, experience, and understanding you have gained over the years by being tall yourself, and to help them to build the self-confidence which will make the difference between them being a tall person or a person who just happens to be tall.

On a grander scale, think about all the other tall people in this world. Most will simply live with and adjust to their height and, in many cases, learn to love it, and to capitalise on it. In advocating treatment you are saying to the retailers, designers, manufacturers, and standards setting bodies of this world, 'don't worry about making things fit the people, we'll make our children fit your products'. Dumb, or what?

Do We? Don't We?

You've made your decision, and think it's a good idea to have your child's height restricted. What now? Off to the doctor for a referral to a growth clinic? First things first: talk to your child as openly and as impartially as you can about what you propose. You may be surprised at how even a ten year old child can reach an informed decision, as long as you do give them all the information, without trying to bias them to your way of thinking. Don't be tempted to think that they are only children, and that they won't understand. They can and they will, and they will respect you for consulting them.

It cannot be stressed strongly enough how important it is to involve your child in the decision making process. Many tall people who have had the treatment have commented how it was imposed upon them and how, given the choice, they would have been happy to have been left alone, and not been treated. Some, of course, are happy with the decision made by their parents, but are already thinking about whether they are going to have their own child's height restricted; in some cases they had already decided.

Whatever decision you eventually reach between you, make sure that you reach it in good time, i.e. before puberty starts. It is too late when your offspring is singing baritone in the church choir, or is off to university; an eighteenth birthday present it ain't!

If you opt for growth restriction for your child, make sure it is for the right reasons, what is best for them, and not to exorcise your own troubled childhood ghosts. Talk to other tall people, parents of tall children. The Tall Persons Club has a section called "Little Big Ones", which is a great source of info among parents of tall children, especially for parents who aren't tall themselves. Talk to other tall children about their feelings, and then make your decision. Be aware that the treatment is not reversible. Once you go with it, there is no turning back.

Above all remember that the height restriction you may decide upon is not for your benefit, but for that of your child. Restricting a child's height can be the right thing to do, but it has to be for the right reasons.

I have encountered several parents who made the decision on behalf of their children, without ever consulting them. From the conversations I had with them it became clear that they were treating their own insecurities rather than doing what was best for their child in the long term.

Among those who had undergone the treatment the general feeling seemed to be one of 'well, it's done now, and I don't know any different'. Most were uncertain whether they would ever consider having their own children treated when the time came.

It is also true that medical professionals are only human, and subject to the same failings as we all are. They may encourage a decision in line with their own feelings or motivations about height, rather than the best course of action.

On a TV show I took part in an audience member raised the point that if someone is treated the genes remain unchanged, and did that mean that the person's children would also be deemed to need treatment when the time came? The question was directed at the expert on the show, a doctor who specialised in height restriction. He said simply: "Well, we have to stay in business."

You can imagine the audience reaction for yourself. I think that the remark may have been a flippant one, not meant to be taken too seriously, however inappropriate it was at the time, but I wouldn't put money on it.

Height Reduction

If you are squeamish, you should now go and make a cup of tea or something, and come back in a page or two.

Once an adult has achieved their full height, there is only one way to reduce it, lending credence to the old joke about having your legs shortened.

The femur is shortened by surgically removing a section, typically between two and four inches, of the bone. This is effectively all but the same as fracturing the leg. Because the cuts are made under controlled circumstances the break is clean, not ragged as it might be as the result of an accident, so setting and healing is usually relatively straightforward.

Following healing, extensive physiotherapy is required to get the muscles back into shape. The person has to learn to walk again, as the body's centre of gravity will have been shifted by the operation, thus affecting balance.

In some cases it has been necessary to carry out similar operations on the arms, in order to maintain the body's proportions. These may be done one arm at a time, so as to not affect the person's ability to function in day to day life any more than is absolutely necessary.

Some Case Histories:

During my time running the TPC I encountered many people who had either had or were considering height reduction surgery. They in no way represent a comprehensive study, and I offer the following only for illustration purposes.

In most cases, the surgery was carried out in the 1960s and 1970s. One had his operation in the mid 90s.

A woman who had previously been 6ft 6in and was now 6ft 2in told me she was glad to have had the operation. In her case her height and the difficulties it caused led to severe depression. Without the surgery she is convinced that she would have committed suicide. At the time we spoke, in the early 1990s, she was happily married and running a retail business together with her husband.

A man of 6ft 2in had previously been 6ft 5in. He made it very clear that he now considers his decision to have the surgery to have been a huge mistake. During our conversations I discovered that he had not been offered much in the way of counselling and support.

A woman in her sixties had been 6ft 2in, and was shortened by three inches. The surgery had been carried out while she was a young woman, in her early twenties. She was now in a wheelchair, due to numerous problems that had developed in her legs, beginning in her forties. How much of this was down to the surgery and how much would have occurred anyway no-one can be sure, although her doctor advised her that without the surgery her current difficulties would probably have been much less severe. In her own words: "I am now dependent on a wheelchair to get around. I wish the Club had been around when I was a girl. If it had been, I don't think I would have had the operation. Tell anyone from me that it's just not worth it in the long run."

A man of 6ft 4in had previously been 6ft 6in, and was happy with the results of the surgery. He was resident on a small island on which most buildings are quite small with low doors and ceilings. As he was happy living there, and had no intention of ever leaving the island, he made the decision to fit into his chosen environment as best he could.

A woman in her late twenties contacted the Club to ask for details of any surgeons willing to carry out height reduction operations. She firmly believed that all her problems would be solved if only she were three or four inches shorter. I suggested that she meet some Club members to share experiences before taking such a drastic step. The woman refused all suggestions to meet or talk with other tall people; she also refused to undergo any counselling. When I pointed out that no surgeon would proceed without her having undergone counselling she told me that she would simply have the surgery done privately.

The last case is an example of someone who, I believe, had chosen to see her height as the cause of all her ills, and didn't want to risk being persuaded otherwise. I doubt that, for her, height reduction was the answer.

I came across many more people who had undergone surgery, but whether it had been the right thing to do was rarely clear. For some it certainly was right, while for others the physical problems that began to develop twenty years later led to regrets. Several suffered with reduced mobility or, at the least, constant pain and discomfort. One cannot be sure that was caused solely by the surgery, but one cannot rule out the surgery as a contributory factor. Old injuries - and that is what height reduction is: both legs broken on purpose – can often lead to unforeseen difficulties later in life.

Of all the people I spoke with who had undergone height reduction about two thirds regretted their decision.

The isolation many tall people feel, the sense of being the only person to be so tall, of being an oddity, has led some to make a decision they would later regret. I have lost count of the number of times I heard or read the words: "If only the Club had been around when I was young, my life would have been very different."

It seems that all too often we resort to surgery not because we should, but because we can, and I would apply that to not only height reduction surgery, but to most, and I do stress most, cosmetic surgery.

Where height is concerned, surgery is rarely the answer, because however you change the packaging, the contents will remain the same.

Part Three

Some General Musings

Philosophical Moments

In some societies I would be seen as having achieved the status of wise elder. In ours I have achieved the status of boring old fart. Whichever way you choose to view it, I offer here a few dollops of the wisdom I like to think I have gained in the course of the last half century or so. This is not intended to be one of those self-help guides, nor a free commercial for some deity or other during which I start scribbling in tongues. It's just my view of the world and life in general.

You may feel that this has nothing to do with height, but it does. For those of us who are unusually tall the way we deal with our most outstanding feature is reflected in our attitude to life in general.

Most of the quotes are far from original and someone is sure to say that they have heard them all before from other sources, but I don't care. It is part of the human condition that each new generation feels the need to reinvent the wheel. I have attributed quotes where I am able to, and I trust you will pardon me for occasionally paraphrasing others.

I can't recall where I first heard this one, but it is so true, if only we allow it to be.

Happiness is wanting what you have.

Learning to differentiate between 'want' and 'need' is the first step to freeing yourself from the drudgery of chasing things that you are told you ought to want, but could quite comfortably live without. Chasing money, status and possessions is all very well, as long as that is what you really want. If, however, dedication to that goal means you miss your children growing up, end up divorced and stressed out with a dicky ticker, then even with all the cash in the world you will never know true happiness.

In conjunction with the previous one, always remember that...

Money is the measure of a person's wealth, not of their worth.

Does that one really need an explanation?

Here's a really old one, originally coined by King Arthur, way back in the middle of the first millennium:

In times of prosperity a man forgets himself. In times of hardship he is forced to look in on himself, even though he be unwilling.

Anyone can deal with prosperity. It's how you deal with adversity that reveals your true character.

For those who follow the maxim that if at first you don't succeed give up, I offer this little gem:

**Even while you are falling flat on your face,
you are still moving forward.**

If everyone gave up after a failure or two, we would never remember Winston Churchill (poor school reports), Fred Astaire ("Can't act, can't sing, can dance a little."), Walt Disney (went bankrupt before starting the Disney Studios), Henry Ford (bankrupt twice before starting Ford Motor Company at age 40) nor Henry Heinz (went bankrupt, then 'invented' ketchup).

On the other hand, some of the greatest failures are not remembered as such. Christopher Columbus was searching for the western route to India, and made a total mess of it. That's why we still refer to parts of the Caribbean as the West Indies. Alexander Fleming was a sloppy lab technician, whose cultures became contaminated with a fungus that killed the bacteria he was trying to grow. Now he is remembered for having discovered penicillin (erroneously, as it turns out, but that's another story). Post It Notes came about thanks to a chemist who made a batch of glue that wouldn't set. Charles Goodyear accidentally dropped some rubber on his wife's stove, thus discovering the process of vulcanising rubber. Add to that list William Roentgen (X-rays), Louis Pasteur (various bit and pieces), and Mr Kellog of Corn Flakes fame to name but a few, and you begin to see that failure isn't necessarily a bad thing.

One of the most famous and prolific failures of all time has to be Thomas Alva Edison. When asked by a journalist how it felt to have failed over 2000 times in his attempts to produce a viable light-bulb, he answered: "Young man, I did not fail 2000 times. I successfully discovered 2000 ways that would not work!"

Now that is the right attitude!

In fact, it's always worth remembering that…

No-one ever learned anything by doing it right.

It is only by getting things wrong that we learn to do them correctly, as we refine our techniques, and practice, practice, practice.

This one is an original. It's mine, all mine, so there!

Most of us try so hard to live the kind of life that we think others expect us to lead, we fail to realise that they are far more worried about what we think of them.

The funny thing about life is that we spend most of our time trying to live up to impossible ideals. We actually believe that we are in some way superior to animals, that we have overridden all of the basic instincts that exist throughout the animal kingdom. How wrong can we be?

Within any group of animals a pack order is established, usually with displays of physical force. Because we have learned that it isn't socially acceptable to smack someone in the mouth to prove that we are superior to them we instead buy houses, cars and other assorted goodies to show how wonderful we are. Birds strut their stuff with impressive displays of plumage or intricate songs. Drop into the average night club on any weekend and you will see the same thing going on. Plumage has become designer clothes and the latest fashion in hairdos and accessories, the display is dancing and posturing.

Once we realise that we have not shaken off basic animal behaviour, but merely modified it, we are free to appreciate the basics so much more. What does take to keep the average animal happy? Shelter, warmth, enough food to live on, something to stop them getting bored and the odd bit of rumpy pumpy. Oh how simple life can be.

"But what will people think of me?"

Quite frankly, who cares? As long our behaviour and our actions cause no harm to others why should we care? Most of the people we look up to and admire are more concerned with how long they can maintain the pretence, how long it will be before we rumble them. And no matter how high a social or professional position you might achieve, it is only a matter of time before you are usurped.

Few of us are destined to leave the mark of a Plato, Copernicus, Da Vinci, Newton or Nobel on this world. In a couple of generations' time our great great grandchildren will barely know our names, much less what kind of life we led. If we are lucky, we shall be names on a family tree, with perhaps our life span and profession noted, tucked away in the bottom of a rarely opened drawer.

You might think this to be a very depressing view of life. I find it to be incredibly liberating. Whatever I do in this life it is unlikely to impact greatly on the future of humanity. On the other hand, we can never know what effect our actions will have on others, and whether they or their descendants may be the ones to have that great impact. However, considering the odds, all I can do is my best, and if it has a positive effect that is wonderful; and if not then so be it. In the overall scheme of things I understand that I am potentially useful but, ultimately, expendable.

Yet, although I am expendable, I shall continue to play my role, even after my demise. It is a fact that every atom and molecule in my body, which is after all nothing more than an extremely complex set of chemical and electrical reactions, has existed since the beginning of time. What's more, they will continue to exist until the end of time, just not in their current coherent form. What's that if not eternal life?

It is part of the human condition to attach much greater importance to our existence and to our actions than we merit; take global warming. Whilst I do not doubt that our actions may influence our climate, I am not so sure that the effect we have is as great as we like to imagine. 10,000 years ago much of the Northern Hemisphere was in the grip of an ice age, covered by a blanket of ice and snow. The climate changed, the ice melted, and yet there was not a factory or internal combustion engine in sight. Yes, the climate is certainly changing, but then it always has done, courtesy of an elliptical orbit of the earth and a wobble to its axis.

Natural disasters – I prefer to think of them not as disasters but as natural occurrences – ultimately have a far greater effect than mankind ever will. Massive volcanic eruptions in several locations around the world during the early nineteenth century caused planet wide climate change, the effects of which endured for more than a decade afterwards. Harvests failed, snow fell in June at latitudes not known for this phenomenon, and 1816 became known as the year without a summer.

In the end, our planet will always find its own balance. Whether we like it or not, that might include the demise of Homo sapiens. Impossible? Well, climate change due to natural occurrences saw off the dinosaurs and many other species, so why not the human race?

Now that we are all thoroughly depressed by the prospect of an uncertain future, we can all rejoice in the fact that we all face an uncertain future. It is what provides the sense of mystery, the reason to go exploring, to discover what we can do and experience in whatever time we have available to us on this Earth. Uncertainty offers excitement, intriguing possibilities and unlimited potential.

Life is out there ready to be grabbed with both hands and lived to the full. Safety is all very well (and largely sensible) but it's the venture into uncharted territory that provides the adrenalin rush, those moments of undiluted exhilaration – or terror – which let you know that you are really alive.

I know that I could have accrued great wealth, had I chosen to do so. Instead I chose to do whatever felt right at the time. Which life would have been more fulfilling and more rewarding I can't begin to speculate. All I know is that I do not regret the choices I made.

When you are all tucked up in a big box and a bloke with a screwdriver is getting to work on the lid, if you can think 'That was fun, and I did ok', then yours is a life well lived. You should have no regrets. Members of TPC might even indulge in a smug little snigger as they think of the poor bloke who has to dig that 7ft+ hole.

Life is always good if you allow it to be, and the hard times will help you to appreciate the good times all the more.

Without bad there can be no good, without negative there can be no positive, without dark there can be no light.

The Epilogue

Well, since I started with The Prologue it seems appropriate that I should end with one of these.

Whether you have found what precedes this useful, vaguely entertaining, or a complete waste of time, I thank you for sticking with it this far.

Although this volume has concentrated on height it is true that all of us are at some time or other inclined to fixate on one particular aspect of ourselves, be it physical or psychological, and to view it as the source of all our ills.

Whatever problems you may or may not encounter in your life, it is how you face them and how you deal with them that determines the kind of life you will have. For better or worse, it is largely in the mind.

For most of us today, life is just too darned easy. We don't realise how well off we are. We did not endure the horrors of World War II or of one of the many other armed conflicts. Anyone mention the Gulf Wars? Excuse me, but the members of our armed forces who have served and continue to serve in troubled areas of the world today joined voluntarily. They were not conscripted as were those who preceded them. I do not mean to belittle their experiences, only to put them into context.

How would you have dealt with surviving the atrocities of concentration camps, the hardships of drought ridden Africa, the aftermath of volcanic eruptions or tidal waves?

If your biggest worry is that you don't have the latest designer trainers or mobile phone, ask yourself how you might feel if you had no idea where the next bowl of rice was coming from, or why your children were dying from diseases which could be easily cured? Compared with that, the difficulties faced by tall people on a daily basis in the Western World pale into insignificance.

I am not saying that we shouldn't continue to actively work towards improvements, but let us never forget that the lot of the tall person is just one very small part of life in the overall scheme of things.

If you have been, thanks for reading. If not, then this book can still be useful to prop up that wobbly table, or to jam open a door. If soaked in paraffin it also makes a terrific fire lighter.

Best wishes.

Phil.

Appendix

Appendix

Make an Event of it

I wasn't going to include this originally but, when we were ready to go to the printer, there was a load of empty pages waving about in the back. It seemed a shame to waste them, so I thought I would add this short guide, mainly for any TPC members who fancy a go at organising the annual event.

Each year the Club celebrates its anniversary with a weekend in a nice hotel somewhere, with outings and events which are meant to provide something for everyone. Many organisations like the TPC organise similar events, but very few achieve either the best prices or a suitably varied programme of events.

Right then: let's look at the various stages of initial planning.

1. Location

I make no apologies for emphasising the importance of "Location, location, location." It should always be within a good road and rail network, and my preference in Britain would always be within an area encompassed by the M62, M6, M5, M4 and M1. Two exceptions to this rule are Liverpool and Cardiff, but only because they are still within half an hour of that, and both have outstanding transport connections.

The average urbanite seems to consider anything outside that area a suburb of the Hebrides, and will be less inclined to make the journey. During my tenure I chose locations for ten national events. The three lowest attendances were in Glasgow, Newcastle and Grantham. Need I say more?

2. The Outline

I always tried to ensure that first timers are made to feel part of everything from the time they arrive, and that all levels of fitness are allowed for. The age range can be from 12-80, and I have known it to be even greater. Most are likely to be between their late twenties and early fifties.

A good balance of on-site and external events also helps to prevent the feeling of enforced holiday camp style jollity. There is a big difference between a weekend that is well organised and one that is regimented.

It is also important to allow for some relaxation time for those whose energy levels aren't what they once were.

3. Budgeting

Putting a weekend together is not difficult. Getting the prices right requires some hard nosed negotiation. Making a profit is desirable. Getting it wrong is a doddle.

I always aimed to break even with a minimum of 60 people attending the gala ball. Two thirds of the actual total would attend the whole weekend, three quarters for two nights, 90% for one night, with the remaining 10% attending the dinner only.

If we had 100 people attending the gala evening I expected the weekend to show an overall profit of £1000-£1500. This profit helped to keep subscriptions down, covered the cost of organising the event, and contributed to the cost of representing the TPC at overseas events.

Some organisers find the idea of making a profit from members abhorrent. I don't know anyone, who having enjoyed excellent value for money and having had a good time, would object to £10 profit being made on their £200 spend. After all, those who attend events are using more of the Club's services and had good value for money, so isn't it right that they should be contributing more to the Club's operating expenses?

4. The Process

A weekend can be divided into four separate elements: accommodation, the gala dinner, outings and events, additional services.

Having decided on the area in which I wanted to place the event that year, I would shortlist three hotels. The selection of the hotel is always the first priority, as it is easier to arrange events around the hotel than it is to arrange a programme of events and to then find a suitable hotel.

Next I obtained a copy of the hotels' brochure including their weekend break offers. Most three and four star hotels have special BB&D rates for weekends throughout the year, which give a general indication of the prices which are achievable or, more accurately, can form a starting point for negotiation – downwards.

From 1995 to 1999 the job was easy. We used Swallow Hotels, and word got around within the group that ours was an event which attracted plenty of good publicity. Hotels like good publicity, especially when it's free. This made others within the group much more receptive, and more willing to be flexible on price.

If a relationship can be built with a particular group of hotels it will ultimately be to everyone's benefit, the Club, the participants and the hotel.

That said, there has been one major change between then and now: Hotels are now wedding venues. Many of the business hotels which once clamoured for our business are now busy with weddings at weekends, with the August Bank Holiday in great demand. Even so, especially the larger hotels will still fight for the business. If they have 200+ rooms of which 40 or 50 have been booked for a wedding that still leaves a lot of capacity. Of course they may have more than one wedding that weekend, so it may weaken our hand, but how many weddings have you seen that generate national media coverage?

I arranged to visit to each short-listed hotel and to meet the Conference and Banqueting Manager. If the hotel was too far away to make travelling there and back in a day practical I would tell them that it was my practise to never book an hotel that I hadn't stayed in. I only once failed to get a free night B&B, and even then I was given a fantastically reduced rate. I would always promise to have dinner in the hotel. It's a great way of having a weekend away in nice hotels without it costing the earth. I always took Carol along on these weekends. She provided another set of eyes, and would often pick up on things that I missed.

A tour of the hotel and its facilities I take as routine. I would also ask to see the kitchens, providing it was convenient. The cleanliness of the kitchens can say a lot about an hotel and it's the little things that matter. For example, if I saw grease caked around the base of any of the appliances or tables it would put me on high alert for everything else I saw in the rest of the hotel, and significantly reduce the chances of making the booking.

5. The Negotiations

And so to the negotiations, which sometimes took place over a complimentary lunch. Yes, these preliminary visits were tough, but I had to endure them for the benefit of the Club and its members. Carol admits openly to being embarrassed at how tough I could be when it came to getting the best price. I came away from most of those lunches with extremely sore ankles.

Appendix

Make no mistake: Conference and Banqueting Managers are not there to do you any favours. They are there to take your money. They have targets to meet, and failure to do so results in memos from Head Office which include words like "...terminate your employment...", which is all ammunition to the hard negotiator.

Our host would give me prices for accommodation and for the gala dinner, and I would promptly tell them that they would need to improve on them, regardless of how good they might already have been. I knew they would never offer their best price from the off.

When they showed reluctance to reduce their rates any further I would make a big thing of the Club's non-profit status and of its record of generating publicity, and then tell them the budget I was working to. Needless to say the figure would be a fair bit lower than I knew they would accept. Their reaction would indicate clearly just how great the gap was, and I would tell them that, of course, I had some room to manoeuvre and that I was sure we could reach an agreement.

We would discuss the gala dinner, and I would mention that several of the attendees were likely to have special dietary requirements, and ask if it might be possible to meet chef. Eager to please, they would always comply – big mistake on their part.

The manager might have told me that, for example, the £27.50 dinner was not negotiable. However, once chef was sitting with us at the table, and we had discussed some of the options for vegetarian and gluten free meals, I would tell him that budget was a major constraint, and ask whether he could put together a decent dinner for say £22.

Hotel chefs are great with food, but rarely too hot when it comes to striking the best deal. Chef would propose a suitable menu at, or very close to, that budget, while the manager's teeth could be heard gnashing behind the fixed professional smile. Usual attendance for the dinner was around 100, so I now had an extra £500 or so to play with.

At this point the ability to do mental arithmetic faster than the person you are negotiating with can make a huge difference.

Consider that our usual room requirements for the three night weekend would run to at least 40, 50 and 60 rooms for Friday, Saturday and Sunday nights respectively. I costed in a profit for the Club of £5 per person per night. I also had to allow for a single supplement, which I always passed on at cost, and which was usually £10-£12 per night.

Work it out – that's a bare minimum of (40x3) + (10x2) +10 = 150 room nights, times £5, or £750 base line profit. About two thirds of the rooms would be twin or double occupancy, so the real figure was nearer £1250. If I had to concede £3 per head on the dinner to get the room rate I wanted we were still about £950 to the good. I win; the Club wins!

Always be prepared to give little to get more back. A useful phrase in any negotiation is: "If I could…, would you…?"

Most hotels have their own DJ for dinner and dance events. I would rarely haggle too much over the price for that service, as the hotel is unlikely to be making much profit on the deal. A local entertainment agency, usually one recommended by the hotel, could provide a specialist act. Close up magicians or a speciality act generally worked well. A good agency will have other ideas too.

6. The Programme

I always think of the days in sections. 09.00-17.00 is action time, 17.00-19.00 get ready time, 19.00-01.00 main event, and 01.00 to 03.00+ wind down time.

During my time, I favoured ten-pin bowling for the Friday evening. It was always a great ice breaker, provided competition and could be booked in conjunction with food. A small local coach operator would always be much cheaper than one of the nationally recognised companies, and so the whole event could be put together for around £15 per head. As this event was offered as an extra, it did not impinge on the budget for the weekend, and might even generate a profit of £30-£50.

There are plenty of alternatives for the Friday evening, but budget constraints will always influence whether or not it should be a chargeable extra. I believe it is acceptable to make an additional charge for an event that does not take place in the main hotel, but not for one that does.

For the rest of the programme, the hotel concierge is the best source of information about which local venues are worth a visit, and which offer the best value for money. Mediaeval style banquets are a great Saturday night out. The hotel may suggest a suitable in-house event aware that, by keeping the drinks trade in the hotel, they will recoup some of what they have lost in earlier negotiations. As long as everyone was likely to enjoy themselves and it fitted into the budget I was happy with that. Bear in mind too that an event in the hotel eliminates transport costs to and from an external event

One day had to incorporate free time for people to explore and to do as they pleased. I favoured Sunday for the outing, as in those days – jeez that makes it sound so long ago – most shops would be shut. Now that it is almost impossible to tell the difference between the two days as far as the shops are concerned, I don't suppose it makes that much difference. An additional, chargeable activity, such as go-karting or quad biking, which will only attract the most fit and active, helps to fill the weekend nicely.

The main outing was determined by the location of the hotel. If it was in or very near a city centre it was usually possible to allow for a range of activities or places to visit which people could get to under their own steam, and in their own time. Liverpool was a great example. A tourist ticket to seven attractions (it may have been more) was relatively inexpensive, more than filled a day, and therefore gave very high perceived value. For group outings our Sunday outing in Newcastle is a good example. It included two venues, Lindisfarne and Alnwick Castle, and a light lunch on Lindisfarne.

7. Controlling the Budget

And so to another important point: never pay in full in advance for venues and meals on the day out. I used to agree with each venue to pay for actual numbers attending only. We achieved this either by entering as one group, counting the number and then paying, or by giving each person a voucher for admission or food, and paying the venue on presentation of vouchers with invoice, whether on the day or upon later presentation.

Now here's the sneaky bit. I shall tell the story in relation to our Newcastle weekend, as that was the one to which it is most relevant. Attendance was the lowest we had ever had, with only 65 people scheduled to attend the gala dinner, and 60 booked for the Sunday outing.

As I have already said, these weekends were budgeted to break even at around that level and that left no margin for error. I didn't want to book and pay for two coaches if we could get away with one. I had a quiet word with the hotel manager, and arranged for the bar to remain open until at least 03.00. It was a small room, very cosy, and ideal for about thirty or so people.

A large bar for that small number would have felt like rattling around in an aircraft hangar, which was not the atmosphere I wanted to create. It worked.

The next morning, with the solitary coach I had booked due to pull out of the car park at 09.00, quite a few of the late night revellers were nursing sore heads, and had still not appeared for breakfast. Not wanting to appear totally unreasonable I allowed two minutes of grace, and the coach departed at 09.02, with just 47 people on board.

I had arranged to operate either group payment or the voucher scheme at both venues as well as for the pub lunch on Lindisfarne, so not one unused place was paid for. In the end, even that weekend generated a modest profit.

8. Additional Services & Benefits

We generally needed a meeting room on the Monday morning, and I usually got it for free. One conference manager did want to charge 50% of the usual fee for the room. I asked who else she thought she might be able to let it to on a Bank Holiday Monday, and offered to pay for tea and coffee for the attendees instead. She still wasn't totally happy, but found the idea of us holding our meeting in the residents' lounge even less acceptable. I couldn't bring myself to tell her I was going to order the tea and coffee anyway.

Carol and I always received a complimentary room, which is customary for the organisers of a major event. On a couple of occasions I even managed to blag a suite, to accommodate all of the extra materials we had to bring for the weekend. You see how we suffered?

9. Summary

So there you have it. That was how I put the weekends together. I will not claim that everything was an unbridled success, because I did make the odd mistake, but overall everyone seemed to have a good time and feel that they got value for money.

The full programme for three nights accommodation sharing a twin or double room., usually in a four star but never less than three star hotel, worked out at around £165. Single supplement took that to around £200. It included the Sunday Gala Dinner with additional entertainment, a Saturday evening event with food and the Sunday outing. Bowling and go-karting were extra. Considering that the usual room rates for these hotels were rarely less than £100 per night, and often considerably more, I think we did pretty well.

With the passing of time, I would revise my target budget for today to around £190, with single supplements taking it to about £225.

I suppose my top tips to anyone organising this type of event are these:

- Always negotiate final prices face to face – you will squeeze out an extra pound or two
- Never pay more deposit than you absolutely have, preferably none at all.
- Keep attendees busy so that they have no chance to get bored
- Only pay venues for actual numbers attending
- If an event looks and feels expensive the actual cost doesn't matter – it's called high perceived value
- Run to schedule – if people oversleep for whatever reason it is their problem
- Don't be ashamed of making a profit as long as you have given value for money.

Whether organising an event for the TPC or for another organisation, the principles are the same.

10. ...and Finally

Organising a weekend event isn't rocket science, although some professional Conference Organisers would have you believe that it is. Specialist Conference Companies used to call to offer the Club their services. One man assured me that with their buying power they could offer prices far better than I could ever negotiate directly, so I invited him to quote prices for the very hotel we had used the previous year. His best room price was over 20% higher than the one I had achieved, and of the events that were included in the weekend he managed to match the price of only one. Our conversation ended with him offering me a job whenever I might happen to want one.

Follow my tips and I am sure that you will be able to put together a great weekend for a good price.

Have fun!

Useful Resources

Most of the organisations listed below are run on a voluntary basis, and therefore change their postal address from time to time. The website is more likely to remain constant. This information was compiled in Spring 2008.

All telephone numbers are UK telephone numbers. If calling from abroad you should use the country code 44 and omit the first "0" from the number.

The fact that an organisation is listed here should not be taken as an endorsement recommendation or implication that it is a substitute for the advice and services of a suitably qualified specialist physician.

Tall Persons Club GB & Ireland

www.TallClub.co.uk

07000 825512 (07000 TALL-1-2)

Marfan Association UK
Rochester House
5 Aldershot Road
Fleet
Hampshire
GU51 3NG
Tel: 01252 810472
www.marfan-association.org.uk

Child Growth Foundation
2 Mayfield Avenue
Chiswick
London
W4 1PW

Tel: 020 8995 0257 or 020 8994 7625
www.childgrowthfoundation.org

Sotos syndrome
Contact the Child Growth Foundation.
A support group exists with the structure of the CGF

Klinefelter syndrome
www.ksa-uk.co.uk

Acromegaly/Gigantism
Pituitary Foundation
PO Box 1944
Bristol
BS99 2UB

0845 450 0376 Administration line
0845 450 0375 Support and Information Help Line
www.pituitary.org.uk

For conditions related to unusual height which are not listed here the World Wide Web has a large number of resources.

The quality of the information varies significantly. Check the credentials of the organisation or individual operating the website. Unless you are sure of the website's credibility, treat information with caution. Consult a suitably qualified and experienced physician or health professional.

The Tall Persons Club GB & Ireland and the Child Growth Foundation are both excellent organisations for information and support, and are good points of first contact. Both should also be able to recommend alternative and specific sources of information and support.